THE PRINCIPLES OF EPISTEMOLOGY IN ISLAMIC PHILOSOPHY

SUNY Series in Islam
Seyyed Hossein Nasr, Editor

THE PRINCIPLES OF EPISTEMOLOGY IN ISLAMIC PHILOSOPHY

Knowledge by Presence

Mehdi Ha'iri Yazdi

Foreword by
Seyyed Hossein Nasr

State University of New York Press

Published by
State University of New York Press, Albany

Printed in the United States of America

For information, address State University of New York Press, State University Plaza, Albany, N.Y., 12246

Production by Dana Foote
Marketing by Bernadette LaManna

Library of Congress Cataloging in Publication Data

Hā'irī Yaxdī, Mahdī.
The principles of epistemology in Islamic philosophy : knowledge by presence / Mehdi Ha'iri Yazdi ; foreword by Seyyed Hossein Nasr.
p. cm.—(SUNY series in Islam)
Includes bibliographical references and index.
ISBN 0-7914-0947-3 (acid-free).—ISBN 0-7914-0948-1 (pbk. : acid-free)
1. Knowledge, Theory of (Islam) 2. Knowledge, Theory of.
I. Title. II. Series.
B745.K53H35 1992
121'.0917'671—dc20 91-11999
CIP

10 9 8 7 6 5 4 3 2 1

CONTENTS

FOREWORD

The Principles of Epistemology in Islamic Philosophy: Knowledge by Presence by Mehdi Ha'iri Yazdi is not an ordinary book on Islamic philosophy, a simple addition to the already existing library of works on the subject in European languages. Rather, it is one of the first works in English belonging to the living tradition of Islamic philosophy and written by a person trained in the traditional method of philosophical study. It is a major expression of the Islamic philosophical tradition in a language that is contemporary and written by an author who is not only a master of the philosophy of Ibn Sīnā, Suhrawardī, and Mullā Ṣadrā but also a thinker who displays complete familiarity with Russell and Wittgenstein, Kant and James.

Despite the efforts of a number of scholars such as Henry Corbin and Toshihiko Izutsu to make the integral Islamic philosophical tradition better known to the West, most readers are probably still unaware of what is meant by the "living Islamic philosophical tradition." In the prevalent intellectual map of the Western world, Islamic philosophy is equated with what the Latins called Arabic philosophy and is relegated to the medieval period. Most of even those who have some interest in Islamic philosophy identify it with Latin Averroism, the disputations of St. Thomas and Duns Scotus, or the arcane art of Raymond Lull. They hardly ever think of this philosophy in later centuries and outside the Arabic zone of Islamic civilization in Persia, which has remained the main site of philosophical activity in the Islamic world during the past eight centuries. To situate the work under consideration and its author, it is therefore necessary to cast a brief glance upon that "living Islamic philosophical tradition" to which they belong.[1]

The Living Islamic Philosophical Tradition

Islamic philosophy, although eclipsed in the 5th/11th century in Persia and other eastern lands of Islam with the attacks of Shahristānī, Ghazzālī, and Fakhr al-Dīn Rāzī, did not simply journey to Spain to enjoy a brief Indian summer with Ibn Bājjah, Ibn Ṭufayl, and Ibn Rushd and to finally die out in the Western extremity of the Islamic world. The philosophy of Ibn Sīnā was revived by Naṣīr al-Dīn Ṭūsī and his circle in the 7th/13th century, while two generations earlier, a new intellectual perspective was inaugurated by Suhrawardī who named it the School of Illumination *(ishrāq)*. Furthermore, the "science of mysticism" or gnosis became formulated about the same time by Ibn 'Arabī and soon began to interact in a very creative manner with the Islamic philosophical tradition as well as with theology or *kalām* which itself was becoming ever more "philosophized."

The result of all these cross-fertilizations was several centuries of extensive philosophical activity in Persia marked by such figures as Quṭb al-Dīn Shīrāzī, Dabīrān Kātibī, Athīr al-Dīn Abharī, Ibn Turkah Iṣfahānī, the Dashtakī family, and many other figures about whom very little is known in the Western world. This period of rapprochement and intermingling, lasting for some three centuries, culminated with "the School of Isfahan" that was founded by Mīr Dāmād in the 10th/16th century and which reached its apogee with Mullā Ṣadrā, his student, whose ideas are reflected in many pages of this book.

Despite many ups and downs in the late Safavid period and the destruction of much of Isfahan as a result of the Afghan invasion in the 12th/18th century, the torch of Islamic philosophy lit anew by Mullā Ṣadrā continued into the Qajar period when once again Isfahan, under Mullā 'Alī Nūrī, became a great center for this philosophy, while Tehran also began to rise as a center of philosophical activity from the 13th/19th century onward. During this period a number of significant philosophers such as Ḥājjī Mullā Hādī Sabziwārī and Mullā 'Ali Zunūzī appeared upon the scene and wrote important treatises that are read in traditional circles in Persia to this day. They also trained many students who carried the living tradition of this school with its emphasis upon oral teaching as well as the written word into the Pahlavi period and the contemporary world.

Such masters as Mīrzā Mahdī Āshtiyānī and Mīrzā Ṭāhir Tunikābunī were among the most important of these figures, succeeded later by Ayatollah Sayyid Abu'l-Ḥasan Qazwīnī in Qazwin and Tehran, Sayyid Muḥammad Kāẓim 'Aṣṣār and Ayatollah Sayyid Aḥmad Khunsārī in Tehran, and Ayatollah Rūḥallāh Khumaynī and later 'Allamah Sayyid Muḥammad Ḥusayn Ṭabāṭabā'ī in Qum. It was with such teachers and masters that Mehdi Ha'iri Yazdi studied, benefiting from their oral instruction as well as their vast knowledge of the texts of Islamic philosophy interpreted within a living intellectual tradition that covers the span of well over a millenium and goes back to the origins of Islamic philosophy. He is the product and spokesman of that tradition while representing one of its most important interactions with Western philosophy.

Mehdi Ha'iri Yazdi

It is necessary to discuss the educational and intellectual background of the author of this volume in order to understand better the relation of this work to the traditional Islamic philosophical tradition to which it belongs. Mehdi Ha'iri Yazdi was born into one of Iran's foremost families of religious scholars in 1923 in the city of Qum. His father, Ayatollah Shaykh 'Abd al-Karīm Ḥā'irī Yazdī, was the most celebrated and influential religious scholar of Shi'ism of his day and the person emulated *(marja'-i taqlīd)* by the majority of Shī'ites. It was he who established Qum, the holy city situated a hundred miles south of Tehran, as the major center of Shī'ite studies in Persia during the reign of Reza Shah and made this center a serious rival to Najaf in Iraq.

The young Mehdi was thus brought up in a family of devout religious scholars known for their piety and religious fervor. He received his earliest training at the hands of his father and then commenced his formal traditional studies in the city of Qum, mastering both the transmitted *(naqlī)* and intellectual *('aqlī)* sciences, reaching the level of highest authority *(ijtihād)* in Islamic Law as well as in theology and philosophy. Since the role of the teacher is paramount in traditional Islamic education, it is necessary to mention some of his famous teachers here. Mehdi Ha'iri studied jurisprudence *(fiqh)* with Sayyid Muḥammad Ḥujjat Kūh Kamari'ī and the famous Ayatollah Burūjirdī who succeeded Ayatollah Shaykh 'Abd al-Karīm Ḥā'irī Yazdī as the supreme leader of Shī'ism.

From his youth, however, Mehdi Ha'iri was attracted especially to "the intellectual sciences" as traditionally understood, at the heart of which stands Islamic philosophy. He thus began to seek the best teachers in the field, men who had kept alive the millenial tradition of Islamic philosophy in Persia. He studied the *Sharḥ al-hidāyah al-athīriyyah,* the commentary of Mullā Ṣadrā upon the Peripatetic opus of Athīr al-Dīn Abharī, and the *Sharḥ al-ishārāt,* the commentary of Naṣīr al-Dīn Ṭūsī upon the famous *al-Ishārāt wa'l-tanbīhāt* of Ibn Sīnā, with Ayatollah Sayyid Aḥmad Khunsārī in Tehran. He also studied traditional mathematics based on the texts of Euclid with the same venerable master. Mehdi Ha'iri studied the *Shifā'* of Ibn Sīnā, that most advanced encylopedia of Peripatetic philosophy, with one of the greatest of the recent authorities in Islamic philosophy, Mīrzā Mahdī Āshtiyānī, who taught the eager young student in both Qum and Tehran. As for the philosophy of the School of Mullā Ṣadrā, Ha'iri studied the *Asfār* of this master and the *Sharḥ al-manẓūmah* of his Qajar commentator, Ḥājjī Mullā Sabziwārī, with Ayatollah Rūḥallāh Khumaynī, who at that time taught philosophy and gnosis *('irfān)* in Qum. Ha'iri also journeyed to Meshed in Khurasan to study traditional astronomy with Sayfallāh Īsī.

This long period of apprenticeship with reputable masters made Ha'iri well versed in traditional Islamic philosophy, but it did not mark the end of his formal education. Wishing to master also modern disciplines and current methods of approach to the study of Islamic subjects, he entered Tehran University where in 1952 he received his doctorate from the Faculty of Theology *(ilāhiyyāt)*. That Faculty has tried to wed traditional Islamic learning and new methods of research and study that had reached the Persian scene from the West. This experience whetted the appetite of Ha'iri for a more genuine and direct experience of Western thought. To this end he set out for the West itself where he was to spend over a decade in the formal and systematic study of Western philosophy in such universities as Michigan and Toronto, where he received both a master's and a doctorate degree in philosophy, the latter in 1979. Having mastered the English language and the intellectual medium of Western thought, he also taught over the years at such universities as Harvard and Georgetown in America, McGill in Canada, and Oxford in England. In 1979 he returned to Iran to resume his post as professor of Islamic philosophy at Tehran University and his association with the Iranian Academy of Philosophy. Today, although formally retired, he continues to teach a number of advanced students at his home in Tehran.

There have been several figures belonging to the tradition of Islamic philosophy who have dealt with Western philosophy and thought such as 'Allāmah Ṭabāṭabā'ī, the great master of traditional philosophy, gnosis, and Quranic commentary, whose *Rawish-i falsafa-yi ri'ālizm* is a major response of Islamic philosophy to Marxist dialectical materialism. One can also name in this list his student Ayatollah Murtaḍā Muṭahharī and the gifted Iraqi Islamic philosopher Bāqir al-Ṣadr. None of these figures, however, knew Western thought first-hand, but rather through translated texts, some of which were far from being accurate. As far as I know, there was only one figure before Mehdi Ha'iri who was educated and brought up in the traditional *madrasah* system, had received the traditional training in Islamic philosophy, and who also knew Western thought firsthand. That figure was Sayyid Muḥammad Kāẓim 'Aṣṣār, another of the venerable recent Persian masters of *falsafah* and *'irfan*. The latter, however, confined his writings to traditional Islamic subjects. Ha'iri can be considered as the first person who, nurtured from his early days in traditional Islamic learning and then in the thought of Ibn Sīnā, Suhrawardī, Ibn 'Arabī, Naṣīr al-Dīn Ṭūsī, Mullā Ṣadrā and others, then immersed himself in the world of Kant and Hegel, Russell and Wittgenstein, and wrote of problems posed by Western thought. His writings are therefore of particular significance in the contemporary Islamic intellectual scene.

Mehdi Ha'iri Yazdi is in fact himself an important representative of the Islamic philosophical tradition. He is an Islamic philosopher belonging to the living tradition of Islamic philosophy but dealing with problems and issues raised by Western thought and accepting fully the intellectual challenge of the West. His writings are not simply of historical interest. Nor are they simply a faint echo of Western philosophical concepts in the garb of Persian or Arabic as is to be seen in the case of so many so-called modern Islamic philosophers. He is an important contemporary intellectual voice that is at once thoroughly Islamic and profoundly philosophical in the authentic meaning of this term. Furthermore, he writes in a language that is comprehensive to both the traditional student of Islamic philosophy and the person nurtured upon the Anglo-Saxon or Continental schools of philosophy of recent decades.

Mehdi Ha'iri Yazdi has written numerous articles and a number of major books in Persian and Arabic and a few works in English, among which the present work is perhaps the most important. His books include *'Ilm-i kullī (Universal Knowledge); Kāwishhā-yi 'aql-i naẓarī (Investigations of Pure Reason); Āgāhī wa guwāhī (Concept and Judgment),* which is a translation of and commentary upon *al-Taṣawwur wa'l-taṣdīq* of Mullā Ṣadrā; *Kawishhā-yi 'aql-i 'amalī (Investigations of Practical Reason),* which deals with certain problems of the philosophy of ethics in a manner unprecedented in Islamic thought; *Hiram-i hastī (The Pyramid of Existence);* and *Metaphysics*. He has also written an Arabic commentary upon the *Shifā'* of Ibn Sīnā that has not as yet been published.

These works and numerous articles and essays reveal Ha'iri to be an important philosopher who stands firmly in the tradition of Islamic philosophy, yet deals with many issues in a manner that one cannot find in the works of the earlier masters. He is an original thinker in the traditional and not trivialized sense of the term in that he goes back to the origin, to the principles which he then applies to problems and situations many of which were not confronted by the Islamic masters of old. He deals on the one hand with well-known issues of Islamic philosophy and on the other with new problems arising from the challenge posed by modern Western philosophical thought to all non-Western intellectual traditions. He is also a master comparativist, and his oeuvre contains some of the best works written in comparative philosophy as far as Islamic and Western philosophy are concerned.

The Principles of Epistemology in Islamic Philosophy Knowledge by Presence

The present book, which is one of Mehdi Ha'iri's most significant, turns to a subject first elucidated in Islamic philosophy by Shihāb al-Dīn Suhrawardī. The founder of the School of Illumination *(ishrāq)* based his epistemology on the distinction between knowledge by concept or conceptualization *(al-ʻilm al-ḥuṣūlī)* and knowledge by presence *(al-ʻilm al-ḥuḍūrī)*. Ha'iri begins with this distinction and then amplifies the meaning of knowledge by presence and its consequences for epistemology, cosmology, theodicy, and mysticism. He makes a rigorous distinction between a knowledge based on the concept in the mind of something that is itself absent from the mind and a knowledge based on something which is itself present in the mind and whose very existence is inseparable from the knowledge of it.

The author deals in a masterly fashion with the deeper meaning of knowledge by presence as it concerns the knowledge of the self of itself or self-knowledge, God's knowledge of the world, and the very existence of the world as "presential knowledge" by God. He debates extensively with Kant, Russell, Wittgenstein, and others who developed their epistemology without awareness of the reality and meaning of knowledge by presence. He also opposes the view of certain Islamic Peripatetics who considered the world to be the result of God's contemplation of Himself rather than presential knowledge. On the basis of the theory of knowledge by presence and as an extension of the teachings of Suhrawardī and Mullā Ṣadrā, Ha'iri expounds further the meaning of emanation in cosmology as being related to God's presential knowledge and of *fanā'*, or the annihilation of the Sufi, as being its reverse process whereby the human self returns to God.

This book is also concerned to a large extent with the philosophy of mysticism. Ha'iri distinguishes between the language *about* mysticism and the language *of* mysticism and then in a masterly fashion provides a critique of the philosophy of mysticism as discussed by

William James and W. T. Stace. Ha'iri's discussion of ineffability in mysticism demonstrates not only his intellectual but also "existential" familarity with mysticism, while his philosophical analysis of the language of mysticism in the light of presential knowledge opens a vast vista upon the philosophy of mysticism in the ambience of Western thought.

*

* *

In this work of Ha'iri one observes comparisons and contrasts between Ibn Sīnā and Kant, Ibn 'Arabī and James, and Suhrawardī and Russell in a manner that is in total contrast to the shallow comparative studies one often observes among Oriental scholars who display a sense of inferiority towards Western philosophy, as well as among Western scholars with no sense of the meaning of traditional teachings and the difference between a traditional metaphysician and a modern secularized philosopher. Ha'iri journeys between the two worlds of Islamic and Western philosophy in a masterly fashion and constructs an edifice that is a notable addition to the long tradition of Islamic philosophy. One sees infused in this work piety with intelligence and philosophical rigor with mystical insight in a manner that makes the author a worthy successor to the Islamic sages and philosophers of old.

The author himself is in fact an embodiment of the teachings he writes about. He combines humility with logical acumen and penetrating philosophical knowledge with profound religious faith. His person testifies not only to great mental powers but also to a heart full of love for God and man. He possesses a knowledge which is not simply cerebral but which belongs to the realm of the heart-intellect. He typifies the traditional Islamic philosopher who was at once a learned man and a sage, a source of knowledge and a fountainhead of love and humanity, a being in whom philosophy and spirituality were intertwined in a dazzling bi-unity. It is fortunate, therefore, that this important work is now made accessible to the general Western public. May it be studied seriously by students of both Islamic thought and Western philosophy, for it is certainly one of the significant recent products of the "living Islamic intellectual tradition" that continues to survive to this day despite all the vicissitudes of time. It has a most important role to play in making available that millenial wisdom of which contemporary man is in such dire need.

Seyyed Hossein Nasr
Bethesda, Maryland
January 1991
Rajab A.H. 1411

Introduction

Despite the prevalence of sundry epistemological considerations in the study of human knowledge, the fundamental preepistemic question regarding the relation between knowledge and the possessor of knowledge remains unresolved. Succinctly put, what beckons the attention of philosophical inquiry is the reason as to why and how a knowing subject, with or without knowing itself, becomes united with or otherwise related to an external object as the thing known. The assertion: "I know something," certainly presupposes the fact that 'I' as the knowing subject is already, in one way or another, *acquainted* with itself. If such is the case, then it will become necessary to ascertain the nature of this acquaintance, and more specifically determine whether such an *acquaintance* is anything other than the very being of the self. In the light of this fundamental introvertive question, and by means of laws and principles of logic, the inquiry into the nature of the relation between knowledge and the knower can lead to the very foundation of human intellect where the *word knowing does not mean anything other than being*. In this ontological state of human consciousness the constitutive dualism of the subject-object relationship is overcome and submerged into a unitary simplex of the reality of the self that is nothing other than self-object knowledge. From this unitary simplex, the nature of *self-object consciousness can, in turn, be derived.*

In the language of illuminative philosophy, this consciousness is referred to as "knowledge by presence." The prime example of this knowledge is that which is apparent to the knower performatively and directly without the intercession of any mental representation or linguistic symbolism. This knowledge manifests itself through all human expressions in general and self-judgments in particular. Hence such assertions as "I think," or "I speak," become in particular the vehicles for the manifestation of this knowledge. The active subject of these judgments is the performative 'I' as distinct from the metaphysical 'I' or the Self which has been the fundamental issue in any philosophical inquiry.

The very nature of the performative 'I' leads to the conclusion that, in all of our self-judgments, there is necessarily a pragmatic unity and a self-continuity. This impetus, in itself, acts to unify and objectify all that it encounters within the external world.

Furthermore, the notion of a performative 'I' has served as the basis for the concatenations of ideas from which the general theory of mysticism was derived and logically explained. Now, we can properly show that the intellectual foundations of mysticism rest in the systematic analysis of 'knowledge by presence,' and its prime example and ramifications: the performative 'I'. This is the 'I' that by way of facilitating mystical experiences catalyzes the attainment of the vertex by the self's unitary consciousness. The result is the ultimate stage of knowledge by presence: the stage of absolute existential unity with the One.

The primary aim of this study is to introduce the notion of knowledge by presence, as nonphenomenal human consciousness that is identical with the very being of human nature, to the epistemological study of philosophy. Having touched on this aim, we are legitimately prepared to utilize philosophical analysis in formulating the mystical theory of the *unicity* of the whole world of Being as the prime proposition of mystical theory. Moreover, on the basis of knowledge by presence, the truth and substantiality of the performative self as distinct from the transcendent self can be established. Most important of all, through this analysis the paradoxical problems inherent in the theory of mysticism can be examined through the logic of philosophical thinking. In this regard, the theory of knowledge by presence permits a systematic approach to the whole subject matter of mysticism and the formulation of a philosophical approach to mystical thinking free of the intellectual idiosyncracies which have, thus far, typified the relations between mysticism and philosophy. Therefore, knowledge by presence, as instantiated by the reality of the performative 'I', is the focus of this study, given its central position of the understanding of the relations between knowledge and the knower and the identity of the very being of human consciousness with its self-knowledge, as well as to mystical approaches that are premised on this relation.

This inquiry will begin with an examination of knowledge by presence. On the basis of this knowledge, we will also try to establish the truth of the performative self-identity in the human being. Then we will turn to its most important implication, which is the philosophical solution to the paradox of mystical unity of the self with the One, and the One with the self. The analysis of the nature of knowledge by presence will then be extended: first, to specify the connotation of the concept of knowledge by presence as identical with the concept of the unqualified meaning of the being of the self-identity of human nature; and second, to bring to light its radical implication, which is the rational explanation of mystical experiences. Hence, mystical unity taken as another form of knowledge by presence is expressed through the notion of the annihilation *(fanā')*, and the annihilation of annihilation *(fanā' al-fanā')*, which results in unity with the absolute truth of Being.

However, heuristic exigencies, as well as the attempt to relate mysticism to philosophy, has led this study to view the mystical annihilation and absorption as forms of knowledge by presence, yet depicted as two separate notions, interrelated in a unitary simplex, where God and the self are existentially united. While this unitary consciousness signifies an absolute oneness in truth, intellectual reflection on it yields a material equivalence between God and self. In that case it can be inferred that the formal equation of mysticism is:

"God-in-self = self-in-God."

Once the above equation is carefully constructed, it may justify holding mystical assertions as meaningful and self-objective in philosophical inquiry, far from being hallucinatory, emotional, or as Stace put it, transubjective.[1]

One

Knowledge by Presence: A History

It is clear that philosophy, if it is to establish the integrity and systematic unity of human reason, is obligated to coalesce all forms and manifestations of awareness and subject them to the overriding power of the judgment of human intellectual consciousness. In attempting to accomplish this feat, modern Western philosophy has, since its inception, been compelled to exclude certain claims of awareness from the domain of human knowledge, and to brand them as mere expressions of fervor or as leaps of imagination. This was done lest the flow of philosophical logic be disrupted and force the disintegration of primary awareness. For instance, given that mystical experiences are characterized by a noetic quality in the sense that they make a certain claim of awareness of the world of reality, philosophical inquiry is compelled to ascertain the truth or falsehood of these experiences as a possible alternate dimension of the human intellect. While the same can be said concerning the problem of self-consciousness, the problem of our knowledge of our sensations and feelings, and our knowledge of our faculties of apprehension, and our knowledge of our bodies, theoretical reason is beckoned to examine their place in the comprehensive philosophical account of human consciousness. More often than not, modern philosophy has disparaged the inclusion of these species of knowledge into the corpus of its thinking for the sake of maintaining its uniform understanding of awareness. Yet, the exclusion by philosophical thought of these matters does not, *ipso facto*, prove the falsehood of these types of knowledge.

In fact, this study will make clear that these forms of knowledge do submit themselves to philosophical inquiry, and that, far from being anomalies to logical thinking, they stand to further the search for the nature of being. Examination of the history of the concept of knowledge by presence will both attest to this truism and serve as a prelude to the examination of its inner logic and its implications for philosophy. The notion of knowledge by presence not only possesses a historical legacy but has itself acted as the agent of history in bringing about the separation of Islamic and Western philosophies, both of which had emerged from the bosom of the Hellenic philosophical tradition. The reason as to why Islamic philosophy was given to the primacy of such a primordial mode of knowledge, which has thus far evaded the Western analytical tradition, is itself a question of great interest and importance. A possible clue may lie in the manner in which the Islamic and the Western philosophical traditions understood Greek thought. A cursory review of the formation of Islamic philosophy will be instructive in this regard, and will also shed light on the primary importance that the notion of knowledge by presence holds in Islamic philosophy, and the manner in which early philosophical thinking led to a coherent doctrine of knowledge by presence *(al-'ilm al-ḥuḍūrī al-ishrāqī)*.[1]

Since the time of Plato and Aristotle the mainstream epistemological tradition has been divided on the most fundamental problem of human intellectual knowledge, precipitating diametrically different strands:

First, there is the Platonic view in which intellectual knowledge is an intellectual reflection by the human mind on unique, simple, universal, immutable, and immaterial objects. In this view intellectual knowledge is, in fact, an intellectual *vision* of these "transcendent" objects.[2] The Forms, as intelligible objects of our transcendental knowledge, have a real and metaphysical existence, and are things or beings in and of themselves, independent of the process of the human mind and of the sensible physical objects that exist in the world of "becoming." On the basis of the dualism inherent in 'being' and 'becoming', Plato developed his notion of a "true reality" as the field of objective reference for our intellectual knowledge. This true reality is characterized by the power of being the source of knowledge in our minds and also by constituting the reality of things in themselves, or as they really are.[3] In contrast to this, Plato described a "symbolic reality" as the field of "belief," which is, as F. M. Cornford has stated, placed by Plato himself "between reality and non-reality," such that, "one cannot form any stable conception either as being or not being, or as both being and not being, or as neither."[4] As a matter of fact, Plato's theory of knowledge may be seen as a pattern of "intellectual perception" instead of "intellectual theoretical abstract conceptualization."

Plato explains what this intellectual perception would amount to:

> The ascent to "see" the thing in the upper world you may take as standing for the upward journey of the soul into the region of the intelligible; then you will be in possession of what I surmise, since that is what you wish to be told. Heaven knows whether it is true; but this, at any rate is how it appears to me. In the world of knowledge, the last thing to be 'perceived' and only with great difficulty is the essential Form of Goodness. Once it is 'perceived', the conclusion must follow that, for all things, this is the cause of whatever is right and good; in the visible world it gives birth to light and to the lord of light while it is itself sovereign in the intellect and in truth. Without having had a 'vision' of this Form no one can act with wisdom, either in his own life or in matters pertaining to the state.[5]

Secondly, there is an antithetic view to this Platonic way of thinking. This view, as Aristotle argues, asserts the fact that there is no identification of "seeing" and "knowing,"[6] since knowing is never seeing if there is no intelligible object to be seen. Thus the central issue for Aristotle was: What is knowing, if it is more than seeing, and if there are no antecedent objects in the objective world to be seen such as the Platonic Forms?

If one agrees with Aristotle that Plato's "Ideas" do not exist, and that the consequent "intellectual vision" of these antecedent Ideas is not what really constitutes the essence of human intellectual knowledge, one is faced with the problem: What then are the true objects of human intellectual knowledge? If for instance, the pure reality of a triangle does not exist in the world of real being, and our intellectual knowledge of triangle *qua* triangle is not obtained by an intellectual perception of the pure reality of a triangle, then how can one have an intellectual knowledge of a triangle at all? Since the pure reality of a triangle does not exist among sensible objects, the Aristotelian conception confronts a problem. It is with a view to addressing this problem that Aristotle presents his renowned analysis of intellectual knowledge in these words:

> Knowledge and sensation are divided to correspond with the realities, potential knowledge and sensation answering to potentialities, actual knowledge and sensation to actualities. Within the soul the faculties of knowledge and sensation are potentially these objects, the one that which is knowable, the other that which is sensible. They must be either the things themselves or their forms. The former al-

> ternative is of course impossible: it is not the stone which is present in the soul but its form. It follows that the soul is analogous to the hand; for as the hand is a tool of tools, so the mind is the form of forms and sense the form of sensible things.
>
> Since according to common argument there is nothing outside and separate in existence from sensible spatial magnitudes, the objects of thought are in the sensible forms *viz.*, both the abstract objects and all states and affections of sensible things. Hence (1) no one can learn or understand anything in the absence of sense, and (2) when the mind is actively aware of anything, it is necessarily aware of it along with an image; for images are like sensuous contents except in that they contain no matter.[7]

Succinctly put, since Aristotle evidently denies the existence of any intelligible objects outside of human nature and separate from sensible spatiotemporal magnitudes, he did not agree with Plato that intellectual knowledge is, in fact, the intellectual perception of those separate objects. Therefore, when there is no objective reference for an intellectual vision to be found, that vision proves to be a figment of the imagination. The conclusion is that the true objects of thought exist in sensible forms and are intellectualized through "abstraction."

The discrepancy between these two approaches has, since the beginning of the history of philosophy, led to the examination of the problem of knowledge through the two divergent approaches, those of Plato and Aristotle. Over the course of the unfolding of the Western philosophical tradition, this division became so distinctive, overriding the ultimate unity of objective of the two schools, that many modern philosophers have concluded that the Platonic and the Aristotelian philosophies are absolutely antithetical in nature, and therefore any attempts aimed at bringing them into systematic unity would be in vain. In the face of this great philosophical division, the epistemological problem concerning human intellectual or transcendent knowledge remained unresolved. Therefore, while both the Platonic and the Aristotelian philosophical traditions have sought to arrive at intellectual knowledge as distinct from sensory empirical awareness, their disagreement over the path adopted—either as the intellectual "vision" of intelligibles or the architectonic "abstraction" of our sense-experience—has obfuscated the search for the fundamental preepistemic foundation for human transcendent knowledge.

From the véry beginning of its history, there has existed in Islamic philosophy a unanimous concern for establishing a common ground between Plato and Aristotle on the matter of human knowledge. In principle, the Islamic approach shows that the two ostensibly contradictory systems of epistemology, the Platonic and the Aristotelian, can be employed in a simple philosophical framework for the purpose of arriving at a satisfactory solution to the problem of human knowledge. In this regard, Islamic philosophy maintains that the mind is constituted by its nature to function in different ways at the same time; being perceptive of intelligible substances on the one hand, and speculative about sensible objects on the other. Yet, Islamic philosophy extends beyond attempts at a resolution of the differences between Plato and Aristotle, and points to their analytical shortcomings. Islamic philosophy is of the belief that, just as the Aristotelian analysis of "abstraction, " though not to be refuted, does not account for a final and satisfactory resolution of the problem of intellectual knowledge, Plato's theory of intellectual "perception" cannot be regarded as the complete treatment of that problem either. Islamic philosophy, while based on the fusion of the Platonic and the Aristotelian approaches, ultimately extends beyond the confines of the two, asserting that both Plato's and Aristotle's views can be reestablished on a primordial sense of knowledge, the meaning of which is to be so fundamental and so radical that all forms and degrees of human knowledge can be reduced to it. There is some conception of this primordial sense of consciousness in the simplicity with which all applications of the word knowledge meet, like lines converging upon a common center. In other words, there must be an ontological foundation for both 'abstraction' and intellectual 'vision' so that all varieties of human awareness can flow from it.

Of course, we must admit that this method of philosophy was pioneered by "pagan" Neoplatonists starting with Plotinus and ending with Proclus in the West. They originated the notions of "emanation," "apprehension by presence," and "illumination," all of which served as steps toward Islamic philosophy's view of the ultimate ontological foundation of all knowledge. The Neoplatonists undoubtedly contributed significantly to the resolution of important problems in philosophy, and especially provided new insights into the problem of mystical knowledge and the apprehension of the One and Unity. Without this significant precedent, it would be hard to conceive that Islamic philosophy would have later been able to successfully systematize its approach.

In the philosophy of Dionysius, in particular, there exists a treatment of certain advanced principles of illumination that can facilitate the constitution of a philosophical system. Therefore, while it was Muslim thinkers who engaged in the systematization of the precepts of their predecessors, the principles of illumination utilized by them in their formulations—such as those based on the idea of emanation and the theory of knowledge by presence—were initated and developed exclusively by the Neoplatonists. However, the Neoplatonists were not, in general, concerned with the basic question posited here, namely, whether or not there are existential grounds for all modes of human apprehension and epistemology, that is, grounds for all modes of human knowledge. Is there common ground for the Platonic intellectual vision, Aristotelian abstract knowledge, knowledge of the self, sensory knowledge, and mystical knowledge? This earlier school of philosophy did not explicitly identify the primordial mode of knowledge with the very existential states of the reality of the self, although when encountering the problem of mysticism it touched the ground and spoke of a kind of knowledge by presence, as opposed to ordinary knowledge pertaining to the subject-object relation. Moreover, Neoplatonism did not characterize its understanding of knowledge by presence through the actual existential truth of mystical consciousness of the One that can occur in the human mind as an instantiation of knowledge by presence.[8] But in Islamic illuminative philosophy all these steps are manifestly present, making clear what is meant by knowledge by presence. Yet, the full understanding of knowledge by presence was predicated upon the historical unfolding of Islamic philosophy. The elaboration of the mainstream of the Islamic interpretation of Hellenic and Hellenistic philosophy eventually leads to the emergence of the illuminative system in Islamic philosophy, based on the logical truth of knowledge by presence. The very vicissitudes of this historical process itself provides an important insight into the examination of the concept of knowledge by presence.

Al-Fārābī's Theory of Divine Forms and God's Knowledge

Abū Naṣr al-Fārābī (ca. 870–950) is known as the Second Master and the greatest authority after Aristotle. His fame comes from having introduced the doctrine of the "Harmonization of the opinions of Plato and Aristotle," and he began his discourse with Plato's ideas concerning the necessity of placing such a harmonization at the very foundation of philosophy. Al-Fārābī believed that Aristotle had categorically rejected the existence of the Platonic Ideas, but that when Aristotle had reached the problem of theology and the notion of a "first cause" of the universe, he found himself faced with the difficult problem of the Divine Forms, the existence of which must be, beyond any doubt, presupposed in the Supreme Mind of the First Being. This kind of existence, of course, is characterized by all those descriptions given of the real being of Forms by Plato. Having understood Aristotle's predicament, al-Fārābī, in one of his famous tracts, described the manner in which the Aristotelian notion of "efficient cause" necessarily leads to the divine existence of Forms. He began his discourse by stipulating the principle of the "applicability" of all the univocal words such as "existence," "essence," or "living," to the Divine Reality. Al-Fārābī pointed out that the univocality of the meaning of these expressions can be preserved by considering variations in degrees of their meanings, rather than requiring uniformity or otherwise similarity in the observable references of these expressions. The fluctuation of exactness and "nobility" of a principle does not violate the essential unity of that principle. Thus, al-Fārābī concludes that existence, essence, living, or knowing can be equally applied to God as to other-than-God in the same sense, although they are true of God in the highest and noblest degree of the same sense, and of other-than-God in a lower one.

On the basis of this linguistic theory, al-Fārābī proceeded to explicate the central theses of his philosophy of the divine existence of the Forms in these words:

> Thus, we say, since God has been proved to be the living "cause" for the existence of this universe with all varieties of beings in it, it is therefore necessary for Him to hold in His Essence all those "Forms" that He is supposed to bring into the world of existence. If there were not in the essence of God these Forms as the patterns of existing things, then what would be the preexistence design of those which He brought into *real* existence? And in what order has He given effect to what He has brought into being?[9]

Concerning the problem of knowledge, al-Fārābī describes his opinion in the following manner:

> A Ring *(faṣṣ)*—The human soul is that which is capable of conceiving a meaning by definition and by understanding the pure reality of that meaning from which all extraneous accessories are shaken off and the sheer reality of it has remained as the common core, to the simplicity of which all variation of instances is reduced. This simplification has been made by a power commonly known as the "theoretical reason" *(al'aql al-naẓarī)*. This state of the soul is analogous to a mirror, and the theoretical reason is the power of the transparency of that mirror, and the intelligibles appearing in that mirror are reflections from the realities existing in the divine world; like the features of corporeal objects that reflect on the transparent surface of a

> mirror. This will be so if the soul's transparency has not been corrupted by nature or it has not happened that in the upward relationship of the soul that transparency has become blurred by some downward preoccupations such as passion and wrath.[10]

It must be stated at this juncture that al-Fārābī's theses on Plato's Ideas and the problem of human knowledge have been the subject of renowned criticisms throughout history, and especially by modern historians. Muhsin Mahdi, a characteristic critic of medieval Muslim philosophers in general and al-Fārābī in particular, writes,

> In many instances his (al-Fārābī's) conclusions depend upon one's accepting as genuine some documents of questionable authenticity, notably the extracts from *The Enneads* of Plotinus that gained currency in Islamic thought as *The Theology of Aristotle*.[11]

While the criticism is valid in principle, it does not hold in connection with the Forms and the intellectual vision of intelligibles. This is mainly because al-Fārābī's first argument concerning the problem of the Divine Ideas is based on the typical Aristotelian notion of the "first efficient cause."[12] However, this is not a reliance upon, or reference to, some extracts from Plotinus' *Enneads* as well as other sources. The fact that al-Fārābī made reference to the "Aristotelian theology" in this argument meant no more than a reference to the Aristotelian theological philosophy of the first efficient cause. It did not imply, at least in this particular place, that al-Fārābī's reference was made to the book of doubtful authorship called *The Theology of Aristotle*.

It is apparent that the cited historian's criticism of Islamic medieval philosophy is based on a confusion of the "use and mention distinction." Very often when Islamic philosophy used *The Theology of Aristotle*, it did not explicitly mention the "Book of Theology," but merely referred to the theological dimension of Aristotelian philosophy.

There are many other places in the works of Aristotle from which one can easily infer that in his philosophy there is an outstandingly theological dimension that allows one to call it the "theology of Aristotle." It was from the Aristotelian doctrine of efficient cause that Avicenna developed his renowned analysis of "emanation." It was out of the Aristotelian "final cause" and "ultimate perfection" in the *Ethics*[13] that Averroes and St. Thomas[14] developed the theory of "beatitude" and "ultimate felicity." Moreover, the famed Aristotelian notion of the "unmoved mover" served as a theological proposition in physics. All this accounts for the "theology of Aristotle" from which these medieval philosophers, both in the East and in the West, drew their ideas about the foundation of the universe and the problem of human knowledge.

It would seem that the philosophy of al-Fārābī, on the whole, attempts to propound these major themes. A systematic philosophy such as Aristotle's cannot confine itself to the limited scope of some particular philosophical problems related to physical objects and yet ignore others. Rather, the nature of the real and unchangeable being of the "intelligibles" in relation to the existence of sensible objects was considered in a logical unity in such a manner that any account of the truth of the one is consistent with the possibility of the truth of the other. Therefore, the order of 'knowledge', like the order of 'being', was described in a unity of causal connection such that just as a set of contingent consequent events implied a necessary antecedent of being, a contingent piece of human knowledge also presupposed a necessary antecedent intelligence behind it. All ostensible human intellectual acts and abstractions could not have more than a receptive part or preparatory role in the act of emanation by the Divine Forms on the transparent tablet of our potential intellect. Yet, such an intellectual act of emanation can possess no meaning except in terms of our prospective theory of knowledge by presence. We shall indicate that Aristotle has, though not explicitly, committed himself to the logical consequences of such an idea, and treated at least some of his metaphysical problems in the light of such an integral unity. The task of an interpreter such as al-Fārābī, however, is to understand the whole comprehensive structure of Aristotelian thought by himself, and to let the philosopher be understood by others regarding the manner of the completeness and consistency of his philosophy.

Avicenna's Theory of Human Knowledge

After al-Fārābī, his interesting philosophical thesis resonated in the thinking of other well-known Muslin philosophers who followed in his footsteps, introducing theories of human knowledge on the basis of a synthesis of the opinions of Plato and Aristotle. These syntheses were made in accordance with different principles and different degrees of reconciliation between the two traditional Hellenic ways of thinking.

Avicenna (Ibn Sīnā, d. 1037), for instance, on account of his renowned analysis of "emanation" *(qā'idat al-wāḥid)*,[15] argued that, while the Active Intellect remains itself in the order of separate being—transcendent, immutable, and absolutely incorruptible—it brings about in the human mind all forms of human knowledge from total potentiality into gradual actuality. In his commentary upon the Quranic "Light Verse" and analysis of the symbolism of this verse, Avicenna declared:

> "Parmi ses facultés, il y a ce qui lui appartient en fonction de son besoin de regir le corps, et c'est la faculté à laquelle est attribué particulièrement le nom d'intelligence practique. C'est celle qui, parmi les choses humaines particulières qui doivent être faites pour arriver aux fins choisies, decouvre les premisses indispensables, premiers principes, idées repandues, fruits de l'experience, ceci avec le secours de l'intelligence speculative, qui fournit l'opinion universelle par laquelle on passe à l'opinion particulière.
>
> "Parmi les facultés de l'âme, il y a aussi ce qu'elle possède pour autant qu'elle a besoin de parachever sa substance en (la rendant) intelligence en acte. La première est une faculté qui la prepare à se tourner vers les intelligibles, certains l'appellent intelligence materielle et elle est la niche. Celle-ci est suivie par une autre faculté qui vient à l'âme lors de la mise en acte en elle des premiers intelligibles. Par cette nouvelle faculté, (l'âme) se dispose à acquerir les seconds; soit par la reflexion, qui est l'olivier, si elle demeure faible, soit par l'intuition intellectuelle, qui est de plus l'huile, si l'intuition est plus forte que la reflexion; elle s'appelle intelligence *habitus* et elle est le verre. Et la faculté noble, murie, est une faculté sainte, 'dont l'huile est presque allumée'.
>
> Un peu plus tard, lui viennent en acte une faculté et une perfection. La perfection consiste en ce que les intelligibles lui sont donnés en acte, en une intuition qui les represente dans l'esprit, et c'est 'lumière sur lumière.' Et la faculté consiste en ceci qu'il lui appartient de realiser l'intelligible acquis, porte ainsi à son achèvement, comme est l'objet de l'intuition, des qu'elle le veut, sans avoir besoin de l'acquerir (à ce dernier instant), et c'est la lampe. Cette perfection s'appelle intelligence acquise, et cette faculté s'appelle intelligence en acte. Ce qui la fait passer de l'*habitus* à l'acte parfait, et aussi de l'intelligence materielle à l'*habitus*, c'est l'Intellect actif. Il est le feu.[16]

In this analysis, as is clearly established, the focus of the exegesis is to free the human mind altogether from possession of any kind of initial activity by attributing all intellectual operations to the separate Active Intellect. Avicenna, in quoting the Quranic expression, referred to this separate intellect as the "fire" *(nār)*. On this account, all that the human mind can and is designed to do is to prepare itself, through coordination of the powers of perception and apprehension, to receive its own proportionate degree of light from the fire. This proportion varies in degrees, so that the greatest intensity of light is the overabundant light bestowed upon a soul that enjoys the greatest degree of proximity to the fire; or, as in another Quranic expression in the "Light Verse" used by Avicenna: "light upon light" *(nūr 'alā nūr)*.[17]

Al-Ghazzālī's Treatise on Light

A philosophical interpretation of the aforementioned Quranic verse was, in fact, the critical factor that led the orthodox theological mind of al-Ghazzālī (1058–1111) to the light of mysticism. Under the influence of the rather mystical interpretation of the scriptural text, introduced by Avicenna, al-Ghazzālī developed a systematic approach to Sufism, reflected in his famous work *The Niche of Lights (Mishkāt al-anwār)*.[18]

Although defiant *vis-à-vis* the conclusions of the philosophers who preceded him, and especially critical of Avicenna, in his book, *Incoherence of the Philosophers*, al-Ghazzālī enthusiastically committed himself to the mystical implication of this Avicennian thesis of the "niche of lights." Based on the Avicennian theory, al-Ghazzālī developed a significant linguistic account of the expression 'light' veritably and literally applied to God as the source of lights, and to the existence of the universe as an emanative light, emerging from the Light of Lights.

Al-Ghazzālī's achievement in the *Incoherence* is for the most part semantic, for he is among the first philosophers, at least in the history of Islamic speculative thought, who distinguished the problem of using a word in its meaning with reference to its applications from the problem of using the word in its meaning without reference to its applications. At the stage of setting a standard meaning, there cannot be any reference to a particular application—empirical or transcendental. Since this is a stage of the registration of the relationship of words and meanings, there is no preference for one particular application of the word over another. It is only in the case of an application that the problem of reference arises.

Concerning the word 'light', it is, al-Ghazzālī states, "an expression for that which is by itself visible and makes other things visible, such as the sunlight. This is the definition of, and the reality concerning, light, according to its first signification."[19] Subsequent to delineating the standard meaning of the expression 'light', al-Ghazzālī further explicates that as regards the application of 'light' the only unquestionable and indubitable reference for the word is when applied to the One, which is by itself visible, and makes other things visible.

Other applications of 'light', including the physical light of our sight, are incomplete and involve many defects which make them far from being pure applications for the meaning of light. Al-Ghazzālī writes in this regard:

> If, then, there be such an Eye as is free from all these physical defects, would not it, I ask, more properly be given the name of light?[20]

It is clear that in Avicennian epistemology, as well as in the manner in which al-Fārābī deals with epistemological problems, there is no complete submission to the Platonic intellectual vision of the Ideas, nor is there absolute resignation to the Aristotelian theory of abstraction. Instead, as can be seen in al-Ghazzālī's formulations, there is a radical move to answer the question: If epistemology should presuppose, or correspond to, ontology, what might the ontological features of our intelligible universal objects be; and how and where do these universal objects exist? Philosophers often claim to know universal entities that are ostensibly universal, but different from individual physical objects. Should this be the case, a subsequent question can be posed: What is the nature of the being of these entities and how do they relate to our individual consciousness? Briefly put in metaphorical terms, a possible answer to these puzzling questions is that the human mind is like the niche of a light which, due to conjunction with an external transcendent fire, obtains illumination and reflects in itself whatever is given to it, and depending on the degree it can approximate the fire, it becomes closer to the source of light that is intellectual knowledge.

Whether or not this kind of metaphorical language is an adequate solution to the problem of intellectual knowledge is not the point at issue here insofar as we are dealing with the history of knowledge by presence. It must be further added that a metaphorical answer, such as the one discussed above, to such a fundamental question is really an oversimplification and does not do justice to the philosophy of human knowledge. However, the objective of our inquiry at this juncture is to present a well-documented survey of the historical background of the theory of knowledge by presence in Islamic thought. Once the central argument of the inquiry into this mode of knowledge is elucidated, this study will engage in a logical examination of the failure or success of the theory of apprehension in general, and the Islamic approach to a nonphenomenal or preepistemic awareness of the self in particular.

It is clear that both al-Fārābī and Avicenna, though profoundly affiliated with the Hellenic system of thought, have developed their ideas on the basis of the philosophies of Plato and Aristotle. Yet, the two Muslim philosophers' hypothesis of intellectual knowledge is founded on an emanation from, or unification with, separate entities. These entities are Divine Ideas or Forms that may be already present in the First Cause, according to al-Fārābī's analogy of the "mirror"; and as formal knowledge, they are identical with and present in the separate substance of the "Agent Intellect," in the terminology of Avicenna. Both al-Fārābī and Avicenna tried to impute their own theories to the Hellenic language of their master in philosophy—Aristotle. However, their approaches in this regard were different; one utilized the notion of the First Cause, and the other an interpretation of the Agent Intellect, two concepts which, beyond any doubt, are typically Aristotelian. It has therefore been understood that both of these medieval Muslim philosophers had gained some sense of knowledge by presence, although neither of them ever managed to present a thorough analysis of this fundamental concept.[21] Clearly, each of their two systems points to a peculiar identity of the knowing subject with the Divine Objects. However, the nature of the identity is open to question; a problem to be discussed only within the framework of our theory of knowledge by presence.

Averroes's Theory of Man's Ultimate Happiness

By the time Averroes (Ibn Rushd 1126–98), known to medieval Western philosophy as "the commentator of Aristotle" appeared, this general pattern of epistemology had gained more of an Aristotelian structure than a Platonic one. Both in his commentary on the *De Anima* and in his commentary on the *Metaphysics*, Averroes strongly advocated Aristotle's position concerning the distinction between the Agent Intellect (or Active Intellect) and human intellect. Averroes argued in this regard that the Agent Intellect is not part of the nature of the human intellect; rather, the latter is designed to set out from potency to act through the process of unification with the former as the exogenous source for the actualization of intellectual knowledge. What this unification implies and how the manner in which the nexus between the Agent Intellect—as a completely separate substance—and the human intellect—as a material, spatiotemporal one—can be understood, are questions to which Aristotle, according to Averroes's interpretation, does not address himself. Averroes, however, did seek to answer these questions, but failed to provide satisfactory responses. Instead, he merely resorted to establishing an analogy between "form-like" and "matter." Here, Averroes argued that the Agent Intellect, being a type of form, is united with the human possible intellect as its matter, forming what may be termed material intellect. On several occasions, Averroes presents his proposition in an emphatic manner, arguing that the independent Agent Intellect becomes united with the human material intellect making an existential union between form and matter. Averroes's thesis reflects the Aristotelian treatise on the problem of the "surviving soul" and "man's ultimate happiness."

In his long commentary on the *Metaphysics*, Averroes wrote: (*Comment* 17.d.)

> We, however, have already examined these two opinions in the book, *De Anima*, and we said that the agent intellect is, as it were, the "form" in the "material intellect." And that it brings about the intelligibles, and receives them at the same time, inasmuch as it is involved in the material intellect. And that the material intellect is generable and corruptible.[22] We have explicated there in the *Book De Anima* that this is the opinion of the philosopher, and that the habitual intellect has a generable part and a corruptible part. That which is corruptible is only its action, but the intellect in its essence which enters into us from the outside is not corruptible. For if it were generable, its emerging would be subject to the law of change and transmutation as considered in the essays of that science, *De Anima*, in the discussion of substance, where it was explained that: if something should emerge without transmutation, then something would come to being out of nothing. And therefore that intellect, which is in potency, is, as it were, the locus for this intellect which is in act, not as a matter for the subsisting form. If, however, the action of this intellect, that is, the Active or Agent Intellect, inasmuch as it is joined with the material intellect, were not generable, then its action would be identical with its substance and it would not have been compelled in this action to join and unite with the material intellect. But since it has in fact joined with and acted upon the material intellect, its action will be considered from the standpoint of something other than its substance being joined with it. And for that reason whatever action it achieves as a separate substance in us, it does not achieve for itself but for other than itself. Thus, it is possible that something eternal understand something generable and corruptible. Then if that intellect becomes free from potency at the time that human perfection reaches its climax, it is necessary that this action, which is considered as other than the substance of the intellect itself, be eliminated from it. And then at this time we are either not to understand this intellect at all, or we understand it such that its action is nothing other than its substance. And since it is impossible to say that

> in the state of final possible perfection we lose altogether our understanding of it, it therefore remains to be said that since this intellect becomes absolutely free from potency, we understand it inasmuch as its action, that is our understanding, is nothing but its substance. It is the ultimate felicity.[23]

How this analogy works, what its accurate interpretation is, and whether it really answers these questions—all must be understood within the scope of the theory of knowledge by presence and unity by emanation and absorption that will be developed in this study.

It appears that Averroes's argument, in its entirety, indicates how a peculiar relation of the corruptible and unseparate possible intellect to the Agent Intellect which, unlike the possible and habitual intellect, is absolutely incorruptible and wholly separate from human existence, is possible.

Reflection upon this proposition leads us to the consideration of a number of fundamental points, which are most significant for the purposes of this study. These points can be elucidated as follows: First, the Agent Intellect is analogous to a form for the material intellect functioning as its matter. This leads to a kind of unity between the two substances, material and immaterial, though the analogy is not strong enough to confirm such a projected unity. However, in point of fact, the material intellect is related to the Agent Intellect, as a locus or a stage to an unseen agent. Second, the Agent Intellect through its intellectual illumination comes to us from without *(dākhil 'alaynā min al-khārij)*; it is not originally a part of the human mind. Third, the highest possible degree of perfection in intellectual knowledge on the terrestrial realm is our understanding of the Agent Intellect; namely, our intellectual communication with intelligible objects, once our intellectual consciousness is no longer mediated by any intellectual contemplation and reflection on the Agent Intellect. Rather, our knowledge is achieved by an existential unification with the very substance of the Agent Intellect. In our interpretation, this unification can only be understood through a form of knowledge by presence which we shall call annihilation or absorption. Fourth, this "existential unitary awareness" is the mystical consciousness, which is not only philosophically possible in terms of knowledge by presence but is also attained through the ultimate felicity of human logical contemplation in this world. Fifth, this argument underlies Aristotle's belief in the survival of the human soul after death; for, if the ultimate unification is to be purely existential with no material potency involved, then no corruption or decomposition of the human body can ever have an impact on such a highly purified unification of the human soul with the Agent Intellect.

The interesting argument that led Averroes to this rather peculiar conclusion—"existentially unitary consciousness"—will be discussed later with a view to addressing the question: How can an individual soul become existentially united with the One or with the divine intelligible natures?

Now, for purposes of reference and analysis we shall summarize the pertinent arguments here: When our intellectual potentiality of contemplation and introspection is exhausted due to the actualization of the highest possible degree of intellectual perfection—a perfect self-realization—it means that there is no longer potentiality in reserve. When there is no "potency" there is no meaning for "act." The empirical operation, as well as the logical application, of the dichotomy of the "act–potency relationship" comes to an end. This is also given by the rule of the opposition of privation and aptitude, as will be demonstrated later. In view of what has been considered here, there is no meaning for "act," such that the notion of knowledge can no longer be accordingly interpreted as an "immanent act" of the human mind. In these circumstances, we should either be left absolutely ignorant, that is, knowing nothing of intelligible objects, or, on the grounds that we are in fact in the perfect condition of our knowing, we should be supposed to know better than ever.

The first supposition is impossible, because it is contrary to the state of intellectual perfection that we have just obtained. It remains therefore to be said that we, in these circumstances, know the intelligible substance. As a result of this knowledge, we know everything in the intelligible world, but not through mediation of the act of perception or conceptualization, and not even through vision and reflection or any kind of intentional representation, but only by unity with, or *presence* in, the reality of that Divine Substance. In fact this argument intitiates the discussion of the theory of knowledge by presence and its essential feature of self-objectivity.

At this stage of awareness, it should be pointed out that knowledge is no longer an intentional or transcendental phenomenon of mind, but rather it may be put forward as a kind of self-realization transcending representational knowledge, "reaching" the self-awareness of the reality of the self. This process takes place by virtue of an existential unification and not by an intellectual or phenomenal act of knowing. Other questions as well as a number of objections may be raised to this interpretation from different angles, but we shall consider their implications at a later time.

As has already been illustrated, the common feature in all of the three aforementioned Islamic approaches to the problem of intellectual knowledge is to pass through the Aristotelian sensory intelligence, arriving at a kind of Platonic vision. The preview of their careers extends further to incorporate a sense of knowing, which is essentially identical with the truth value of human personal identity.

Moreover, the principal position of the three philosophers discussed above is that they are all fully convinced that the Agent Intellect is divine and absolutely separate from our spatiotemporal existence and that the relation between such a Divine Being and our existence is established through illumination[24] in the sense of intentionally acquired intellectual knowledge, and as a consequence of union by absorption[25] in the sense of our self-realization, when the self is in some way united with the Divine Realities. This unity has been expressed through the analogy of a mirror, through the analogy of a niche of light and finally through the transubstantiation of man's material intellect into a Divine Being. This transubstantiation, according to Averroes, takes place through frequent unification of man's material intellect with the action of the separate substance that is illumination or emanation.[26]

This common feature continued to be the foundation of the whole structure of Islamic philosophy, eventually culminating in the complete system of the illuminative philosophy of Suhrawardī (1155–91) and later to the Islamic "existentialism" of Ṣadr al-Dīn Shīrāzī (Mullā Ṣadrā, d. 1640).

It may be added here that Averroes's commitment to the problem of "beatitude" and to unity by emanation and absorption does not contradict his critical stance against the Avicennian thesis of emanation. While in examining the descending order of existence in the world, Averroes categorically condemns this rather Platonistic theory of emanation as entirely non-Aristotelian, in the matter of human knowledge he appeals to an illuminative union of the human intellect with the divine Agent Intellect. This radical change of attitude is mostly due to the fact that the range of the overflowing of the light of existence from the simplicity of the First Cause to the multiplicity of the universe suggests a variation to the ascending process based on man's intellect progressing from the multiplicity of this world to the simplicity of the Divine Radiance.[27]

Averroes himself sheds light on his thinking. His explication is particularly instructive regarding the fact that despite his position on the problem of divine causality, he chose to reestablish the problem of human knowledge on the basis of the principle of the "illuminative" relation between human knowledge and the separate Agent Intellect. In his long commentary on the *Metaphysics*, Averroes writes:

> The reason that Aristotle has taken this move to bring forward the Agent Intellect separated from matter as the cause, not for all, but for the occurrence of our intellectual powers is the fact that in his opinion these intellectual powers are unrelated to matter. For that matter, it becomes obviously necessary that that which is not in some way associated with matter must come into existence from an absolutely separate and immaterial cause, in just the same way that those material objects must be generated from their material causes.[28]

This passage gives a clear account of Averroes's commitment to an instantiation of emanation that ultimately has been denoted by illuminative Muslim philosophers as knowledge by presence. From this passage, as well as from many other instances in the words of Averroes, it can be inferred that in principle, Averroes distinguished between divine causality and causation in the material realm. The final conclusion of Averroes in this regard is reflected in the statement that the cause for immaterial objects must be absolutely divine and immaterial—through emanation, while the causes for material things ought to be material ones—and by generation and corruption.

The Element of 'Irfān in the Theory of Knowledge by Presence

A fundamental factor in the plausibility and wide popularity of illuminative philosophy is the linguistic science of mystical apprehension (*'irfān*).[29] This science was pioneered and developed by Ibn al-'Arabī (1165–1240). As this study will show, *'irfān* is to be understood as the linguistic science of mystical apprehension, and the expression of mystical ways of experience both in the introvertive journey of ascent and the extrovertive process of descent. Attempts have been made to identify the science of *'irfān* as an independent science distinct from philosophy, theology, and religion. The great achievement of Ibn al-'Arabī in this new well-organized science was his famous doctrine of the absolute "oneness of existence"[30] (*waḥdat al-wujūd*). This doctrine is based upon the proposition that the whole reality of existence and that which really exists (*al-wujūd wa al-mawjūd*) are absolutely one and the same, and that all the multitude in the world of reality, whether they be sensory or intellectual, are merely "illusory": playing in our minds as the second image of an object plays in the eyes of a squint-eyed person. It is the opinion of this study that Ibn al-'Arabī's doctrine of the oneness of existence is neither pantheistic nor monotheistic, as interpreted by almost all scholars. Rather, this doctrine should be understood as *monorealistic,* adhering to the invariability and the strict sense of the unicity and oneness of the world of reality.[31] Through variegated types of mystical experiences by means of his invented device of a linguistic science called *'irfān,* Ibn al-'Arabī attempted to present the mystical truth of the doctrine of the oneness of existence and to outline its principles, problems, and consequences. Ibn al-'Arabī's successful explications of the fundamentals of this doctrine not only greatly influenced philosophical and theological circles but, in addition, brought forth an alternative pattern of life for the social and political structure of Muslim communities.

Later on this mystical version of the ontology of the world of reality also influenced profoundly the philosophical principles of the Islamic philosophy of existence (existentialism), although there is undoubtedly a great difference between such a purely mystical monorealistic view and the philosophical approach to the characteristic "unity-in-difference" and "difference-in-unity" of the notion of existence proposed by Ṣadr al-Dīn Shīrāzī.

To return to the topic of the historical background of illuminative knowledge, reflection upon the early interpretations of the Aristotelian ideas of the Agent Intellect and the efficient cause, as well as those of mystical considerations, seems to suffice in leading to the conclusion with which this study is concerned. For the growing importance of illuminative knowledge was due to the common involvement of these aforementioned philosophers in approaching the problem of human intelligence in connection with divine intelligence.

On the basis of this system of philosophy of knowledge, it is not a mere arbitrary judgment on the part of theoretical reason to prove or disprove the hypothesis of mysticism and the truth or falsity of its paradoxical statements, but it is entirely reasonable to undertake an analytical approach to the problem of mysticism. Moreover, it is not philosophically unwarranted to deal with the question of the self and personal identity, as well as with the most private relation of the self to its sensation, its faculties of apprehension, and its body. All this is logically available in principle through knowledge by presence.

The Illuminative Account of Knowledge by Presence

While Averroes was driven ultimately toward a kind of knowledge by existential unification with the divine separate substances, he did not succeed in giving a complete account of the theory of knowledge by presence. A philosophical account of "presential knowledge" *(al-'ilm al-ḥuḍūrī)* appeared for the first time in the history of the Islamic tradition in illuminative philosophy, the chief exponent of which was Shihāb al-Dīn Suhrawardī (Shaykh al-Ishrāq) (1155–91). Also important in this regard was Naṣīr al-Dīn Ṭūsī (d. 1274), whose great achievement concerning knowledge by presence centers upon the problem of God's knowledge of Himself and His knowledge of the universe. In his commentary on Avicenna's emanationism, Ṭūsī's main concern was to account for the question: How does God as the Necessary Being, who is also necessary in His act and His knowledge, know His emanation? Suhrawardī believed that one cannot make any inquiry into the knowledge of others who are beyond the reality of one's own self before getting deeply into the knowledge of one's selfhood which is nothing other than knowledge by presence.

In his dream of Aristotle, Suhrawardī's opening remark was his complaint about the great difficulty that had been puzzling him for a long time concerning the problem of human knowledge. The only solution that Aristotle taught him in this mystical trance was: "Think of yourself before thinking of anything else. If you do so, you will then find that the very selfhood of yourself helps you solve your problem."[32] However, Suhrawardī's illuminative philosophy was based entirely upon the dimension of human knowledge that is identical with the very ontological status of being human. He furnished the foundation of our intellectual consciousness as well as our sensory experience with a profound philosophical analysis of "knowledge by presence." The word "presence" or "awareness-by-presence" appeared, with great frequency, in the works of Plotinus, and, for that matter, in other Neoplatonic philosophical expositions. Why this form of awareness should have a seat in the very reality of an individual self in the first place is, however, a question that was not explicitly probed in the Neoplatonic philosophical corpus.

The primary question with which Suhrawardi began his inquiry was: What is the objective reference of 'I' when used in an ordinary statement like "I think so-and-so," or "I do this-and-that?" Suhrawardī's doctrine of knowledge by presence was marked by the intrinsic characteristic of "self objectivity," whether in mysticism or in other manifestations of this knowledge. For the essential nature of this knowledge is that the reality of awareness and that of which the self is aware are existentially one and the same. Taking the hypothesis of self-awareness as an example, he posited that the self must be absolutely aware of itself without the interposition of a representation. Any representation of the self, empirical or transcendental, must necessarily render the hypothesis of self-awareness contradictory. It is, rather, by the very presence of the very reality of the self that the self is aware of itself in absolute terms. Consequently, the self and awareness of the self are individually and numerically a simple single entity. This train of thinking arrived directly, and inevitably, at the very notion of the self-objectivity of knowledge by presence. Self-objectivity, however, is the chief characteristic of the theory of knowledge by presence discussed in this study, to be distinguished from any other species of human knowledge.[33]

The Islamic Philosophy of Existence (Existentialism)

Long after Suhrawardī, the history of this philosophical tradition, proceeding in the same direction, gave rise to another achievement that was as fundamental as the previous one. This was the rise of an Islamic type of "existentialist" philosophy, formally called *aṣālat al-wujūd*. The founder of this school of philosophy was Ṣadr al-Dīn Shīrāzī (Mullā Ṣadrā), who called his methodology of thinking "metaphilosophy" *(al-ḥikmat al-muta'āliyah)*.[34]

The basic nature of the metaphilosophy of Mullā Ṣadrā was that it provided a metalinguistic method in philosophy by the use of which independent decisions on the validity and soundness of all philosophical issues and logical questions—be they Platonic, Aristotelian, Neoplatonic, mystical, or religious—may be made. The process of decision making can be implemented without becoming involved in the particularities of each of these systems. Mullā Ṣadrā's first attempt was to give a primordial, immediate, and univocal meaning to the word "existence."[35] By this he meant to assert that the concept of existence can absorb and accommodate in itself all forms and degrees of reality in general, and overcome the Platonic distinction between 'being' and 'becoming' in particular. Accordingly, the word existence is equivalent to the world "reality," and is applied to the existence of God with the same univocal meaning as when applied to the existence of any phenomenal object. In Mullā Ṣadrā's opinion there was no good reason for separating the order of being from the order of intelligence, or from any kind of knowing. In brief, anything that comes out of absolute nothingness into a degree of realization—no matter how weak it may be, or which *is*, from eternity, in the world of reality, is truly to be considered as an existence. Existence, therefore, is absolutely immediate and a most applicable concept.[36]

This univocity of existence in the philosophy of Mullā Ṣadrā is what makes up the innermost feature of that concept. On the outermost of the same concept, there is nothing but gradation and variation of the same sense of univocity for the sufficient reason that this outermost variation belongs to the very innermost univocity; it does not therefore jeopardize the univocal application of existence. In this sense existence is true of appearances as well as realities and "unseen" entities or separate substances, should they, in themselves, really exist. The light of this existence is so luminous and so radiant that it sheds light on everything, even on its own denial and negation. To cite an example, when someone in his imagination is thinking of "nothingness" as a mental entity, this phenomenon of nothingness is a true instantiation of the most comprehensive concept of existence. The phenomenon of nothingness is thus a form of existence belonging to the world of reality.[37]

What has been discussed thus far constitutes the matter of the historical background of the theory of knowledge by presence, and its immediate consequences, such as self-objectivity. The aim of this historical presentation has been to show that there is no contradiction when we arrive at the basic ontological reality of awareness, where the existential truth of the knower and his "unitary consciousness," and the thing known, are united. This existential truth, which will be discussed fully later on, may be considered as the objective reference of this particular type of awareness, as well as awareness itself. Also, this historical survey confirms the fact that it is not only the philosophy of mysticism that leads us to the logic of self-objectivity, but that the very nature of the philosophy of the self as well as any approach to the metaphysical theory of human knowledge will also lead us to the position where we must ask the question: How can a form of knowledge by presence be a necessity in philosophy, and how does its self-objectivity underlie all our phenomenal knowledge? Therefore, the concept of the self-objectivity of presential knowledge must be made subject to exacting consideration and systematic analysis.

Two

Immanent Object and Transitive Object

The Meaning of Immanent Object

If it is by any means justified or plausible for the Aristotelian understanding of 'intentionality'[1] to distinguish two kinds of human action, 'immanent action' and 'transitive action', then nothing, it seems, can prevent us from taking a similar line, distinguishing two kinds of corresponding objects, 'immanent object' and 'transitive object'.

This distinction is not based on any arbitrary identification of the renowned Aristotelian account of the two different actions with our provisional distinction between two systems of objectivity. We understand *prima facie*, that such an unwarranted identification is not admissible, since an action, be it immanent or transitive, can never be applied to the objects of that action. Yet, it is certain that an immanent action such as our knowledge can quite logically be analyzed into a knowing subject and the object known. As such, the anatomy of the object known is in turn analyzable into an internal and external object. When our analysis arrives at this stage, we may, beyond any doubt, feel entitled to legitimately characterize the internal object as immanent object and the external object as transitive object.

Turning to the analysis of the concept of knowledge itself, among various distinctions which have so far been made regarding the notion of human knowledge, the distinction between 'subject' and 'object' is the most widely accepted one. Given this antecedent, one of its logical consequences would be the development of another distinction already made by some philosophers between 'subjective object' and 'objective object',[2] or in our terminology, 'immanent object' and 'transitive object'.[3] It is with this latter distinction that we are concerned here. Those who are unfamiliar with philosophical speculation may be inclined to dismiss such a distinction; yet reflection on the very concept of knowledge itself proves that there must be an immanent object as distinct from the transitive object.

In the analysis of the theory of knowledge, the term "subject" signifies the mind that performs the act of knowledge through knowing something, just as the term "object" refers to the thing or the proposition known by that subject. However, since in a known proposition there is always something involved, be it particular or universal, it is consequently true to say that the object of knowledge is always what we call the thing known. It is also observed that because the relation called knowing is constituted by the mind as the subject associated with the thing as the object, both of which are knitted together into one complex whole, the subject and the object are to be called the constituents of the unity of knowledge. The terms "subject" and "object" are two essentialities of the unity of knowledge.

Intentional by its essence, the act of knowing is always motivated, determined, and constituted by its object. The object therefore has a share, together with the subject, in the organization and determination of the act of knowing,[4] but differs from the subject by having a unique role in motivating the act of knowing. Therefore, whereas the main characteristic of the object is to motivate the action of the subject, the subject, on the other hand, cannot take part in the procedure of motivating its own intentional act, for the simple reason that one who is ever present to himself cannot be the object of himself. In other words, the mind is designed to serve as the efficient cause for the intentional act of knowing something, and the object serves as the final cause for the completion of such an action. The efficient cause is not supposed to be absolutely identified with the final cause in the Aristotelian system of causation. Thus, a subject cannot be identical with its object.

Putting the subject-object relationship within the context of the Aristotelian system of causation, one can further infer another characteristic distinction between the knowing subject as an efficient cause and the thing known as a final cause for the act of knowledge. While the efficient cause is defined as the acting agent, that is, that which brings about the act of knowing,[5] the final cause functions in two different ways depending on its external and internal existence.[6] The external existence of the object, being *prima facie* independent and absent from the mind, can only motivate the intellectual activity of the subject from outside and cannot be identified with it. But the mental existence of the same object being present in the mind is the cause of the subject's causality. That is to say, the knowing subject as the efficient cause is in its turn caused and actuated by the mental image of the object in the operation of the act of knowledge. For it is the idea of the object that first effectuates the potential causation of the subject by bringing it from the state of potentiality to the state of being an actual agent. Had the idea of the object not been present in the mind of the knowing subject, the potential subject would never come to the act of knowing at all. Therefore, in this sequence of causation the idea of the object comes first, and is regarded as the prime cause or the cause of causation in the system of causality. And the objective reality of the same thing constitutes the last and final cause of the immanent act of knowledge. In this sense it is not surprising that one thing stands at the same time for the first and the final cause when viewed from different perspectives. While the mental representation of that reality is the first and the prime cause of knowing, its objective reality is the last and the final one.[7]

The Double Sense of Objectivity

In accordance with the above analysis, we can legitimately suggest a double sense of objectivity that characterizes a single entity as both an immanent and a transitive object. As has already been elucidated, the immanent object comes first, and counts for a mental representation of the thing known. This is the mere idea of the object manifested by the subject in the subject itself. This mental representation stimulates the intellectual power of the subject by driving it into the act of knowing. From this standpoint, the idea of the object has priority over all the other causes in question, because it takes effect before the other causes can do so. The transitive object, on the other hand, comes last because it is the prospective reality of that ideal object. Since the transitive object is not present in the mind of the agent, it naturally lies beyond the frame of his mind, as well as beyond the intellectual existence of the immanent object.[8]

All this is the case if one interprets the intentional epistemic act of knowing as a mental sequence of natural events analogous to a set of external events dominated by the law of causation. When, however, an act of knowing occurs, there is a complex unity in which knowing is the uniting relation, and the subject and object are arranged in a certain order such that the sense of the act of knowing governs over the whole as a form of unifier. In this structure both of the two terms—the subject and the object—function as bricks, and not as cement. This cement is the uniting relation itself, that is, knowing.

This threefold theory of knowledge, namely, the subject as the knower, the object as the thing known, and the relation among them as knowing, accounts for the whole constitution of the intentional act of knowledge. Just as the complex whole of the relation is characterized by being immanent and intentional, so also each and every part of it has the character of immanence and intentionality. Thus, from this point of view it follows that there must be an immanent object essential to the very structure of our knowledge apart from the object that lies independently outside of our mind and has no identical relationship with our knowledge.

Cunningham[9] elaborates upon this kind of object, the immanent one, and shows how minds are bound together and are never separate in their phenomenal status:

> . . . the objective reference of judgement means that, in the act of knowing, mind and object are bound together and are not separate and distinct. Knowledge, then, is primarily a relation between mind and objects, and exists only when that relation exists. No object, then no judgement; no judgement, then no knowledge.[10]

Ducasse[11] has quite clearly and accurately developed this idea by placing it within a dualistic sense of objectivity. Thus:

> The comment suggests itself here, however, that if with Cunningham we say that whatever the mind knows is an object, then we are forced to distinguish between what might be called, "subjective objects" (viz., states of mind, such as our feelings called pain, or nausea, or our conception of Julius Caesar, or of the seventh decimal of, etc.) and "objective objects" (such as Julius Caesar himself, or the seventh decimal of itself etc.)
>
> The relation of the mind to "subjective objects" perhaps constitutes no problem, but the mind's relation to "objective objects" is in any case a radically different one and is specifically the subject under consideration when "objective reference" is discussed.[12]

The prominent point of this discussion is that the term object in relation to knowing has to be understood in two different ways: one is that which is immediate, immanent, and identical with the existence of the knowing subject; and the other is that which is transitive and independent, the existence of which lies outside of, and is exterior to, the existence of the subject. The former is that which has been quite accurately marked by Ducasse as "subjective object" and the latter as "objective object."

The distinction between subjective objects and objective objects does not merely serve to show how these two kinds of objects are bound together, providing a communion between the external and internal worlds of existence. In addition, the distinction enables us to understand that in our knowledge of the external world there is always an essentiality combined with a sense of probability in the relation between these two kinds of objects. The essentiality is that of the subjective objects, and is understood by the very definition of the notion of knowledge. The probability is that of the objective object. They both have to join together in order to make up our knowledge of external objects. Probability here means that those objective objects may or may not truly correspond to the subjective objects. Probability, however, characterizes our phenomenal knowledge.[13]

Double Objectivity is Characteristic of Phenomenal Knowledge

The double sense of objectivity, however, is the essential feature of our phenomenal knowledge, or in Kantian terminology, "discursive knowledge," be it perceptual or conceptual, empirical or transcendental. That which the mind immanently possesses—representation—is the necessary subjective object, such as our conception of Julius Caesar or the conception of the seventh decimal of, but not necessarily an objective object such as Julius Caesar himself, or the seventh decimal of itself. In the case of sense perception, if I perceive of a physical object, for instance, the shape of a television set, there are two objective entities to be distinguished from each other. There is on the one hand an external object existing independently outside of my mind, the reality of which belongs to the reality of the external world, and has nothing to do with the constitution of this episode of my perceiving. This is the objective object which is the physical reality of the shape of my television set itself regardless of my perception of it.

On the other hand, corresponding to this, there is also an object that is present in and identical with the existence of my perceiving power. This is the subjective object that constitutes the essence of my immanent act of perceiving, the reality of which belongs to the reality of my perception. The relation of knowing or perceiving, however, with regard to the objective object is accidental and with regard to the subjective object, essential.[14] The former relation is accidental because the external object as an independent existence lies outside of my mental power and is exterior to it. It is only the matter of the coaccidentality of the existence of our mind along with its knowledge and the existence of the objective object that brings them together in the unity of the act of knowing. But, in the very definition of knowledge as such, the subjective object is necessary and essential, because insofar as the relation of knowing is concerned, it is impossible to have an act of this kind without having, or even with a possibility of having, a subjective object. But there is no absurdity in having an act of this kind while having no objective object in the external world. Thus, it makes perfect sense to say that the subjective object is the constitutive given in the essence of the notion of knowledge as such, but the objective object is accidental, lying outside of the conception of knowledge in the extramental world and serving as the final cause in the factual case of our knowledge of an external object.

Conformity in the Sense of Correspondence

This is all very well, so far as preliminary remarks to our prospective theory of "correspondence" knowledge are concerned. Yet, we should assert that the Aristotelian conception of "causation" as interpreted here does not necessarily establish another theory of "conformity" as opposed to the theory of "correspondence," a conformity in the sense of identity of the thing as an external object with the thing as a mental entity which then appears to us. Taking an external object as the independent reality of the final cause, and its mental image as the internal one, there is no possibility of any kind of identity of one of these two entirely different types of existence with each other. Therefore, no matter how strongly this Aristotelian notion of causality has to be interpreted, it can never bring us to a sense of conformity, which ends in some kind of identity between things in themselves and things as known to us. The meaning of correspondence, therefore, is inevitably taken as a negation of the idea "identity," and thus the notion of conformity, regardless of what it may be attributed to, can only be construed as something closer to correspondence than to identity.

Therefore, we are not challenging the focal point of the renowned Aristotelian[15] thesis of identity of the understanding and the thing understood: *idem est intellectus et intellectum*, the intellect and what is understood are identical.[16] On the contrary, we are quite willing to legitimately interpret it in such a way that it can stand up to Kant's devastating criticism of the idea of conformity in the sense of identity. In this regard, Kant said:

> If, then, on the supposition that our empirical knowledge "conforms" to objects as "things in themselves", we find that the unconditioned cannot be thought without contradiction, and that when, on the other hand, we suppose that our representation of things, as they are given to us, does not conform to these things as they are in themselves, but that these objects, as appearances, conform to our mode of representation, the contradiction vanishes. . . .[17]

It seems obvious to me that the whole weight of this Kantian argument hinges upon the point that should things in themselves ever be conformed to or identified with—things as they are given to us—there would be a flat contradiction. Succinctly put, if the transitive, independent, external object becomes, in the case of knowledge, existentially identical with the immanent object totally dependent on our mind, then that is a precise contradiction. The only answer to this contradiction, it seems, would be: firstly, the conformity between external and internal objects should not be understood as any form of existential identity, but rather as a correspondence relation of the immanent object to the transitive object; secondly, the Aristotelian thesis of identity, quite possibly, calls for a strong sense of the existential identity of the act of understanding with the immanent object being understood essentially, and not with the transitive object being understood only accidentally.

Looking at the matter in its totality, we have so far reached the conclusion that even in our ordinary knowledge, which we call phenomenal knowledge, there are inevitably two senses of objectivity; one is the immanent object, and the other the transitive object. On the other hand, in our conception of knowledge by presence there is only one sense of objectivity and that is solely the immanent object.

What Kind of Object is Involved in the Concept of Knowledge?

A further account of the dualistic sense of objectivity requires the presentation of an analysis of the proposition usually given, when one has ordinary phenomenal knowledge of an external object, the kind of knowledge that we will later call knowledge by correspondence.

Suppose we have a prime statement:

A. S knows P

As this prime statement stands, it is analyzable into three analytic substatements, each of which describes a constituent component of the essence of knowing. These are:

a. S is the subject who knows P.
b. P is the object which is known by S.
c. The act of knowing P has been operated by S.

The fact that the prime statement logically implies all three statements means that substatement b like a and c is essential to statement A such that if one posits statement A and denies substatement b in a logical conjunction, one will commit oneself to a flat contradiction.

The conjunction would be:

A_1. "S knows P" and "it is not the case that P is the object known by S."
Given this supposition, the conjunct:
"it is not the case that P is the object known by S" is equivalent to the statement:
"it is not the case that P exists in S's mind" which is certainly equal to:
"it is not the case that S knows P," and we reach the conclusion that:

A_2. "S knows P" and "it is not the case that S knows P."

Since the denial of substatement b leads to this contradiction, it follows that the denial of this denial is the case. Thus, it is the case that b is a necessary truth of the prime statement. Thus P, as it stands for the subjective object in the definition of the relation 'knowing', is a logical component of this relationship, and as contained in that relation, is an essential object and not an accidental object.

All this points to the intrinsic immanent object called the subjective object in the relation of knowing. Yet, the above analysis does not hold when the objective object is considered. That is because if we substitute objective objects for subjective objects and take:

B. S knows P

as our prime statement where by P we mean an independent existence such as a physical object, say a table, it is also analyzable into three statements as follows:

d. S is the subject who knows P,
e. P is an external object which is known by S,
f. The act of knowing P is initiated by S.

But, contrary to the former case, we do not get a logical contradiction if we posit the prime statement B, and deny substatement e in the following conjunction:

> B_1. "S knows P," and "it is not the case that P is really an external object known by S."

The reason that B_1 is not inconsistent is that one can quite possibly be informed that S eventually knows P, while one disagrees with S that P is the case. Succinctly put, it is not a self-defeating question to ask:

> B_2. "S knows P," but, "is P really the case that is known by S?"

On the contrary, it seems to be an open question as to whether a certain external object exists, even though we know with certainty that S believes that such an object does exist. Thus, we do have two senses of objectivity—essential and accidental.

For these two fundamentally different senses of 'object', one of the leading figures in Islamic philosophy, Ṣadr al-Dīn Shīrāzī, uses the terms "essential," "actual intelligibles," and "accidental intelligibles" in the case of transcendental knowledge, as well as the words "essential," "actual sensibles," and "accidental sensibles" in the case of empirical knowledge. He wrote:

> The forms of things are of two kinds, one is the material form the existence of which is associated with matter and position and is spatiotemporal. With respect to its material condition placed beyond our mental power, this kind of form cannot possibly be "actually [and immanently] intelligible," nor for that matter "actually [and immanently] sensible" except by "accident." And the other is a form which is free and separate from matter, from position, and from space and location. The separation is by a complete abstraction, like an "actual intelligible," or by incomplete abstraction such as "actual imaginables" and "actual sensible objects."[18]

In this passage there are apparently two fundamentally important dichotomies involved. First is the actual or essential intelligible object versus the accidental or material one. The other is the actual imaginable or sensible object, distinguished from the accidental or material one. In both dichotomies the first range of object is characterized by actuality and essentiality, and the second by materiality and accidentality. An object is said to be "essentially and actually intelligible" only if it is existentially identified with, and present in the mind as being a constituent of the mental phenomenon of the act of knowing. The object is believed to be "actually sensible" or "actually imaginable" when it becomes part of our sensation or imagination in act. But when the object lies existentially beyond our intellect or beyond our sense-perception and imagination, then it has an exterior relation of correspondence with its representation in our mind. It will be very much an aspect of chance and accidentality that characterizes the appearance of the material object represented in our mind at the time we imagine it or sense it in a sense-perception. This means that there is no logical certainty such that the correspondence relation must hold up, for there is always room for the logical possibility that S's knowledge of P does not turn out to be true. Thus, it seems fairly acceptable to say that since the correspondence of the mental object to the material object is accidental, the material object should be called an "accidental object." In effect, accidentality here means the probability that scientific truth always involves.

Man possesses, accordingly, "essential intelligible" as well as "essential sensible" faculties, both of which are referred to, in Ducasse's terminology, as "subjective object," and in our terminology, as "immanent object." Likewise, humans have "accidental intelligible objects," as well as "accidental sensible objects," both of which Ducasse might refer to as "objective object" if he could come to consider the matter metaphysically; we have called these accidental objects "transitive" and "absent" objects. It is the assertion of this study that, of these two major kinds of objects, the immanent and the transitive, the immanent object alone is constitutive of and essential to the theory of knowledge *qua* knowledge.

Double Objectivity of Sense-Data

It is not just the analysis of the double sense of objectivity that is based on the theory of correspondence. The Russellian thesis of "sense-data" also involves the same theory of double objectivity, though Russell himself may not admit such an implication. This suggestion, however, becomes clear when he contends that there must be a correspondence relation between the sense-data and the independent existence of the physical object perceived. When there is a correspondence, there is double objectivity. Bertrand Russell wrote:

> On the matter of sense-data, we have seen that, even if physical objects do have an independent existence, they must differ very widely from sense-data, and can only have a correspondence with sense-data, in the same sort of way in which a catalogue has correspondence with the things catalogued.[19]

Russell is by no means prepared to further admit that there is an implication to be considered in the very notion of correspondence. The implication is that if there are supposedly physical objects the existence of which is independent from sense-data, they are inevitably entitled to be objective objects corresponding to the mental entities that are to be called subjective objects, or as Russell puts it, sense-data. If physical objects enjoy correspondence with sense-data in the same sort of way in which a catalogue has correspondence with the things catalogued, then on both sides of the correspondence relation there should be corresponding objects so that the diadic correspondence relationship can make sense. This is a logical implication.

Just as on the one side of the relation there are some physical objects that can be objective objects, there should also be, on the other side of that relation, some mental objects which are to be regarded as subjective objects. It is evidently true that a catalogue, in order to make sense at all, must subjectively hold a sense of objectivity of the things it has catalogued, relating the latter to the objects that constitute the former. But, as is evident, Russell is reluctant to accept, in any case, that there are any mental or subjective objects at all. He describes the matter in this way:

> There is on the one hand the thing of which we are aware, say the colour of my table, and on the other hand the actual awareness itself, the mental act of apprehending the thing. The mental act is undoubtedly mental, but is there any reason to suppose that the thing apprehended is in any sense mental?[20]

If the sense-data are not to be mental objects, one wonders what else they ought to be.

To return to the system of illuminative philosophy, we must now discuss why all physical objects that are existentially independent of our mind are treated in that system as "absent objects" as opposed to "present objects." Considering the existence of physical objects as entirely independent from and unaffected by our mental act of knowing, the point becomes clear that the nature of such an existence always lies beyond the radiance of our existential mentality, and is never identical with it. This state of "independence," "unaffectedness," and "beyondness" is expressed by illuminative philosophy as the state of "absence," and the objects belonging to this state as "absent objects." This deals with the word "absence." As for the word "presence," illuminative philosophy has, on the same basis, taken it to mean the condition of identification of the existence of the mind with the existence of its mental acts and mental entities. Those entities presented under the condition of identity in the mind of the knowing subject are marked as "present objects." "Presence" therefore, in a positive sense has a connotation similar to the meaning of "identity" in existence with the mind, just as the word "absence" signifies the sense of difference in existence from the existence of the mind. In a negative sense, "present objects" are those objects which are not absent from the existential radiance of the mind.

For so long as we maintain the viewpoint of the pure terminology of illuminative philosophy, there will seem little or no difference between illuminative philosophy and Ducasse's empirical approach to the double sense of objectivity. It should be noted, however, that there exists a further step in the above mentioned subject in which Ṣadr al-Dīn Ṣhīrāzī's (Mullā Ṣadrā) analysis goes much deeper than Ducasse's. This is the expansion of essential subjective objects from being restricted to mere sense-impressions as the objects of sense-experience, on which both of them agree, to intelligible transcendental objects that appear only in Mullā Ṣadrā's philosophy of existence. It seems quite obvious that, as an empiricist philosopher, Ducasse did not appear obligated to take a further step on the matter of transcendental objects, these being far beyond Ducasse's scope of sense-impressions and his subjective objects. But in Mullā Ṣadrā's system of philosophy, the distinction between essential and accidental objects is primarily designed to apply to all kinds of epistemic acts, be they empirical or transcendental, that is, the transcendental understanding of intelligible objects. "Intelligibles," said Ṣhīrāzī's, "are actual objects of our mind, the kind of objects that are completely free from matter and essential to the intellectual act of knowing."[21]

Transitive Objects Are Absent Objects

From all this we are now able to understand how these circumstances justify suppositions by illuminative-oriented thinkers, such as Mullā Ṣadrā, who asserted that things belonging to the order of the external world are to be held as absent objects as opposed to present objects. These external objects are not, in a true sense, present to, and identified with, us in the order of being, but their conceptions and representations are. Mullā Ṣadrā wrote in this regard:

> A treatise on the theory that the knowledge of these objects whose existences are absent from us is possible only through the intermediary of the representations of these objects in us.[22]

In his opinion, however, it would be absurd if the objective reality of these objects were ever present to our mind such that an external object became totally internal, and an independent existence fell from its order of being to the order of conception subsisting in the state of our mentality. Yet, in this philosophers's view, we can, nevertheless, achieve communication with these absent objects only by virtue of having perceptual or conceptual representations of them in our mind. These representations belong originally to us and have been raised and set up by our intellectual power.

Let us sum up the discussion of the distinction between immanent and transitive objects. Objects of our knowledge are to be understood as being two kinds: (a) immanent, intrinsic, and necessary objects constituent of the act of the knowing subject; and (b) transitive, extrinsic, and accidental objects absent from the mind and extraneous to the act of knowledge. The relation of these two distinct objects is through correspondence, and not identity.

The immanent object being free from association with matter can be exemplified as sensible, imaginable, and most transcendentally intelligible, depending on the degree of the abstract knowledge and our mental power of apprehension. In this project even an immanent sensible object in our empirical knowledge enjoys a primitive degree of abstraction and transcendentality because it is free from matter. That is, it subsists not in matter, but in mind.

The transitive object, on the other hand, is an external, material, or immaterial form of the object, which is existentially independent of and separate from the state of our mentality and has no susceptibility to any degree of abstraction. In the case of a material object, it is associated with matter, space, and time. Moreover, in the instance of a nonmaterial object, if there be any, it stands by itself with no passive relation to matter, space, or time. These transitive objects can be communicated with only through initiating representations of them in our mind. These representations, therefore, being in the order of conception, are to be regarded as immanent objects proper, and those which have been represented by them—the existence of which has remained in the order of being—are to be held as transitive and accidental objects.

Finally, one should notice that on the matter of subjective essential objects, which we have just characterized as being free from matter, the question as to whether they are free, hence, "abstract," or essentially free, hence, "innate," can easily be decided. Although it does not principally concern us, we have already indicated that "abstraction" is not to be taken to mean another intentional act added to the act of knowing, perceiving, or conceiving. Rather, it is none other than the act of knowing itself, such that even in its primitive form it represents the pure form of the material object through sense-experience. Abstraction, therefore, is not to be construed as the sum of perceiving the whole material object, then separating its form from the matter keeping the form in the mind, and leaving the matter in the external world. The subjective power of knowing does not, and cannot, import anything from outside of itself. It is rather the innate power of representation of the pure forms of things that makes the simple essence of our knowledge possible. On this illuminative basis, all kinds of our knowledge enjoy a proportionate degree of transcendentality. An empirical sense-perception, for instance, because of being a sense-representation of the pure form of a physical object, counts as an imperfect primitive form of the transcendental object.[23] The existential status of a sense-perception can never be classified as a material object; it is, rather, an immaterial entity that represents the pure form of the material object. It stands for the form of that material object without having its external matter.

Conclusion

In all this we have been dealing with the following fundamental point: the analysis of the notion of knowledge logically implies that since the object is nothing but the immanent and essential, the meaning of the objectivity of this object is, as we have just shown, analytic and manifested in the very constitution of knowing. The transitive object, on the other hand, being on the whole accidental, does not constitute the essential core of human consciousness. The transitive object is thus constitutive only when the knowledge of an external object is in question. This is a particular species of knowledge that we shall in our terminology call "knowledge by correspondence" as opposed to "knowledge by presence." However, in the primordial form of knowledge that is knowledge by presence, and all the more in the theory of knowledge, the external transitive object does not serve as a constituent part of the general concept of knowledge at all. From all this it follows conclusively that our prospective notion of knowledge by presence, as characterized by self-objectivity, is truly and necessarily accounted for by the basic form of knowledge, without having an external physical object corresponding to the essential present object. Knowledge by presence, however, is literally subsumed, as the prime example, in the category of knowledge as such, because it is noetic and objective by its nature and it satisfies all essential conditions of the conception of knowledge, although it has no transitive accidental object. Thus, there is no reason to deny a sense of objectivity for this kind of knowledge simply because it possesses no extraneous object. Likewise, there is no reason to call for a kind of transubjectivity[24] in mystical apprehension which is, as we shall see, a species of knowledge by presence. Succinctly put, knowledge by presence is literally called knowledge by presence, because it is marked by being noetic and having an immanent object that makes it a self-object-knowledge, adequate to the definition of knowledge as such with no need for a corresponding transitive object additional to the immanent one.

THREE

Knowledge by Presence and Knowledge by Correspondence[1]

A GENERAL REMARK

It may be inferred directly from the preceding discussion on the matter of the dualistic sense of objectivity that we may distinguish two species of knowledge corresponding to the two species of objects. The suggestion that knowledge can be accordingly divided into knowledge by presence and knowledge by correspondence with which we are now concerned is quite understandable when we have decided that there is a subjective-essential object and an objective-accidental object.

Knowledge by presence is the kind of knowledge that has all its relations within the framework of itself, such that the whole anatomy of the notion can hold true without any implication of an external objective reference calling for an exterior relation. That is, the relation of knowing is, in that form of knowledge, a self-object relation without the intrusion of a connection with an external object. In this presentation of the notion, however, what we are forced to call the objective object is not in any way different in its existential status from the subjective object. That is to say, the sort of object that we have marked as essential to the notion of knowledge as such, and as immanent in the mind of the knowing subject is, in knowledge by presence, absolutely united with the objective object. Hence the latter object is no longer absent and accidental to the truth value of the former. In other words, in the case of knowledge by presence the objective object and the subjective object are one and the same. Knowledge by presence is therefore constituted of the simple sense of objectivity that is immediately present in the mind of the knowing subject and thus logically implied in the definition of the conception of knowledge itself.

Knowledge by correspondence, on the other hand, is that class of knowledge which enjoys both a subjective object and a separate objective object, and which includes a correspondence relationship between one of these objects and the other. In fact, a combination of the outer and inner objects along with the maximum degree of correspondence between them makes up the essentiality of this species of knowledge. Since correspondence is indeed a dyadic relation by nature, it logically follows that whenever this relation holds, there must be a conjunction between one object, A, and the other, B. The relation cannot hold true if either conjunct is false. If there were no external object, there could be no representation of it. As a result, there could be no possibility of a correspondence relation between them. Consequently, there could be no possibility of the existence of that kind of knowledge at all. As described above, the external object plays a major role in the essentiality of knowledge by correspondence,[2] but has no constitutive part in knowledge by presence. It is now imperative that the characteristics of each of these two major species of knowledge be discussed.

Knowledge by Presence

There is, as we have just indicated, in the very analysis of the relation of knowing a complex unity that constitutes the entirety of the nature of this relation.[3] In its mental existence this unity is originally simple. Reflection on this unity can, nevertheless, legitimately break down its simplicity into a triple multiplicity such that it can be analyzed by reflection into the act of "knowing," the subject as "knower," and the object as "known." This conceptual triplicity with respect to the notion of knowledge by presence is derivable from reflection on the primordial simplicity of the constructive mental existence of the immanent act of knowing itself, the kind of act that is absolutely identical with the existence of the human mind itself. As regards the absolute unity of the act of knowledge with the knower's mind itself, we have in the preceding chapter seen that such an absolute unity is that to which Averroes's theory of "beatitude" and its sense of transubstantiation was committed.[4] In the case of knowledge of the self and the suspended soul, Avicenna too is interpreted by almost all his disciples as aiming at the same version of absolute unity, although Avicenna denies the Porphyrian unity of knowing and known in other modes of knowledge.[5] Moreover, one of the most famous theses of Ṣadr al-Dīn Shīrāzī is the advocation of an existential unity between the knower, the known, and the act of knowing.[6] There is no reason whatsoever why we should not be able in our reflection upon a simple and absolute unity to analyze this unity into different conceptual parts, without this conceptual complexity damaging the original simplicity of the unity.

Take the mathematical central point in a circle as an example. It is mathematically assumed that the point is simple and therefore indivisible in the sense that it cannot be divided into various points at the center. Yet, we are taught that it is possible to divide it up into various sides and directions once we have conceptually reflected upon it and defined it as "a point equally distant from all points on the circumference of the circle." Obviously, it is the same indivisible point that has been now divided into different sides in accordance with the different points that are assigned to it on the circumference of the circle. Yet, we know that this kind of reflected multiplicity in the definition of the center does not violate the simplicity of its mathematical status.

The point of this analogy is that while the original structure of knowledge by presence is simple and indivisible, the conceptual analysis breaks it down into three interrelated components that are all characterized by being essential, present, and mental. It does not, however, go further and embark upon an external object. Yet the analysis of knowledge by correspondence, as we shall see, does so; it takes the external object as the fourth item of its essentiality. Therefore, knowledge by presence is self-evident and has a self-objective object.[7]

One of the main characteristics of knowledge by presence is its freedom from the dualism of truth and falsehood. This is because the essence of this pattern of knowledge is not concerned with the notion of correspondence. When there is no external object, correspondence between an internal and external state, as well as between "external fact" and "statement," is not withstanding. Thus, while it is the case that the principle of correspondence has been widely accepted as the criterion for truth or falsity in a statement about an external object, and while it is also the case that this principle has been accepted as the standard for the examination of truth or error in, as Russell puts it, knowledge of truth,[8] such a principle neither can, nor is required to, be adhered to in the case of knowledge by presence.

Since the dualism between truth and falsehood depends substantially upon the correspondence relation in the first instance between the subjective-essential object and the objective-accidental object, and in the second instance between a statement and its objective reference, there is no application for such a dualism in knowledge by presence. If there is no correspondence, then there is no meaning to the concept of knowledge by correspondence: hence there exists no meaning for a statement about this knowledge, nor for a statement about an external physical object, nor for the truth or falsity of such a statement. Consequently, due to this freedom from correspondence, knowledge by presence is not prone to the logical dualism of truth and falsity.

Another characteristic of knowledge by presence is its freedom from the distinction between knowledge by "conception" and knowledge by "belief." Knowledge by presence is not subject to this distinction, but knowledge by correspondence is.

This distinction was first made by Avicenna in his *Logica* in order to disentangle the problem of definition from the problem of demonstration and confirmation. He wrote:

> Every piece of knowledge and apprehension is either by conception *(taṣawwur)* or confirmation *(taṣdīq)*. Knowledge by "conception" is the primary knowledge which can be attained by definition or whatever functions as definition. This is as if by definition we understand the essence of human being.
>
> Knowledge by "confirmation" on the other hand is that which can be acquired by way of "inference." This is as if we believe the proposition that "for the whole world there is a beginning."[9]

It seems that this is the same, or close to the same, distinction as is made by some modern logicians between "meaning" and "truth value." On the basis of this distinction, a word or a sentence can make perfectly good sense by definition without having any truth value. To have only a meaningful word, phrase, or sentence we need not bring out any demonstration justifying the belief that it is true. All we have to do is to appeal to a verbal or logical definition of that word, phrase, or sentence. But to know a confirmative judgment we are logically obliged to rely upon a justification for the belief that the judgment is true.

No matter how valid it may seem, this distinction does not have any applicability when knowledge by presence is considered. This is so because both of these two alternatives—conception and confirmation—are intrinsic characteristics of conceptualization which belongs to the order or meaning and representation, not to the order of being and the factual truth. But the alleged reality of knowledge by presence does not involve any sense of conceptualization and representation. Therefore, knowledge by presence does not involve any sense of conception and confirmation.

One should notice that by denying the dualism of truth and falsity in considering knowledge by presence, we do not mean that no sense of truth is applicable to that peculiar category of knowledge. For, there is another sense of truth in the linguistic technique of illuminative philosophy that is of relevance to our discussion, and which we can call nonphenomenal.[10] Strictly speaking, however, it is equated with the notion of being. In this system of philosophy, when one says, for instance, "God is the Truth," one is simply saying that God exists or God is the Necessary Being. Here, also, if we can equate knowledge by presence with a sort of "instantiation" of the reality of the object in mind, then we are in a position to legitimately apply such an existential sense of truth to the reality of knowledge by presence. But here the point is that the logical dualism of truth and falsity as well as the logical distinction between concept and belief have no applicability in the domain of knowledge by presence, but rather both of them are appropriate properties of knowledge by correspondence.

Knowledge by Correspondence

If there are two independent existences such that the existential circumstances of the one do not bear upon or derive from the other, and consequently there is no causal connection and no constant conjunction between them, then it seems true to say that the one is "absolutely neutral" with respect to the other. Another way to put this is that each of these two given different beings is existentially distant from the other. Thus interpreted, they are existentially absent from, and not present to or united with, each other.

Here, as already indicated, the word "absence," quite often used in the linguistic technique of illuminative philosophy, means that there is no logical, ontological, or even epistemological connection between the two existences that are supposed to be in two completely different circumstances of being. The expression "absolutely neutral" is therefore a legitimate one for designating such a particular sense of absence.

A mental entity in contrast to an external object would, at first, appear to be two existences that are absolutely neutral to and absent from each other. This should mean that they are not bound together logically, ontologically, or epistemologically. It can be considered therefore that such a neutrality can never be removed altogether and changed to an absolute unity such that the two existences become, at the same time, and in all respects, one and the same. It is an outright contradiction that a mental entity and an external object can ever become absolutely identical, whether logically, ontologically, or epistemologically, when they are supposed to be different in each of these three criteria.

There is only one possibility for these two different existences to come together and be bound to each other through a kind of unification. This is phenomenal unification which is epistemic, and not logical or ontological. An external object may have, besides its factual reality that belongs to the order of being, a phenomenal representation[11] in our mind, which pertains to the order of conception. This does not mean that an order of the external being appears and resides in our mind in such a way that it becomes considered as existentially united with our mind, and deemed as belonging to the order of conception. It can also be said that one of the main characteristics of the order of conception is that by being mental it subsists in us and is produced by our mind within the domain of our phenomenal act, whereas the order of being is characterized by existing not in us, but in itself, and lying outside of us in the external world, which is independent of the radiance of our mentality.

It has been asserted here that the only possible way that can be taken toward the unification of the two initially neutral existences is an epistemic unification. Yet, what the nature of this unification is and how it takes place remain open questions. The answer to these questions lies in the notion of correspondence. The meaning of correspondence used here, in this theory of knowledge is, briefly considered, "resemblance" in content and "identity" in form.[12] That is, the internal form is united with the external material form, but the mental existence is never identical with the external one. The two different modes of existence therefore resemble each other by virtue of a formal unification. If this formal identity did not exist, there would be no possibility of any communication between the human mind and the world of reality.[13]

When we speak of the notion of correspondence it should of course be noted that we are not, at least at this moment, concerned with the question of the criteriology of logical statements that must be either true or false. In illuminative philosophy this question is regarded as a derivative of the primordial question: How can our knowledge correspond to the world of reality? Or, in other words, how can we understand our external world before we are able to speak and make sentences about it? This is the point that concerns us here with regards to the problem of correspondence. The question concerning the circumstances under which a given statement is true or false is, however, a different issue which should be treated in its proper place.

It has already been pointed out that, unlike knowledge by presence, knowledge by correspondence is marked by being involved in a twofold sense of objectivity. It has a subjective object, as the essence of knowledge as such requires, and it also has an objective object that lies outside the order of conception and counts as the objective reference of that knowledge. The former has been called by illuminative philosophy the present object, and the latter the absent object, the reality of which exists in separation from the reality of the mind of knowing subjects.

In the case of this knowledge, the subjective object plays an intermediary representation role in the achievement of the act of knowing. That is to say, the subjective object represents by means of conceptualization the reality of the external object before the mind of the knowing subject. To achieve this act of representation there must be a conformity in the sense of correspondence between the two kinds of objects. As representation, the subjective object, and consequently the whole unity of knowledge, makes sense only if it has conformity and correspondence with the external object. Knowledge by correspondence, therefore, is that in which:

a. There are two kinds of objects: one is internal and the other is external. That is, both subjective object and objective object must already be in the order of the act.
b. There is a correspondence relation between these two objects.

As elucidated before, since the correspondence relation is accidental, that is, our knowledge may or may not correspond with the external reality, the logical dualism of truth and falsity, or error, comes under consideration. If our subjective object truly corresponds to the objective object, our knowledge of the external world holds true and is valid, but if the condition of correspondency has not been obtained, the truth of our knowledge will never come about. This is because the opposition of truth and falsity is of a particular kind. It calls for a relation, the applicability of which is symmetrical even if the relation itself is not. This means that, to whatever proposition or sentence the quality of "truth" is applicable, the quality of falsehood is by the same reason potentially applicable, and to whatever proposition or sentence the quality of falsehood is applicable, the quality of truth is on the same basis potentially applicable.

In illuminative philosophy, according to the appropriate principles, certain oppositions have been developed that one cannot find in the traditional *square of opposition.* Among these, the opposition of what has been called "aptitude and privation" should be specified in connection with truth and falsity. The nature of this opposition, as it is elaborated, suggests a category of opposition wherein there must be something in which there is eligibility for qualification by one or another of the opposite qualitites. An example of this, mentioned by these philosophers, is an animate object that has eligibility for sight or blindness, susceptibility to which is lacking in the nature of inanimate objects. We can say that a certain individual or species of animal is blind because the generic nature of animality has the aptitude for the quality of sight. But we can never say that a certain instance or species of inanimate things, say a rock, is blind, because the generic term of these things does not suppose sight.[14] Thus, whatever object has, by its nature, "aptitude" for qualification by one of these opposite qualities, it has aptitude and susceptibility for being qualified by the other as well, and vice versa. The opposition of truth and falsity is supposed to be of this kind, and it applies only to those judgments and statements that are, through a correspondence relation, eligible for truth or falsity. But where the application of falsity does not make sense, neither does the application of truth.

By virtue of the correspondence that knowledge by correspondence contains through its objective reference, it possesses the aptitude for being true. Therefore, it may conceivably fail to meet this condition and as a result become false. But this aptitude does not hold in knowledge by presence, for in this kind of knowledge, since it has nothing to do with correspondence, there is no possibility of its being false; thus it is not eligible for falsity. As the nature of this opposition stands, if there is no susceptibility to falsity, there is no meaning for truth either. Thus, the dualism of truth and falsehood only holds in an appropriate opposition in which the possibilty of one opposite is the logical standard for the possibility of the other. The impossibility of one also counts as the criterion of the modal impossibility of the other. But, as we have already maintained, in the high existential degree of knowledge by presence there presides another version of truth which like the knowledge itself belongs to the order of being and not to the order of conception and representation.[15]

The Relation Between Knowledge by Presence and Knowledge by Correspondence

In Islamic illuminative philosophy there exists a notable concern for providing an appropriate technique that can help satisfy the need for an adequate language for expressing those complexities peculiar to this system of thinking. One of those all-important technical words is "illuminative relation" *(al-iḍā fat al-ishrāqiyyah)*[16] which can be regarded as the basic term for the illuminative approaches to the problems of ontology, cosmology, and human knowledge.

Unlike the Aristotelian category of relation, the illuminative relation is not of a kind designed to connect one side of the relation to the other, thus binding separate entities in a complex unity. Neither is it akin to the other categories of Aristotle, all of which belong to the order of conceptions and essentialities of beings. Illuminative relation is, moreover, not meant to account for a copulative between one thing and another as the normal sense of relation is designed to mean. Rather, it is designed to be of the order of existence and reflects the very reality of the light overflowing from the Supreme Principle of lights. This relation specifically stands for the grades of the act of being rather than the capacities of potency. In other words, this sort of relation designates the existential status of an illuminative being proceeding from the First Cause of being. Like the reality of existence itself, the illuminative relation varies in degrees of intensity without separation and detachment from the source of illumination.

On the hypothesis that in the absolute vacuum of eternity nothing, not even time and space, existed except God, the following question arises: How and in what manner did God, as the First Cause, relate Himself to another thing as His first effect and bring it into being, while there was nothing of any element of being to start with? Again, by a further hypothesis one can, for the sake of clarity, conceive that the first effect, because of its simplicity, is so absorbed in that overwhelming light of the Principle that it is existentially indistinguishable, and literally undetachable from the existential radiance of the First Cause. If so, how can we possibly account for the relation between one separate existence and the other? Can the relation of two such things be expressed by a language other than that of illuminative relation?

Obviously in the context of this hypothesis there is no alternative to the phraseology of the illuminative relation that clearly describes the causation by illumination and emanation as distinct from causation by generation and corruption. Once we have succeeded in the conceptualization of this form of causation, the relation between any cause and its immanent effect is subject to the overriding question of whether or not an immanent action itself is a mere illuminative relation, or whether it is something in itself related to something else as its cause. This means that the illuminative relation would be an existential monadic relation by nature in which the relation itself and that which is related are one and the same.

This is all very well so far as the hypothesis of the illuminative relation is concerned. Above and beyond this hypothetical analysis, we are now in a position to proceed to our main question as to whether the relation between our knowledge by presence and our knowledge by correspondence can possibly be couched in the form of the illuminative relation. To be more specific, the question is whether the human mind, regarded as the first cause, antecendent to its own phenomenal consequents, illuminates from the depth of its own presential knowledge the rays of its immanent act of knowledge by correspondence? Does the process of this phenomenal causation take place in the same manner in which the First Cause of the universe sheds the light of existence on the first effect and on the world of reality?

In answer to this question consider the following dialogue:[17]

Q.: How can we as human beings ever have knowledge at all?
A.: Think introvertively of yourself. If you do so, you will certainly find out what truly answers your question.
Q.: But how?
A.: If I introvertively consider myself, I will find in all certainty that I am truly aware of myself in such a way that I can never miss myself. This state of self-certainty convinces me that my awareness of myself does not mean anything but the awareness of "myself," "by" myself, not by anyone or anything else. If I were aware of myself "by" anyone or anything else, it would obviously mean that the awareness of myself belonged to another active power which is not myself. In this case there would be a knowing subject operating in myself in knowing myself. Thus it would not be myself that knows myself. But it has been assumed that it is the very performative 'I' as the subject reality of myself who knows myself.[18]

From this point onward the argument proceeds in two different directions. First, that in the case of self-knowledge, the self as the performative subject of awareness, and the same self that is the object of which it is aware, are absolutely identical. This is the very concept of self-objectivity that characterizes our initial theory of knowledge by presence, which can here account for the self-subjectivity of the performative 'I'. Second, that in the event of any correspondence knowledge in which the knowing subject is an "invariable I," (in our terminology a performative 'I') and the object known is an external object, the 'I' already knows itself by presence and knows its object by correspondence. Only the latter extension of the argument is relevant to our present investigation. Since the argument is extremely involved, it is imperative to develop it through a modern linguistic approach so as to reach a satisfactory conclusion concerning the problem under consideration—the relation of knowledge by presence to knowledge by correspondence.

In the case: I truly believe that "I know P," the question arises, "I know an external object P, but do I, at the same time, know myself?" If I do, then there must be another form of knowledge unintrospectively involved in my knowledge of P. On this supposition it is imperative to ask this question: What is the nature and character of this underlying knowledge of myself implied in the very case of my knowledge of an external object P?

Both of these questions follow from the supposition that the 'I' as the knowing subject does indeed know itself at the very moment that it experiences knowledge of an external object P. Taking the alternative that the 'I' does not really know itself while knowing an external object P, there result some paradoxical questions from various perspectives.

From a logical standpoint, when I say, for instance, "I know P," the word 'I' as the subject term in this statement represents, or refers to, the knowing subject of the proposition. The knowing subject is that which has made up and held within itself this knowing relation to the object P. Just as the word 'I' is a constituent term in the form of the sentence "I know P," so the mind of the agent, as the knowing subject, counts as an integral part of the knowledge on which the whole conception of the knowing relation is based. Thus, a constitutive part of knowledge, the 'I', is subsistently implied in the whole. Given as it is, the 'I' cannot be unknown to itself. Ruling out the knowing subject from the complex whole of the relation of knowledge would cause the meaning of that relation to break down completely, and as a result, human knowledge could no longer remain meaningful. Consequently, that which is an integral part of knowledge cannot remain unknown.

Besides, the act of knowing is designated as being intentional and immanent in contrast to the physical and transitive acts of human beings. Being an intentional act, the whole complex unity of the act of knowing as a relationship is placed within the scope of "intentionality" which implies that each and every element of such a relationship is known by the knowing subject. As thus posited, the 'I' as the knowing subject of such a form of knowledge must be known in its context. Subsequently, based on this hypothesis, the subject term is known, just as the predicate is in all certainty known. If the subject 'I' is known to itself, and it is the knowing subject who knows itself immediately, then the knowing subject knows itself by presence. This is because if the 'I' is known, not by itself, but by a representation of itself, then it is not the 'I' who knows the external object, but in this case it is the representation of the 'I' that knows that external object. Thus, if the 'I' really must know some external object in a self-judgment, it must know the very reality of itself in the first place. When it is seen that the reality of the 'I' should know the very reality of itself, one has an instance of knowledge by presence. A knowing 'I' is known to itself by presence and acts like an active intellect to provide in itself the form of its external object so that it can know it by correspondence.

We can therefore understand from all this that knowledge by presence has creative priority over knowledge by correspondence. In fact, knowledge by correspondence always emerges from its rich and ever-present source, which is knowledge by presence, and which is none other than the very being of the active and performative 'I'. For, if the active 'I' were not present in all of its intentional correspondence knowledge, all human intentionality, such as believing, thinking, wanting, and so on would become meaningless. That is, there would be no sense in saying "I believe so and so," "I want so and so," etc. The relationship of knowledge by presence to knowledge by correspondence should be taken as a cause-and-effect relationship in terms of illumination and emanation. This kind of relation is nothing more than a typically efficient cause-and-effect relationship, but to distinguish this intellectual causation from a physical one, illuminative philosophy places it in its own terminology as an illuminative relation.

To complete our analysis of the illuminative relation between knowledge by presence and knowledge by correspondence, let us turn to a comparative study of Descartes, "*cogito ergo sum*" ("I think therefore I am"), and what some Muslim illuminative philosophers say on the same subject, that is, the knowledge of the self as personal identity.[19] After being troubled by his famous philosophical scepticism, Descartes arrived at a point where he found himself no longer susceptible to doubt. Focusing on his indubitable principle, *cogito*, Descartes said: "I am really doubting; whatever else may be doubtful, the fact that I doubt is indubitable."[20] The certainty of the existence of my doubt leads me up to the certainty of the existence of myself. It seems quite obvious that Descartes managed to establish the knowledge of his selfhood through his self-certainty regarding the state of doubting. In other words, he brought one phenomenal act of his mind as evidence to account for the truth of the existence of his personal identity.

There are on the other side to this argument some observations of which some Muslim philosophers who, though they lived long before the time of Descartes, seemed to be quite conscious. Their position took cognizance of the impossibility involved in this argument. The founder of the Islamic philosophy of existence, Ṣadr al-Dīn Shīrāzī, appears to take issue with Descartes on his *cogito*. But before entering into the details of this debate, a brief introduction would seem to be in order. As we shall see later, the characteristic of Muslim illuminative philosophers, unlike most classical metaphysicians, was their empirical approach to the central issues of illuminative thinking. This is clear in their theory of perception and their theory of light. In this particular matter they also placed considerable reliance on perceptual data in proceeding to their illuminative conclusion. Starting with our particular sense-perceptions, Ṣadr al-Dīn argued:

> No particular sense-perception or phenomenal state of mind, even though in the form 'I', can ever bear witness to the truth value of the existence of myself. This is because any phenomenal event which I attribute to myself, such as my feeling cold, or warmth, or pain etc., must be, and is, presupposed by an underlying awareness of myself. With this underlying awareness alone can I appropriate cold, warmth, pain, pleasure, etc., to myself. If I suffer from severe cold weather, or escape from the flame of a burning fire, it is only because I already am aware of something which, in one way or another, belongs to myself. This is true in doubting, thinking, believing, etc. Thought, doubt, or belief, in general, can never be appropriated to myself, nor can they be a subsisting phenomena in myself. But as particularly applied to myself and possessed by myself in terms of my own thought, doubt, or belief, it involves the underlying awareness of myself. This is the case no matter how the reality of the self is to be understood, and how the problem of self identity is to be handled by philosophy.[21]

Ṣadr al-Dīn Shīrāzī elaborated the issue further in his more formal language:

> Were it the case that I, through my own action, whether it is intellectual or physical, could become aware of myself, it would be as if I

> should bring forth from myself evidence to bear witness to myself. It would obviously be a vicious circle in which the knowledge of my action functions as a cause of my knowledge of myself which is itself already implied in, and serves as the cause of the knowledge of my own action.[22]

The only solution to this dilemma, the illuminative philosophers suggest, rests with the reality of knowledge by presence, insofar as the knowing subject, in our terminology the performative 'I', is concerned. In this system of personal identity the self knows itself in the manner of knowledge by presence, which is existentially identical with the very being of the self itself. In this regard, no representation of the self is needed, let alone a representation of an object or a perception of an action such as doubt, feeling, or knowledge of the other. And the self with its own state of presence provides its doubt about its thought and its knowledge of the other by way of correspondence.

FOUR

An Empirical Dimension of Knowledge by Presence

How are We Aware of our Sensations and Feelings?

Now that the meaning of knowledge by presence and its distinction from knowledge by correspondence have been provisionally described, the time has come to provide an empirical illustration of the former theory. In order to establish that this kind of knowing is primordial and has the principal role to play in the basic formation of the human intellect, we shall first of all proceed to an empirical investigation that will give a sense-certainty of the truth value of the theory of knowledge by presence. When we have made this point clear, we will then move toward the presentation of the transcendental account of this knowledge.[1]

Among several examples that illuminative philosophy offers us for the explanation of its theory is one's empirical awareness of one's sensations and feelings. For example, one knows, by presence and not by correspondence, that one is in pain. Obviously this sort of awareness is privileged with the highest degree of sense-certainty in that when I am aware that I am in pain it makes no sense to say at the same time that I doubt whether I am in pain. This certainty, however, does not account for the property of the truth or falsehood of my awareness of pain. This is so, simply because the logical theory of truth must be given in such a way that the judgment or expression, while making sense, can alternatively admit of the opposite qualities of truth or falsity.

This condition is perfectly satisfied, primarily by knowledge by correspondence, and derivatively by descriptive statements and expressions that are designed to express this kind of knowledge. Why this logical bifurcation, truth or falsity, does not apply to knowledge by presence is a question of which illuminative philosophy is fully aware. We have already mentioned this point among the characteristics of knowledge by presence and will discuss it according to the illuminative system in some detail later on.

As was mentioned, an empirical illustration for knowledge by presence is provided here through the example of our experience with pain. This means that the bare presence of the existential status of pain in our mind is a sufficient and complete condition for being acquainted with pain, without the mediation of a formal representation of the pain experience in the mind. This is ultimately what Russell also had in mind when he tried to sketch out his theory of "knowledge by acquaintance." He had, quite accurately, pointed out that knowledge by acquaintance, unlike our knowledge of truth, is free from the dualism of truth and falsehood. He wrote:

> So far as things are concerned, we may know them or not know them, but there is no positive state of mind which can be described as erroneous knowledge of things, so long, at any rate, as we confine ourselves to knowledge by acquaintance. Whatever we are acquainted with must be something; we may draw wrong inference from our acquaintance, but the acquaintance itself cannot be deceptive. Thus there is no dualism as regards acquaintance.[2]

We have here, in our presentation of the illuminative theory of knowledge by presence, two fundamental points in common with Russell in his theory of knowledge by acquaintance. First, knowledge by presence as discussed here is analogous to Russell's knowledge by acquaintance in being free from the possibility of having truth or falsehood applied to it. Both of them, therefore, have in common that they are neither true nor false. This point is well illustrated in the above passage. Second, that with which we are acquainted and which is present in us must be in itself "something" immediately known, not by "representation" or by an "appearance" of it. To this point Russell has committed himself, not precisely, but by an implicit consequence that can be understood from his argument. For if it were the case that what we are acquainted with is by a representation with which we must be acquainted in its turn, there would be an infinite regression in the range of acquaintances and representations. In order to bring the range of acquaintance to an end the first genuine acquaintance must not be accomplished by means of another acquaintance or representation; it should rather be by presence. At any rate, these are points of agreement and similarity on which we can harmonize the theory of "knowledge by presence" with Russell's views on "knowledge by acquaintance."

Knowledge by Presence is not Knowledge by Acquaintance

We must try now to explain how we gradually come to a position in which we must part company with the acquaintance theory[3] and account for knowledge by presence in the specific sense given above, which is existential and not intentional at all. We must make clear why we cannot confine ourselves to the limits of the connotation of sense-data and the Russellian knowledge by acquaintance. This consideration, however, cannot be achieved unless we comply with our initial aim in this chapter concerning the empirical instantiation of knowledge by presence, and the explanation of how our sensations and feelings cannot be accounted for except through knowledge by presence. We have already pointed out what is in general the meaning of both knowledge by presence and what is knowledge by correspondence. Now we are obliged to discuss why our private states such as sensations and feelings fulfill necessary and sufficient conditions for being empirical instantiations of knowledge by presence and not manifestations of some other category of knowledge, even knowledge by acquaintance.

In the first place, we suggest that an episode of pain or pleasure should be categorized under the title of knowledge by presence and that there is no possibility of considering it as a form of knowledge by correspondence. This is simply because in the acquaintance with sensations and feelings such as pain or pleasure, there is no absent/external object, and thus, at the time of experience, there is no need for a representation of that object. As a result, there is no possibility of a correspondence relation between these two entities, namely, the external object and the internal representation of it, if the external one does not exist. In such a case the possibility of knowledge by correspondence must be absolutely ruled out. What remains is none other than knowledge by presence, which is empirically exemplified through that kind of acquaintance. Pain or pleasure therefore, is sheer existential "instantiation," and not a representation of that with which we are acquainted and is known to us by presence.[4]

Secondly, the thing we are aware of or acquainted with when we are experiencing this sensation is not anything like a sense-datum, which would be a representation of pain or pleasure. It is, rather, a true presentation and not a representation, and hence a real exemplification and not a conception or a perception of pain or pleasure within the power of the mind. We are, therefore, immediately (i.e., without the intermediary of representation) aware of and acquainted with our experience at the time of its occurrence. It is from this viewpoint that knowledge by presence has been understood by definition as self-objective knowledge. For the very objective reality of our pain or pleasure, and not a sense-datum derived from it, is precisely that which we are acquainted with, and that whose entire factual reality is present in us.

At this point we are able to see what makes the theory of knowledge by presence differ in principle from that of knowledge by acquaintance. As regards the latter, what we are acquainted with is supposed to be sense-data, the purpose of which is to represent material objects through our sense-experience to our mind.[5] The sense-data, do, therefore, play an intermediary role between the subject of the acquaintance and the objective references of those things of which the knowing subject is aware. Yet, in considering the former theory, our analysis does not posit any relation or associaton between our mind and an external object or bring out any sense of representation for our real instantiation of feelings and sensations. While we are experiencing pain or pleasure, our actual object of acquaintance, with which we are truly acquainted, belongs to the order of being of our mind. It clearly has nothing to do at the moment of experience, with the order of "conception" and representational "apprehension."

Sense-data, on the other hand, are designed to preserve these two fundamental aspects of correspondence which are incompatible with knowledge by presence. They function (a) as a means of maintaining the correspondence or the kind of association which they have with their external objective references, and (b) as part of the order of conception, and not of the order of being and instantiation. By their nature, they cannot associate themselves with the order of being because they are representations of physical objects. These are sufficient reasons for us not to be satisfied with the theory of knowledge by acquaintance and part company with its consequences. Turning to the theory of knowledge by presence, we may account for the logical validity which was lacking in the Russellian argument. The point of this brief comparative study is to assert the importance and completeness of the theory of knowledge by presence when dealing with private states of mind as opposed to other theories that are in one way or another related to an external object and cannot provide us with self-object knowledge.

Here it is necessary to remind ourselves of the fact that our description of empirical cases of knowledge by presence are always qualified by the phrase "at the time of immediately experiencing our sensation and feeling." This is essential for indicating that we are dealing with a case of knowledge by presence if, and only if, we are in the act of experiencing our sensations and are not engaged in the act of "reflecting" upon our experiences. Conclusions are drawn such that knowledge by presence is not experienced by reflection, for the very meaning of "presence" and its nature which pertains to the order of being as distinct from the order of conception and perception necessitate such an eventuality.[6] If we reflect upon our sensations, say by relating our experience with pain or pleasure last night, or even at this very moment, to a friend or a doctor, we try to conceptualize our feeling and transform it from its order of being into a sort of representation which is of the order of conception. By doing this we move from the existential realm of knowledge by presence to the conceptual state of knowledge by correspondence. This is, in our opinion, what reflection is, because whenever there is room for representation there is possibility for correspondence. What this correspondence necessitates is none other than knowledge by correspondence, which may, in turn, be either true or false.

The Presence of our Sensations is Nonrepresentational

After the above argument, it is hardly surprising that one arrives at the conclusion that knowledge by presence is not a type of phenomenal intentional act of knowing, whether it be discursive or intuitive. We use "intuitive knowledge" here in the ordinary sense of the term, in which the meaning involves spontaneous conception and instinctive representation. As opposed to discursive knowledge, intuitive knowledge is not attained through a process of inference, for intuitive knowledge takes for its truth and objective validity immediate application to external objects. It, however, still has to be placed in the order of conception corresponding to its external object rather than the order of being. In other words, although intuitive knowledge as commonly understood is not "inferential," it is nevertheless "referential," taking external objects as its corresponding objective reference. This is the reason why we have to distinguish knowledge by presence from knowledge by intuition, just as we have differentiated it from discursive knowledge and from knowledge by acquaintance. Another attempt must be made to make it clear how our sense of knowledge by presence is vastly different from the peculiar notion of intuition suggested by Bergson in his work *The Creative Mind*.[7]

Knowledge by correspondence provides us with a representation and conception of its external object and serves as an intentional act of knowing. It initiates in us the whole range of intentionality; but the mode of knowledge by presence, in the state of pain and pleasure, operates in a completely different way. It brings about and gives rise to the real instantiation of the object, which is the actual reality of the object. Instead of objectifying its intentional form of object by virtue of conceptualization, it rather brings to the fore our acquaintance with the reality of the object itself. In this manner, it compels us to identify, under certain conditions, the reality of our mind with the objective reality of the object, these two being bound together in an existential unification. If I say for instance, "I know I am in pain," it simply means "I am in pain." The words "to know" therefore play nothing more than an emphatical role for a certain state of being. This is, however, what we mean by "nonrepresentational knowledge."

In this context, a linguistic observation made by Wittgenstein seems quite striking. He has accurately pointed out:

> In what sense are my sensations private? Well, only I can know whether I am really in pain; another person can only surmise it.—In one way this is wrong, in another nonsense. If we are using the word "to know" as it is normally used (and how else are we to use it?), then other people very often know when I am in pain.—Yet all the same not with the certainty with which I know it myself!—It cannot be said of me at all (except perhaps as a joke) that I know I am in pain. What is it supposed to mean—except perhaps that I am in pain.[8]

Wittgenstein arrives at the point of saying, even though with a sense of uncertainty, "that I know I am in pain . . . is . . . to mean . . . that I am in pain," through his realization of the fact that our acquaintance with our sensations need not be achieved by an intentional form of knowledge nor through the ordinary sense of knowledge. It is thus the case that for any sensation and feeling such as pain or pleasure to be known by the agent, the being of that sensation and feeling must be present in the mind of that agent in such a way that the ontological and epistemological differences between them become absolutely nonexistent. This is because the ontological and epistemological status of a present object and that of the mind in which the object is presented are in fact one and the same. When ontological and epistemological values are united, it is not surprising (and for Wittgenstein there should be no room for doubt or hesitation) that "to know" I am in pain must definitely mean that "I am" in pain.

Concerning our acquaintance with our sensations and feelings, or in Wittgenstein's terminology, pain language, there are two discussions which would seem appropriate if we wish to clarify the matter.[9] One is with Wittgenstein in connection with the above passage. The other is with Russell concerning his famous distinction between knowledge by acquaintance and knowledge by description. Let us start with the first.

What is Pain Language Other than Pain Ontology Language?

We have already encountered Wittgenstein's conclusion that "I know I am in pain" is, in his words, "to mean perhaps that, 'I am in pain'." On the face of it, this statement amounts, linguistically speaking, to saying that "knowing" in this context is either redundant or synonymous with the word "being" which is understood by the next phrase "I am in. . . ." Thus interpreted, the sentence:

"I know I am in pain,"

can really mean only:

"I am in pain,"

eliminating the phrase "I know."

If this is truly the case, the sentence will no longer stand for the "reflection" or "introspection" of my feeling pain, but rather is, as it were, a typical expression of the empirical instantiation of knowledge by presence, insofar as it means that I really am in pain. In that case, my pain, as the object of my acquaintance, is "instantiated," and not represented in my mind in the form of "existential unification."

The matter, however, would be quite different in essence if this statement were given as the formal expression of my "reflection" upon my pain experience. In a case of introspection like this, I reflect upon that with which I have already been acquainted. Through this reflection, moreover, I conceptualize my pain in such a way that, by being objectified in mind, the concept of pain experience functions as the representation of the objective reference, which is in this case the reality of my pain experience. As we have said before, as soon as we get into the intentional act of conceptualization and representation, the problem of knowledge by correspondence comes into view. We have been driven from one type of knowledge, that which is by presence, to another, that which is by correspondence. Now, when we are led to knowledge by correspondence, Wittgenstein's theory no longer seems to hold, because on this presupposition the phrase "I know" does not necessarily have to mean that "I am in . . .", and "to know" is consequently not synonymous with the verb "to be." It makes perfectly good sense to say that, "I know I am in pain," means that, "I have knowledge of a past or present experience, when I was or am in such and such a state of pain."

It is customary in matters concerned with description that I conceptualize further knowledge about my pain in order to assure both myself and my doctor that I am in such and such a state of pain, especially when two states of pain have certain similarities. Through introspection and by reflection on my experience, I place it into its determinate constituents of pain experience in general for the sake of clarity and unambiguous explanation. As soon as this reflection is made, my presence-knowledge of pain falls into the category of knowledge by correspondence. Such as it is, it is hard to agree with Wittgenstein that "I know I am in pain" should mean either that "I am in pain," such that the first subject term "I know" is used redundantly and can be eliminated with no change in the meaning of the sentence, or that "to know" in this usage means "that the expression of uncertainty is useless,"[10] as he suggested later. Neither of these two alternatives sounds agreeable, because none of them could satisfy the normal use and meaning of the verb "to know."

The correct suggestion appears to deal with those sentences such as "I know I am in pain" as an introspective piece of description, which conveys my corresponding acquaintance with the presence of the real instantiation of my pain. That is, when we are experiencing pain, we are already acquainted with pain in terms of knowledge by presence; but when we are furthermore testing our experience by reflecting on it, we then have a corresponding acquaintance with the original instantiation, which forms our typical knowledge by correspondence. This would account for the knowledge of our pain by correspondence, and for the meaningfulness of the whole sentence: "I do know I am in pain."

There is thus no reason whatsoever to delete or interpret in some peculiar way our normal introspective expression that is considered to be part of human consciousness.

What is the Meaning of Acquaintance?

Similarly, Russell's distinction between knowledge by description and knowledge by acquaintance can be made subject to critical examination. We have in the past discussions established that there exists a tangible difference between our knowledge by presence and Russell's knowledge by acquaintance. The difference emerges mainly in the fact that there is an implication in knowledge by acquaintance of reference to an external object that does not appear necessarily in the aforementioned empirical instantiation of knowledge by presence. The pertinent question is: Is it possible to consider that this difference is trivial and that these two theories can ultimately meet in principle, and if not in all cases, at least in the above suggested empirical example, setting aside any verbal or semantic dissimilarities? Let us try to see if there can be a possible harmonization between our theory of presence-knowledge and that of knowledge by acquaintance.

To distinguish knowledge by acquaintance from knowledge by description, Russell has clearly explained:

> Thus in the presence of my table I am acquainted with the sense-data that make up the appearance of my table—its colour, shape, hardness, smoothness, etc., all these are things of which I am immediately conscious when I am seeing and touching my table. . . .
>
> My knowledge of the table as a physical object, on the contrary, is not direct knowledge. Such as it is, it is obtained through acquaintance with the sense-data that make up the appearance of the table. We have seen that it is possible, without absurdity, to doubt whether there is a table at all, whereas it is not possible to doubt the sense-data.[11]

Should the sense-data be considered as the "appearance" of a physical object, like my table, when I am seeing and touching it, then they quite naturally have a kind of "association" with the table as a physical object which causes them. Once we have established this association, the question is, what kind of association or relation could it be, apart from the relation of correspondence? As we have said before, as soon as the relation of correspondence occurs, we must consider the possibility that the sense-data are deceptive in their correspondence with the physical objects. It is true to say that it is not possible to doubt whether the sense-data exist in my mental state. But it is also true to say that it is quite possible to doubt whether the sense-data are truthful in representing and corresponding to the physical object.

The point of the argument is that the sense-data, by evincing such an intrinsic relation to the physical objects, and from the standpoint that they are characterized by an intermediary function, called by Russell himself "appearance," cannot be considered as the whole reality of the objective object with which we are acquainted. They are rather partly subjective, presented in our mind, and partly objective, related to the independent existence of their objective reference. Therefore, as stated, the sense-data fall short of being totally present in the mind together with all this essential relation to the physical object. They have at least one relation that stands for their representation of and appearance as the physical object which depends on the external existence of that object. They instead remain, in this respect, in the order of conception and representation; and with this relation they cannot be in the order of being and have a pure existential unification with the mind.

Given that the correspondence relation to the physical object is part of their nature, the sense-data can never be subsumed in the category of knowledge by presence that we have presented here with the empirical example of that knowledge. It must, however, be admitted that there is a sense of presence in which the acquaintance of the mind with the sense-data, with all their conceptual implications concerning the physical object, can be used.[12] Yet this would require a further ramification of knowledge by presence to be worked out to apply to sense-data and not to be confused with the subject under consideration here.

The empirical analysis under consideration gives us the basis for understanding the major difference between the two kinds of "acquaintance with," or, if you wish, the two kinds of knowledge by acquaintance. One is exemplified by the Russellian sense-data and is typified by having a correspondence implication of a physical object. The other is the acquaintance with our feelings and sensations that is absolutely free from any implication of, or association with, an external object. This is only intended as an explanation of what the illuminative philosophers introduce as an empirical species of their generic notion of knowledge by presence.

Of course, there is a great problem in which almost all fields of philosophy are involved. This is the problem of the mind-body relationship. While there are some very interesting theories within emanationist scheme concerning this problem, this problem is of little or no immediate concern for our major theme.[13]

Another question is how knowledge of our sensations is knowledge by presence through "illumination," and not presence through "unity" or presence through "absorption." We shall speak of this latter problem in detail when we come back to another empirical account of knowledge by presence.

The Empirical Illuminative Account of Sensation

The author of the theory of knowledge by presence, Shihāb al-Dīn Suhrawardī (549/1155–587/1191), gives an empirical illustration of this particular pattern of knowledge by presence, which is quite interesting. He says:

> One of the things that supports our opinion that we do have some kind of apprehensions *(idrākāt)* which need not take a form of representation *(ṣūrah)* other than the presence of the reality *(dhat)*[14] of the thing apprehended *(mudrak),* is when a man is in pain from a cut or from damage to one of his organs. He then has a feeling of this damage. But this feeling or apprehension is never in such a way that that damage leaves in the same organ of the body or in another a form of representation of itself besides the reality of itself. Rather, the thing apprehended is but that damage itself. This is what is truly sensible and it counts in itself for pain, not a representation of it, caused by itself. This proves that, there are among things apprehended by us some things such that in being apprehended, it is sufficient that their reality be received in the mind or in any agent which is present in the mind.[15]

In this passage we can find two straightforward points dealing with the matter at issue, namely, the empirical exemplification of knowledge by presence. The first is what Suhrawardī has indicated by his words, "that we do have some kinds of apprehensions which need not take any form of representation." Mediation and intervention by a representation for the attainment of knowledge is needed and carried out by the intentional act of mind if, and only if, the reality of the object is initially "absent" from the mind of the subject. This is exactly the case when an external object is apprehended. But as regards those objects that are already present in the mind, it seems absurd to "represent" what is in itself "present"; it is more or less like knowing something that has already been known.[16]

The second point constitutes his main argument, which is an empirical analysis of the experience of pain. He seems to be raising this question: From what thing are we really suffering in the case of pain experience—from a cut in our finger, a fracture in our leg, or in his own language, from a representation—*(ṣūrah),* a sense-datum in Russell's words—of that cut or fracture? He believes it would be absurd to put the blame upon the sense-data or the representation and appearance of the pain experience, while the reality of the pain is absolutely present in the mind or in some of the mental powers of the suffering subject, which are all present in that mind. This is simply a physiological fact that one's feeling of a cut in one's finger, for example, is undoubtedly one's acquaintance with the cut in the finger itself, not with the representation or the sense-data of the cut. A cut in my finger is hardly like one in my table that I am seeing and touching. In that experience, it is quite understandable to say that in front of my table I am acquainted with the sense-data that make up the appearance of my table—its color, shape, etc. In the "presence" of the reality of a fracture in my leg, however, it can hardly make sense to say that I am acquainted with the sense-data that make up the appearance of my broken leg; its color, shape, hardness, or smoothness. Does this really account for my pain? No, it certainly does not. Of course, I can see and touch my deformed broken leg from the outside and get acquainted with the sense-data that make up the appearance of my leg, as my doctor does, but this sort of acquaintance is no longer the same as I have already had with my pain itself. It is therefore another kind of acquaintance, with which we are not concerned now. We are talking about the acquaintance with our feeling and our pain, not with the sense-data of the deformation of our leg, which serves as an external physical object and goes with knowledge by correspondence.

Therefore, based on Suhrawardī's approach, it can only be concluded that having established this empirical example we can justifiably say that we do have some kind of apprehension or knowledge that is not attained by any representation or sense-data. It is only through an existential unification that in the system of the aforementioned philosophers is referred to as "presence" that this category of knowledge comes into being. Knowledge by presence therefore is to be understood by definition as that in which the reality of the object known is present in the mind of the knowing subject without any representation or sense-data of that object. This is the meaning of self-object knowledge. The language of this kind of knowledge is also nothing more or less than the language of "being" itself. I believe that the factor that justified Wittgenstein in working out a pain language game, distinct from other language games, was his implicit recognition of the equivalence between, "I know I am in pain" and "I am in pain." This is a theme that will be explicated further in later examples of knowledge by presence.

Five

The Prime Mode of Knowledge by Presence

A Philosophy of Self-Knowledge[1]

In the preceding chapter we have discussed how one can arrive at the truth of knowledge by presence through an empirical experience of one's feelings and sensations. We started with an empirical case in order to avoid becoming bogged down in the Socratic dogma that states that one word always points to one idea and that an *a priori* definition given to a general term such as, in our case, "knowledge by presence," must hold true as the criterion for the truth value of all its specifications and forms. We have thus far tried not to involve ourselves in such considerations. Rather, we began with the factual characteristics of that particular empirical form, regardless of what it might turn out to be by definition. Moreover, an *a priori* definition never was, or will be, our starting point for discussion; and in this chapter again, instead of appealing to an *a priori* definition, we want to concentrate on another exemplification of knowledge by presence. This is the knowledge of the self as performatively expressed by itself in all the forms of our self-judgments.

Here, we wish to proceed toward the prime mode of that knowledge which, according to illuminative philosophy, actively underlies all other modes of human knowledge and apprehensions, and has the rank of superiority over all intentional acts of the self. This feat can be achieved by bringing in some rather practical characteristics and essentialities of this particular mode. This step, moreover, allows us to show that we can ultimately reach the truth of this kind of human knowledge without involving ourselves in a purely transcendental philosophy of the self. This is not simply because we have refused to start with the Socratic dogma of definition, nor is it because we have completely resigned ourselves to the Wittgensteinian dogma of "family resemblance." Our reasoning is rather based on the use of another criterion, which is, like the theory of knowledge by presence itself, Islamic, and which enables us to account for the knowledge of the performative self separately from that of the transcendental self.

This criteriology for establishing definitions and arriving at valid objective ideas does not agree with Socrates' unwarranted *a priori* definitions, nor does it have much in common with the Wittgensteinian notion of "family resemblance"[2] that ultimately must admit to having been based upon the *a priori* idea of similarity. Rather, it takes a stand somewhere in between. It calls, in the first place, for a thorough empirical examination of the prospective factual applications of an idea to find out if they have any practical similarities as well as any differences in their practical aspects. If they do, all similarities are recorded as a list in one column, and all the differences in another. Once they have all been scientifically summed up in this manner, the similarities *in actu* are then made to account for a single uniformity predicated of all particulars in common, and differences accounting for all of the specifications and individuations. This is called, in the Islamic system of philosophy, the method of "composition" *(tarkīb)*,[3] meaning that we must construct the universal ideas of our definitions by way of combining or making a composition of empirical similarities and differences. In this system all universal concepts must be obtained from and warranted by empirical exemplifications, and no pure *a priori* concept is deemed valid or relied on. In his *Logica,* Avicenna provided a chapter in which he elaborated on how no definition can ever be drawn from an *a priori* argument.[4]

In proceeding to the next example of knowledge by presence, referred to here as "the prime mode" of knowledge by presence or "knowledge of the self," we have to show its performative essentialities by resorting to the factual characteristics of what we normally express by the word 'I' as the subject term in a self-judgment. In doing this we must formalize our question.

Before we are able to understand how to know our external world, or in other words, before we can think of anything else other than ourselves, we are obliged, as Suhrawardī believes, to provide a satisfactory answer to the question: How do we really know ourselves?[5] What is the nature, if any, of that kind of knowledge which is commonly known as "self-knowing" or "self-consciousness"? Is it exactly the same as knowing this table, this or that man, the sun, the moon, or the stars on a clear night? Or perhaps the essence of self-knowing should be considered to be not just partly, but entirely, different from that of knowing another thing? The existence of myself is definitely presupposed in any proposition or action of which I am the subject or for which I am responsible. Is the knowledge of myself, likewise, presupposed in any intentional proposition or action of which I am the subject, or for which I am responsible? These are the fundamental questions for the illuminative philosophy of self-knowledge in Suhrawardī's theory of knowledge by presence.

Insofar as the subject matter of this discussion is concerned, we do not intend to examine the historical dimension of this most interesting philosophy, which to a great extent dominates the whole corpus of Islamic philosophy and theology from what Europeans call the Middle Ages to the present time. As an introduction, we have already presented a historical background only to help us understand what we are aiming at. Now, we should, in all honesty, leave this aspect of the problem to interested scholars in the history of Islamic thought. Our intention, rather, is firstly to present a complete philosophical analysis of the theory of knowledge by presence. Secondly, we are interested in extending the applicability of this kind of knowledge to mystical apprehension so as to offer a modern and original explanation for the objective validity or truth value of this particular apprehension called *'irfān*. Only in the light of this illuminative account of the philosophy of the self can we proceed toward our prospective thesis of the "self-objectivity of mystical experiences," which is what we intend to show.

Turning to the analytical consideration of the philosophy of the self that we have already called the prime example of knowledge by presence, we first refer to Suhrawardī's text as the original source of this idea, and then proceed to take issue with him about it. Therefore, we shall present our own literal translation of the text, and then provide an interpretation or illustration in accordance with our understanding, in order to direct our attention somewhat deeper into the core of the subject under consideration. If we occasionally move from our main objective into a comparative study between this philosophy and some famous and well-known philosophies of the West, it is for the purpose of further clarity of thought and the better acquaintance of one system of philosophy with another.

The Invariable Self in the Sense of "I-ness"

Let us begin with a translation of the commencement of Suhrawardī's text, according to the order in which it appears in his major work, *Ḥikmat al-ishrāq*.

Text:

> An Indicative Treatise, concerning the fact that anyone who apprehends his own reality *(dhātah^{u})*[6] is a pure simple light.
>
> Anyone who has a reality of which he is never oblivious is not obscure [*ghāsiq*, lit. crepuscular]. This is so because of the clarity and apparentness of his reality to himself. He is not a mode of darkness inherent in another thing, for even a mode of light cannot be light in itself let alone that of darkness.
>
> Therefore, he is an immaculate purity of light that cannot be located by physical indication.[7]

Suhrawardī has rightly titled his text as An Indication, for this chapter of his work is extremely involved and synoptic. But fortunately by giving some details in the chapter that follows he throws some light upon what he has outlined in these rather peculiar words, which appear to be somewhat unfamiliar to the ordinary language of philosophy. Insofar as our present thesis is concerned, we feel it not only advantageous but obligatory to include some interpretation of these technical words, and to introduce some preliminary technical expressions needed for our prospective argument. Here we shall briefly paraphrase some of these technical terms.

The word "light," as Suhrawardī elaborated upon it at the very beginning of his metaphysics, is not used in an entirely epistemological sense, for what is clearly understood by the intellect does not possess such a restricted sense as when applied to the physical world. It is, rather, intended to encompass a larger meaning of which physical light is primarily a mode. He believed that when something is so clear and luminous that any explanation or practical investigation to make it any clearer is redundant, it should be called "apparent." Therefore, "apparentness" or "appearance" does not, in this language, necessarily mean that there is something else behind this appearance, something showing only its surface to us, not its whole reality. Having said this, Suhrawardī then asks what could be really more apparent than light itself. Would it not be a real absurdity to shine a light on light in order to see it? It therefore becomes true to say that anything of which nothing more apparent can be given in definition or explanation must be truly and even literally called "light."[8] This description is also given for the notion of light when resorting to the empirical essentialities of lights. A physical light is an instantiation of light because it has in common with other lights the feature that, in the case of seeing, nothing is more apparent than the light itself.

Given this understanding and interpretation of light, Suhrawardī appears to have been perfectly correct in considering that physical light, as a mode of light like any other, can have this description predicated upon it; namely, "of which nothing more apparent can be given in definition or explanation." Therefore, that definition or explanation becomes totally redundant. Furthermore, by establishing such a descriptive principle for his illuminative philosophy, Suhrwardī felt quite justified in placing the reality of the human being in this category, and treating it as an actual mode of the notion of light in such a way that it can be easily characterized by all the intrinsic characteristics and qualitites of light such as apparency, simplicity, indivisibility, indefinableness, and so on.[9]

From this, Suhrawardī went on to elaborate further the designation of his principal technique of light in opposition to darkness, which probably points to an ancient Persian religious orientation. First, he divided what he believed to be "light in the very reality of itself" into a mode of light that is genuine, unadulterated, and noninherent in anything else, and another mode of light that is accidental and subsists in something else. What is not light in the very reality of itself naturally falls into the category of darkness. Darkness is also divided into a mode of darkness that does not occur in another thing and therefore is pure and independent, and a mode which does occur in something else and is not independent. The example of the former is "prime matter" *(hylé),* which is called in his illuminative language the "obscure substance" *(al-jawhar al-ghāsiq),*[10] which is the principle of receptivity and passivity. Examples of the latter are all material objects that count as accidents in the Aristotelian manner of thinking.

In Suhrawardī's philosophy there are also things that are counted among the modes neither of light nor of darkness, but are rather dealt with as being somehow in between. They are called "intermediate objects" *(al-barzakh)* as for example, "material substances" that are, in his words, neither light nor darkness, but are rather in such a state that should rays of light be cast upon them by which they can come to light, they thereby become apparent; but should these rays not reach them, they fall back to absolute darkness and disappear.[11]

These remarks should be taken, at least at the present time, simply as a matter of terminology and as a verbal explanation of some technical words. Yet, we must remind ourselves that this sort of philosophical discourse involves some principal implications. In the first place, there exists a linguistic coloring from the ancient Persian dualism insofar as the terminology of light and darkness is concerned. Of course, being conscious of metaphysical and religious consequences, Suhrawradī emphatically and apologetically confined himself to the "language game" of this dualism and conventionally equated the meaning of light with existence and the meaning of darkness with nothingness.[12]

In the second place, this terminology leans firmly in the direction of a reformulation of the famous Platonic distinction between being and becoming in terms of modes of light and modes of darkness. Suhrawardī tried to avoid attaching any positive sense to his notion of darkness and confined that notion to the far side of the square of opposition, which is the direct contradiction and absolute negation of the notion of light and being. Given this linguistic achievement, we are perfectly entitled to suppose, in his favor, that 'light' can be substituted for 'being' in Plato's doctrine.[13] But whether a purely negative sense of darkness can also be accommodated to the other Platonic thesis, namely 'becoming,' is a question to which Suhrawardī, like other Neoplatonists, had committed himself and of which he was acutely aware. For the time being, we are not going to concern ourselves with this question. Let us turn to the main point at issue, that is, the problem of self-knowledge.

Suhrawardī proceeded to the problem of self-knowledge by considering this knowledge as identical with the very reality of the self, and the reality of the self with pure light; therefore the reality of the self serves as the prime exemplification of knowledge by presence which is pure light, and is that from which nothing more apparent can be perceived.

The Major Argument

Text

An Expanded Treatise on What We Have Already Said

A thing that exists in itself *(al-qā'im bi'l-dhāt)* and is conscious of itself does not know itself through a representation *(al-mithāl)*[14] of itself appearing in itself.

This is because, if, in knowing one's self, one were to make a rep-

> resentation of oneself, since this representation of his 'I-ness' *(anā'iyyah)* could never be the reality of that 'I-ness', it would be then such that, that representation is 'it' in relation to the 'I-ness', and not 'I'. Therefore, the thing apprehended is the representation. It thus follows that the apprehension of 'I-ness' would be exactly what is the apprehension of 'it-ness' *(huwa huwa),* and that the apprehension of the reality of 'I-ness' would be therefore exactly the apprehension of what is not 'I-ness'.
>
> This is an absurdity.
>
> On the other hand, this absurdity does not follow in the case of apprehension of external objects, for the representation and that to which that representation belongs are both 'it's.[15]

Before entering into a critical consideration of this highly involved argument of the text, three preliminary remarks are necessary if we are to understand the truth value of this illuminative demonstration:

1. A first glance at the text informs us that there are at least two necessary conditions to be grasped for the correct understanding of the subject matter we are talking about. First, we are dealing with a thing that is existent "in itself," though not necessarily "by itself." That is, the thing must not be a form of being that might, by its nature, be subsistent in something else. Second, that we should concern ourselves with those things that are supposed to know themselves and can be in one way or another conscious of themselves. These things are not from among inanimate beings; rather, they are those beings who can take a position that gives a rational justification for their saying: "I do this and that."

2. In the process of knowing, in general, there is an "agent" standing for the performative 'I' that is established by its very nature of authority to act, not to be acted upon. This "standing for" is just for the subject 'I', and nothing other that 'I' can ever participate in this private inconvertible rank of being. This state of authority is to be called 'I-ness'. 'I-ness' therefore, is the kingdom of the authoritarianism of the subject, which perfectly satisfies the above two conditions. For, as it stands, the 'I' is "in itself," in the sense that whenever it expresses itself in any form of statement such as "I . . .", it means neither more nor less than "I myself . . ." as an active subject. It does not imply that "I am in, or, with another." It is also conscious of itself, because as soon as 'I' has been expressed by itself, it is understood that the 'I' knows itself, whether that expression is direct, "I know myself," or indirect, "I know something" or "I do something," which presupposes

that "I know myself." There is, on the other hand, another sense of "stand for" which is opposite to this 'I-ness' and which is peculiar to what can be truly called "another." Whatever this "another" may be, whether "he," "she," or simply "it," it cannot participate in the authoritarian kingdom of 'I-ness'. This sort of another must then be fitted in its appropriate class—"it-ness." As a result, to know anything, including ourselves, we must proceed by this mode of operation to bring into act and realization an instantiation of the 'I–it' relationship. Consequently, the 'I–it' dictum is to be considered as a law of knowledge, which cannot be violated in any course of events.

3. With regard to all this, if, in a case of a self-judgment such as "I know X," I know myself through a representation of myself, and not by the very "presence" of the reality of myself, we come up against this question: Is this representation of myself identified with the reality of 'I-ness', or does it remain in the state of 'it-ness'? Being a representation, distinct from the reality of myself, it can never be fitted into the realm of 'I-ness', but rather ought to be placed and kept within the boundaries of 'it-ness'. It then follows that the 'I–it' dictum can no longer hold true in the case of self-judgment, and this law of knowledge is violated. For in this case, the representational 'I' falls into the category of 'it-ness' and is no longer within the realm of 'I-ness', and therefore, 'I' by transforming into 'it' becomes "not I" when it should be nothing but 'I'. This is a clear case of contradiction.

Now let us turn to a thorough examination to find out if this argument is valid. There are apparently two ways in which the fact that one is really conscious of oneself can be proved. One is by knowing something other than one's self, such as is the case when one expresses one's knowledge in a statement saying: "I know the objects x, y and z." This means that by attribution to myself I am already aware of myself. Otherwise attributing any knowledge to myself becomes absolutely meaningless.[16] The other is by directly knowing one's self, when one reflects upon one's self and presents one's self-knowledge in a statement by saying "I know myself." In both cases the knowing subject is aware of itself; in the first case by attribution and in the second by reflection.

Concentrating on this awareness, the argument makes the claim that the knowing subject 'I', in itself, is a complete self-object knowledge, and then raises the question as to what the nature of that implied knowledge may be. In other words, any 'I' clause, whether it be in the form "I know myself" or "I know, or do, such and such," is analyzable into a complete self-object knowledge, which can be stated as, "I know myself." Subsequently, the complete judgment, "I know myself," can be reduced, without any loss of meaning, to the self-expressing 'I' as standing for its own ontological reality of 'I-ness'. The question then is: What is the truth value of this self-knowledge, or that greatly simplified 'I'?

In the consciousness of any particular thing, thought, or feeling, there is always an agent that "brings about" that particular act of consciousness. The reality of this agent will be called 'I', no matter what its nature may really be. In the same act of consciousness, there is another thing involved that is not the agent, but is related to it as the thing which has been "brought about" by that agent. The reality of this latter thing is the object of which we are conscious and will be referred to by 'it'. In this manner we can see with Suhrawardī that in the unity of consciousness there is always a predominant dialectical process of the nature of an 'I and it' opposition that must be carefully observed and must not be violated. That is, in this regard neither is 'I' reducible to 'it', nor 'it' to 'I'. In the anatomy of knowledge, 'I' and 'it' make up a unity of opposition.

On the basis of the 'I-ness/it-ness' dictum, Suhrawardī tried to establish his point of argument in the following way: If it were the case that the knowing subject, in order to know itself, objectifies itself, it would set up a phenomenal representation distinct from itself which would be called 'it' and not 'I'. In that case, while, as the law of 'I-ness/it-ness' requires, the 'I' must remain in its unchangeable subject-authority of 'I-ness'; the 'it', being the "self," also falls under this category and becomes united with 'I'. However, once again, as the law of 'I-ness/it-ness' stands, the 'it-ness' can never be converted into 'I-ness' and become totally united with the active reality of 'I'. Nor can the factual reality of 'I' be transubstantiated into the reality of 'it'. Consequently, the 'I-ness' and 'it-ness' turn out to be both different and identical in the same respect. This is impossible. Let us see how they can be different by a sort of opposition, and yet at the same time united in a self-identity, both in the same respect.

They are different because each of them, by the necessity of the law of the 'I-ness/it-ness' relation, stands for a different function and a different component of the unity of consciousness. For while it is true that the 'I' never becomes 'it' in the unity of consciousness, it is also logically and epistemologically true that the 'it' never resigns its own totality to the subject authority of the 'I'. So it does not become altogether identical with the state of 'I-ness' either. In other words, in Islamic philosophical discourse the relation of 'I-ness' to 'it-ness' within the unity of consciousness is considered to be a kind of "correlativity" *(taḍāyuf)*.[17] The standard property of a relation of this kind is that all the related members of the class must be mutually "simultaneous," in act or in potency. That is to say, they are all supposed to be in the state of equilibrium with regard to act or potency in the sense that if one is in act the other or others must be in act as well, and if one is in potency the rest must be in the same condition.

The relationship of fatherhood and childhood, for instance, is of this kind of correlativity. If X is the father of Y at this present time, Y must simultaneously be a child of X at this present time and vice versa. But if X is the father of Y in the past or future, Y must also simultaneously be a child of X in the past or future, but not in the present, and vice versa.

Putting the 'I-ness/it-ness' dictum into this categorical relationship, we arrive at the following conclusion concerning the case of self-consciousness: If we suppose that the 'I' is really in act such that the 'I' can truly say "I know myself," its opposite, 'it', must also be truly in act simultaneously, and to the same degree of certainty. That is, " 'I' know myself" is just another way of saying "I know 'it' " and because the 'I' in this case is in act, the 'it' is also simultaneously in act. Conversely, if the 'I' is not in act but rather in the state of potency, the 'it' also must remain in the state of potency. The conclusion is that in the state of unity of consciousness, the difference and opposition between 'I-ness' and 'it-ness' cannot be eliminated but rather it becomes sharper. They must therefore, by necessity of intercorrelativity and simultaneity, be different, and can never be identical.

But they are, on the other hand, identical, because the 'it' as substituted for "myself" in a self-conscious statement means nothing but the knowing subject itself, the self for which the 'I' has already been designated. By using an equation, we see that the expression, 'it', in a sentence such as "I know it/myself," is equivalent to the object term "myself," such that it can be substituted for "myself" as the object of my knowledge; and the expression "myself" is also, being a reflexive term of the subject, in a way equivalent to the term 'I'; and that therefore, the 'it' is convertible to the 'I' by this formulization: $A = B$, $B = C$, $\therefore A = C$. Furthermore, if I have the right, according to any account or any kind of theory of knowledge, to believe that "I know myself," what has been expressed by "myself" in this statement is nothing other than what is meant by 'I'. Supposing that the expression "myself" as the object known somehow ceases to be identical with 'I', the whole of the statement falls short of being in any way meaningful. Therefore, it must be said that 'I' and 'it' are identical in the case of self-knowledge. The final conclusion is that, in a self-knowledge statement such as "I know myself," the 'I' and 'it' must be both identical and different at the same time. This is an impossibility.

This is the absurdity that Suhrawardī was talking about and wished to attribute to the phenomenalist[18] theory of self-consciousness. He tried to point out that if it were the case that our knowledge of the truth of ourselves is by a phenomenal representation, we would be driven into this flat contradiction. But as we have seen at the end of his argument, he specified that such an absurdity is not involved in, and may not apply to, the knowledge of external beings. For a subjective representation of an external object and the external object itself are both family members of the same class, i.e., 'it-ness'. Hence, one 'it' does not contradict the other, since neither of them is convertible into the opposite state of 'I-ness'. The absurdity surfaces only in the case of self-consciousness where the two opposite and inconvertible terms 'I' and 'it' are involved. They face each other in a state of opposed interrelation, making up together a piece of phenomenal knowledge distinguished from other kinds of knowledge as self-knowledge.

It appears all but obvious that the whole force of the argument is based upon the "invariability" or, if one wishes, the "inconvertibility" of the state of 'I-ness' into 'it-ness' and vice versa. Were the 'I' in one way or another convertible into 'it', there would be two 'it's, and hence a possibility for the two 'it's to be united with each other and judged by the uniting act of the knowing subject without contradiction. 'I-ness' is therefore the court in which "judgment" is made on "other" things and it can never become one of them; it must, at the same time, always remain aloof from judgment as "other" things.

One can, of course, objectify oneself when one reflects upon oneself by saying: 'it' is 'I' who know myself. But by objectification it is meant that one can fictitiously treat oneself as an 'it' and bring one's judgment of unification upon oneself. But this is an objectified fictitious "self" that has nothing to do with the real performative "self," the knowing subject which is the make of the judgment, not the object of it. One should notice that by fictitious self we do not unwillingly commit ourselves to a mystical monistic theory which proclaims that all the plurality of this world is illusory and fictitious. We rather wish to specify that no reflective knowledge of the self can be accounted for by anything but a transformation from the invariable 'I' to the variable nature of 'it'. If such were not the case, the 'I' could no longer be represented at all. Thus any conception pretending to be a representation of the 'I' is fictitious and contradictory. This will then be an "introspective" piece of knowledge that should not be, strictly speaking, called self-consciousness; but grammatically, it is a sort of judgment about a fictitious self similar to those about others.

There is no difference whatsoever between saying "S knows P" and "It is I who know P," or, "I am the one who knows P," provided that the 'I' in the second, and the 'I' in the last statement, are convertible into 'it'. The only difference between the first, on the one hand, and the second and third, on the other, is that the judging subject has not occurred in the first statement but is understood by the act of judgment from the outside, while it has fictitiously occurred in the second and third ones. Since the 'I' in such a place as this is necessarily converted into 'it', the occurrence of the 'I' signifies nothing but 'it'. This is the meaning of being fictitious.

At this point one can criticize this position by raising the following objection: Although Suhrawardī, in this rather ingenious argument, did in fact bring out the danger of absurdity, run by all classical theories of self-consciousness, he hardly succeeded in coming up with the desired result of establishing his own theory of knowledge by presence, which is supposed to be the objective truth of the self.

The answer to this objection is that the form of the argument, rather than its content, must be observed from the beginning to the end. The extensive feature of the argument is one of *reductio ad absurdum*, which in Islamic logic is called *qiyās al-khulf*.[19] Committing himself to a position of proving the proposition that true "self-knowledge" is experienced by presence, Suhrawardī, just for the sake of argument, first supposed that the denial of this proposition is true. Since the denial of that proposition is a simple negation which is positively exemplified in the phenomenologist theory of self-consciousness, he naturally assumed that this theory, the countertheory of his own theory, should be taken, for the sake of argument, as a true premise. Then, putting this premise in a formally valid argument, he succeeded in demonstrating that the above contradiction is implied in this premise. Once this premise has been proven false, the denial of it, which is the theory of knowledge by presence, is finally held to be true. From all this he concluded that the initial proposition, "self-consciousness is a knowledge by presence," is true.

On the whole, focusing our attention on the centerpiece of this *reductio ad absurdum* form of argument, we can put the absurdity demonstrated by this argument in various ways. All of, or at least more than one of, these ways may really have been intended by the author himself, but they need to be explicated in order to be completely understood. They are the following:

First, if my acquaintance with myself were by a representation instead of the presence of my reality to myself, then my acquaintance with myself would be exactly my acquaintance with what is not myself, that is, with a representation, even though it be a representation of myself. This absurdity proceeds from the "epistemic" feature of the problem that can be clearly understood from his words "the apprehension of the reality of 'I-ness' would be, therefore, exactly the apprehension of what is not 'I-ness,' namely 'it-ness.' "

Second, should 'I-ness' and 'it-ness' ever be identical in the case of self-consciousness, while, as the subject-object relation stood, they functioned distinctly, they would be then both identical and different in one and the same respect. This is, of course, a logical form of absurdity that rises from the violation of the law of the subject-object relation in a proposition.

Third, if the expression "myself" in a statement like "I know myself" means 'it' as referential to the representation of myself which is obviously on a par with "not myself," then "I know myself" must have the meaning that "I know not-myself." Now, "I know not-myself" is just another way of saying "I do not know myself." There would be complete chaos and the destruction of human communication should a statement like "I know myself" ever mean that "I do not know myself." This absurdity belongs to the linguistic features of the issue.

At the end of this commentary we must remind ourselves of three important points concerning the objective of this argument and its consequences:

1. For everyone who is, in the manner of his nature, to be acquainted with "himself" in such a way that in the scope of his own acquaintance there remains no logical possibility for anything other than himself, his knowledge of himself is nothing other than himself; his knowledge of himself is nothing other than the very reality of himself. Anything besides the bare reality of selfness counts as "another" that lies beyond, and is foreign to, the true knowledge of oneself. Thus there is, so to speak, a typical equivalence and interchangeability between this kind of "knowledge" of the self and the bare reality of the "selfhood" itself. In other words, in this prime example of presence-knowledge, the meaning of knowledge becomes absolutely equivalent with the meaning of the very 'being' of the self, such that within the territory of 'I-ness', to know is to exist and to exist is to know. This is the meaning of the self-objectivity of knowledge by presence.[20]

In these terms, my most private reality is nothing but the individual fact of my existence, for which the word 'I' has been designated as a direct reference, not to be used in the manner that an ordinary word is used in its meaning. This sort of 'I' can never be converted under any circumstances into 'it' or the like. The language game of 'I' therefore, is radically different from that of anything else expressed by 'it'. We can say, at least at this stage of study, that the former will be called subject language and the latter object language. The subject language is that which can never be used and spoken in the object language, because as soon as the subject 'I' becomes objectified and has been spoken of in the object language, it has already been converted into 'it' and is no longer the 'I'.

But now, the question is how can we manipulate such a radical difference between the two languages? One answer to this question is, if I am not mistaken, the difference between the theory of "meaning" and the theory of "reference." When 'I', as a subject term, is expressed in a sentence, it is not used to mean the concept of the reality of 'I-ness'; rather, it has been designated to refer directly to the factual reference that is the bare reality of the subject. The subject language is therefore referential to the performative 'I' which, by showing itself, makes itself known as a living subject in a self-judgment. The word 'I' accordingly functions as an "arrow" pointing to the kingdom of the performative 'I' in any self-statement, not as a word used for the meaning and conceptualization of the self, though it can do so in an introspective self-proposition.

2. The most significant point that one can conclude from this argument, as well as from other arguments that the author presents later, is that there is at least one thing which is "being-in-itself" in the sense that its being does not subsist in another, and that is known to us by virtue of knowledge by presence. This thing is the reality of my 'I-ness', which has been proven to be in itself, though not necessarily by itself, and present to itself, in the sense that it cannot possibly be more apparent to itself than simply being in itself.

At this crucial point there arises the controversial problem of the Kantian "things-in-themselves" that are supposed to be, in Kant's words, unknowable to us and noumenal in themselves, but in the meantime, conceivable in the manner of our transcendental thinking. We intend to write on this topic later in a place where we can make a comparative study between this illuminative philosophy and Kant's philosophy of noumenalism and phenomenalism. Let it merely be said now in passing that it would be a most interesting subject for investigation.

3. As we have seen, there is no noteworthy mention in the above text of those basic metaphysical and transcendental concepts that generally appear in all the classical philosophical studies, such as "existence" and "essence," or "substance" and "accident" and so on. Instead, great emphasis has been laid on the empirical and active reality of 'I-ness' which, as we have already observed, does not have any

connotation connecting it with the controversial problem of the essence-existence distinction. It seems to me that the main objective of this approach is to consider the truth of the actual reality of the subject that is characterized by the two conditions mentioned above. It does not matter if the kind of subject here under consideration has to be called, in the transcendental language, substance, accident, noumenon, or phenomenon. Nor does it matter if this sense of reality later falls under the heading of existence or of essence when the problem of the essence-existence relation is considered; although, at the end, Suhrawardī does reach the position that such a projected reality of the self is nothing but a pure existence. This is because, according to his illuminative principle that the reality of the self sufficiently satisfies all the empirical essentialities of light, and because light also perfectly applies to pure existence in terms of the greatest "apparency," the self can be defined in terms of a pure existence.[21]

None of these three important points really draws Suhrawardī's attention at this stage of his investigation. When we follow him to the end of his discussion, we shall find him clearly saying that the notion of substance in its conventional positive sense does not belong to the absolute simplicity of the reality of 'I-ness'; neither does it belong to its negative implication which is not to exist in another being. Perhaps substance, as well as other metaphysical concepts, are all, in his opinion, to be understood and considered only after a certain intellectual analysis made by the philosophical mind of the simple reality of the performative, factual 'I-ness'. Thus in the territorial simplicity of 'I-ness', there is no possibility for these manipulated questions such as substance and accident. Indeed it should be admitted that one of the greatest merits of these types of arguments is their careful avoidance of emphasis on any of these delicate metaphysical problems, but instead their examination of the very performative reality of 'I-ness'. This is most characteristic of illuminative philosophy and its realistic posture in its drive to the light of truth.

Argument from Attribute

Now, let us pass on to the presentation of the next argument:

Text

> . . . Again, assuming that it [i.e., self-knowledge] is by representation, then if one does not know that that representation is one's own, one

> thus never knows that one has ever known oneself. But if one supposedly knows that the representation belongs to himself, one must then already have known himself with no representation. However, it is inconceivable that one apprehends himself by means of something superadded to himself, since this superaddition would serve as an attribute to one's self. If this is so, then, one decides that every attribute associated with one's reality, no matter whether it is knowledge or another attribute, belongs to one's own reality, and it then implies that one has known himself before knowing these attributes and even without them.
>
> The conclusion is that one does not know one's self through one's superadded attributes among which is one's representation of one's self.[22]

Whereas the first argument, as we have indicated, was concerned with the logical, epistemic, and semantic function of the state of 'I-ness' as opposed to that of 'it-ness', this argument seems to deal with metaphysical distinction between attributes and that to which these attributes are ascribed, which is prospectively supposed to be the reality of selfness. Still, there has been no interest shown in the manner in which this reality should be interpreted, that is, does it belong to the category of substance, accident, or some other notions?

Although this consideration quite clearly calls for a distinction between attributes and the self to which these attributes are referred, it has been set forth in such a way that even this distinction is to be made by the performative subject itself, and not by an outside agent. This is because a judgment from the outside that makes a distinction between attributes and the thing to which these attributes belong, treats the self as an object which, being converted into an 'it', can easily be analyzed into qualities and the thing qualified. This obviously brings us back to the vulnerable classical argument for the subsistence of material substances, an argument with which Suhrawardī did not wish to get involved.[23]

In other words, this argument must be brought into line with the first one so that it may satisfy the two above mentioned conditions, that is, that the subject under consideration should be something existing in itself, not in another, and that it must have the power to know itself. Given these two conditions, it becomes clear enough that this argument is concerned only with the self that is speaking, doing, or making a judgment of which he or she is conscious. This is what we have already called the performative self. That is because anything other than this performative self could be changed from a knowing subject into an inanimate object which could be referred to as 'it'.

Having made this qualification, there is therefore no possibility of considering this argument among those traditional ones that deal with the distinction between substance and accident on the one hand and attributes and that of which the attributes are predicated, on the other. All those classical arguments spring from the consideration that there is a material substance which acts as a continuous, never-changing 'it' which holds and unites the variety of accidents in the succession of times and events.

The Key Word

Furthermore, it seems obvious to me that there is a key word here that has not been very explicitly indicated in the framework of the argument, but has rather been implied and understood in the notion of "decide," and used as the major step toward the conclusion. This key word is "appropriation" by decision in the sense of taking and using something as one's own. In the case of a self-knowledge given by representation, the knowing subject ought beforehand to have "appropriated" the representation of himself to himself so as to achieve the act of knowing himself through the act of specification. Otherwise, if such an appropriation did not take place properly, he would forever fail to know himself, for a representation that is neither appropriated by decision to himself, nor to any other particular person, is characterized as universal. A nonappropriate representation is to be held universal because it can legitimately be applied to anyone who may be represented by such a nonappropriated representation. Now if this were the case, Suhrawardī asked, how could one appropriate the representation of one's self to oneself in all certainty and be sure that it is one's own representation, while one supposedly does not already know one's self without representation? The representation therefore helps one to know himself if, and only if, one can make it specific and appropriate it to himself so that one can know one's true self through that appropriate representation. On the other hand, if one cannot properly make this appropriation, one can never succeed in knowing himself with any degree of certainty, since a nonappropriate representation remains universally open and applicable to a multitude of individuals as its possible objective references. Such an appropriation implies the awareness of the self-knowing subject, not by representation, but rather by presence.[24]

A counterexample for this argument could be a question like this: In the case of knowing an external object, which undoubtedly exemplifies knowledge by representation, how can one appropriate the representation of the object to the object itself, in order to know that specified object, while one does not already know the object without representation? Whatever the solution for knowledge of an external object by representation turns out to be, it will also be the solution that is proper to knowledge of the self by representation.

The correct answer to this counterexample is that in the course of knowing an external object, say a table, insofar as we are not able to know that object by presence, we cannot with certainty appropriate its representation of it, at least not exactly as we do in the knowledge of ourselves. This is the reason why our knowledge of the external world must remain in the mode of "probability," or in Islamic terminology, in the state of "accidentality," and can never be raised to the logical state of necessity or self-certainty. For that matter, our scientific "truth" is always characterized by degrees of probability and verification. But it is obvious that a necessity and self-certainty are characteristic of our private knowledge of ourselves.

Another Way of Interpretation

There is another way of interpreting this argument. Assuming, for the sake of argument, that our knowledge of ourselves is, like our knowledge of external objects, arrived at by a representation of the reality of ourselves and not by the presence of that reality itself, it then follows that this representation must be appropriated and referred to ourselves as its "objective reference." This appropriation cannot be made except by knowing ourselves through another representation appropriated to ourselves as its objective reference. The other representation also requires another appropriate representation, and so on. This will then go on *ad infinitum*. Therefore, in knowing myself, either I should not know myself at all, or I should know a range of infinite antecedent representations of myself along with the consequent knowledge of myself at the end. The first alternative is completely contradictory, while the second is the absurdity of an infinite number of items of knowledge within the limited scope of a single case of self-knowledge in a limited span of time. This is again another form of contradiction, because it requires an infinity in a finite case of knowing. Notice that in both alternatives we are assuming that, by virtue of self-certainty, we do know ourselves in one way or another. That is, in this interpretation an unspecified sense of knowledge is understood through the assumption of the fact that we do know ourselves with all certainty. Thus we arrive at the conclusion that I cannot know myself by representation at all. But, since I do, with all certainty, know myself, my knowledge must be by presence and not by representation.

Final Conclusion

Text

> Since you are not absent from your own reality *(dhātuk[a])* and from your awareness of that reality, and it is not possible that this awareness be by a representation or any superaddition, it thus follows that in this awareness of your reality you need not have anything besides the very reality of yourself, which is apparent to yourself or, if you wish, not absent from yourself.
>
> Consequently, it is necessary that the apprehension of the reality of the self itself, is only by itself, according to what that self 'is' in its being, just as it is necessary that you are never absent from your reality, and from whatever your reality may consist of. On the other hand, whatever your reality is absent from, like those organs, viz. heart, lungs, brain and all intermediate forms and modes, no matter whether they are modes of darkness or of light, it is not implied in that constant awareness of your reality.
>
> Your constant conscious reality is therefore not a material organ, neither is it an intermediary transcendental one. Had your reality consisted of any of these things, you, as the constant and unfading consciousness of yourself, would never become absent from it.[25]

One way to put this rather long statement is to consider the fact that in the course of all the preceding arguments, Suhrawardī has so far proved at least the negative side of his thesis. That is, the self cannot be absolutely known through anything accessory to the pure reality of itself, no matter whether this accessory thing is a representation made by itself or any other thing that can be referred to as 'it'. From this already proved theorem, together with the earlier presupposition that we are in principle concerned with those beings that are not absent from themselves, he derived two most important conclusions, one following upon the other: (1) That the knowledge of the self must necessarily be through the sheer presence of the reality of the self (this is the positive dimension of the thesis), and (2) that whatever is not known through the presence of the pure reality of the self has neither a basic, nor even a partial, part to play in making up the existential constitution of that reality, and therefore lies beyond the kingdom of 'I-ness'.

As for the first hypothesis, Suhrawardī had pointed out that although we are, in actual circumstances, aware of ourselves, we have clearly understood that it is absolutely impossible to attain this awareness through a representation that would obviously count as something other than the bare reality of ourselves. It must therefore be concluded that our awareness of ourselves is necessarily through the sheer "presence" of the reality of ourselves. The awareness of ourselves means neither more nor less than the very existential reality of ourselves. This is the material equivalence between 'knowing' ourselves by presence and 'being' in ourselves as the objective reality of ourselves, and this is the meaning of the self-objectivity of knowledge by presence, which in fact constitutes the positive aspect of illuminative theory.

Having established all the components of his initial thesis, Suhrawardī immediately moved from this basic achievement toward the other fundamental theories that are of vital interest in illuminative philosophy, as well as in other schools of philosophy.

These theories are as follows:

a. That the self is nothing but an immaterial being.
b. That the self is a most simple and indivisible reality.
c. That the question as to whether or not the self is a substance can be decided, if by "substantiality" is meant the practical, but not the theoretical and categorical, negation of being in another. A thing can be a substance if its actual existence proves not to be in another, and if its act does not depend upon another being.[26]

Since from among three theses the first one is not, for the time being, the object of our immediate concern, we shall leave that topic to its own due place, and focus our attention on the other two, the issue of which is now under consideration.

The Meaning of Simplicity

Dealing with the problem of the absolute simplicity and indivisibility of the self, we can reasonably rely upon the principle of the identity between 'knowing' the self through knowledge by presence, and the 'being' of the objective reality of the self. This is so since, in the domain of that knowledge as has been thus far described, there remains nothing to be pointed to which would be other than 'I-ness'. The pure reality and the absolute presence are governed by nothing other than the ontological state of 'I-ness'. Were there any element that could be understood as constitutive of genus or differentia other than 'I', and which could be referred to by 'it', it would give way to the state of 'it-ness' and, as a result, cause the entire subject-authority of the performative 'I-ness' to collapse. In this case the 'I-ness' would become contradictory. Just as there is no possibility for a transition from the state of 'I-ness' to that of 'it-ness', so also there is hardly any possibility for suggesting any objective composition of 'I-ness' and 'it-ness' when the state of 'I-ness' is in effect. Therefore, to know myself through knowledge by presence is to rule out any element of not-being myself, which would not be present in myself, and to concentrate instead on the absolute purity of 'I-ness', which is wholly present to myself. Since this knowledge remains, at this particular stage, in absolute simplicity, the self also, because of our equation, must remain in the ultimate degree of simplicity.

There are two points to be made here before moving on to the next problem. Firstly, more elucidation is required in order to assure that the applicability of the term "presence" to the awareness of the self on the one hand, and to the objective reality of the self on the other, is philosophically authentic and linguistically literal, and by no means arbitrary or even figurative. Secondly, as far as the manipulated equation of this sort of knowledge with the existential reality of the self known is concerned, we are in a position to say that we do constantly know ourselves insofar as we really are in ourselves; that is, insofar as we exist in the world of reality among external objects, not as we "appear," in Kantian terms, to ourselves in the form of phenomenal knowledge. The most outstanding feature of knowledge by presence, however, is that the immediate objective reality of the thing as it is, is its being known.

An Interpretation of the Words "Presence" and "Appearances"

As for the first point, in this passage Suhrawardī gave his linguistic account of the term presence. This is to provide an interpretation according to which the word can be literally used in the illuminative sense without losing any essential part of its common significance. This linguistic approach is vitally important because it legitimizes the notion of presence as the transition from 'knowing' to 'being'. To be present to myself, Suhrawardī says, is another way of saying not to be absent from myself.[27] If one ever gives the reality of oneself to another, then it becomes true that one has lost oneself to another, and become absent from oneself so that one is no longer oneself with the same existential identity. Knowledge by presence, therefore, means the awareness of a thing whose reality is not absent from itself. This is the negative connotation of the term presence.

There is also another connotation that lies in that negative sense of presence (i.e., not absence) and is equally imperative in the course of the explanation of the theory of knowledge by presence. This is the notion of "apparentness." It has been mentioned that in this theory the self is most apparent to itself in such a way that nothing else can ever be more apparent to the self than itself. It appears all but certain that in the language of illuminative philosophy the word apparent is not used in the sense that has been quite often used by theorists of phenomenology for "showing something" to "something else," but rather as being in the state of ultimate certainty. "I am apparent to myself" accordingly means that I am so sure about myself that it is absurd for me to cast the slightest shadow of doubt on the truth of my being. This is because it would be absurd for me to be at all absent from myself. In this way Suhrawardī identified his terminology of apparentness with the negative sense of presence which is the negation of absence by saying: "It thus follows that in this awareness of your reality you need not have anything besides the very reality of yourself, which is 'apparent' to yourself, or, if you wish, 'not absent' from yourself." Likewise, "not absent from yourself" should in this context mean "not being other than yourself."

Is the Self a Substance?

With regard to the second problem, namely the problem of the substantiality of the self, Suhrawardī considered it with clarity and decided the issue easily on the grounds that he supposed he had already established the proposition of the identity of knowing the self and the objective being of the self. However, dealing with the question whether or not the self is a substance, he wrote:

Text

> Substantiality *(al-jawhariyyah)*, however, whether considered as a complete essence of the self, or given as a negation of a [subsisting] subject or locus for its occurrence, is not something [objectively] independent, such that your reality *(dhātuk^{a})* itself consists of "that" object referred to as an "it" *(hiya)*.

> Assuming "substantiality" to have an unknown meaning, while you constantly know your reality, not by anything superadded to that reality known by yourself, this unknown substantiality which is absent from yourself will not count as the whole, and not even as part, of your reality *(dhātuk^{a})* at all. When you have made your careful inquiry into yourself, you will find out that what you are made of as "yourself" is nothing but that which knows its own reality. This is your own [performative] 'I-ness' *(ana'iyyatuk^{a})*.[28] This is the manner in which everyone is to know himself, and which everyone's [performative] 'I-ness' has in common with you.[29]

On account of knowledge by presence and the identity that he had just engineered between it and the objective reality of the self, Suhrawardī took a further step in this passage toward the solution of the problem of the substantiality of the self. Basing himself simply on the grounds that whatever one knows of oneself by virtue of presence must count as the sole reality of one's self, he believed that it follows that the existence of the performative 'I-ness' is absolutely pure, and that the purity of the 'I-ness' in existence is nothing but its "independence" from being in another. Since in the scope of this knowledge nothing can be found in act other than the 'I-ness' of the self, the objective reality of the self must be in conformity with a mode of being that does not exist in another.[30] This kind of existential independence counts for substantiality.

In point of fact, this argument has been constructed from the two consecutive theorems that have already been proven by the author himself. The first is the identity of 'knowing' and 'being' in the case of self-knowledge by presence, and the other is the purity and absolute simplicity of this knowledge, which decisively and actively excludes any element of "otherness" from the domain of 'I-ness'. Once these two premises have been accepted, the conclusion obviously follows that the self has a form of reality which does not imply any sense of "otherness." This is the meaning of independent reality, which is the equivalent to Suhrawardī's terminology of "substantiality."

The remaining part of the argument is intended to reestablish a warranted and straightforward view of substantiality, and to disentangle this notion from the classical approaches to the controversial distinction between the category of substance and that of accidents. In doing so, Suhrwardī quite ingeniously offered us his own definition of substantiality, a definition that was carefully articulated in the light of his empirical inquiry into the factual circumstances of performative 'I-ness' on the one hand, and the commonly understood meaning of the word subtance on the other. Far from being *a priori* and dogmatic, his definition was characterized by the mere negative import of "substantiality," namely, "not being in another," and by its being based only upon the information suggested by the performative truth value of knowledge by presence itself, regardless of all metaphysical discourse concerning the issue.

When he suggested that if we supposed that the self has an unknown essence, be it substance or accident, such an essence could constitute neither the whole nor part of the reality of the self; he meant that we should not concern ourselves with these controversial problems that are not warranted by the factual reality of 'I-ness'. All we can do, Suhrawardī suggested, is to make a careful inquiry into our performative, and not conceptual, 'I-ness'es to find out what their reality consists of. Of course, by "inquiry" he meant an inquiry into the awareness of ourselves, and into what we are aware of by this kind of knowledge. As soon as the result of this turns out to be nothing more nor less than the unadulterated reality of 'I-ness', there is no reason whatsoever why we should inflict the reality of this 'I-ness' with an 'it-ness', even if such an irresponsible infliction were not to prove to be contradictory.[31]

In conclusion, on the basis of this illuminative theory that the performative knowledge of 'I-ness' is exactly what the reality of 'I-ness' is in truth, together with the simplicity of the nature of this knowledge, a negative sense of substantiality can evidently be established. This negative sense alone is able to describe the reality of the self as a form of being which, while it simply and performatively is, does not exist in another.[32] Now if the category of substance as such can undergo this reduction and simplification and be reinstated in this negative version without calling for a positive, unknown essence, it will be a great achievement for Suhrawardī to have arrived at the conclusion that the objective existence of the self proves to be a substance revealed to us in this sense. But even if this category is not prepared to sustain this reduction in meaning, it still hardly seems possible to challenge Suhrawardī's position in principle that the reality of the self does not subsist in another being. The self is therefore, according to Suhrawardī's philosophy, an independent reality as well as a simple and indivisible being, no matter what category, if any, does *a priori* apply to its essentialities.[33]

Six

An Appendix to the Theory of Knowledge by Presence

Completeness

As the title indicates, we are now, for the sake of completeness, going to trace the issues at hand in detail by sketching out a comprehensive application of knowledge by presence. Since in the aforementioned version of illuminative philosophy this development is based on the fundamentally important treatment of self-knowledge and on the principle that the presence-knowledge of the self has absolute priority over any other kind of human knowledge, we here intend to follow the same train of thought. We have accordingly placed the empirical consideration that follows here as an appendix to our discussion of the problem of self-knowledge in order to further reflect the philosophical ingenuity of our thesis.[1] The reason why we discussed an empirical dimension of knowledge by presence even before we discussed the problem of self-knowledge was simply pedagogical.[2] That is, we tried to start with what was supposed to be closer to our empirical understanding than the problematic issue of personal identity.

In the preceding chapters, we have presented in some detail the two specific cases we have called empirical and prime examples of knowledge by presence, which acted to illustrate the truth and validity of this illuminative theory in the different stages of human apprehension, sense-experience and self-knowledge. Each of the two examples was dealt with according to its own intrinsic characteristics so that it might enable us to know how this kind of knowledge can be verified in these two different stages of apprehension. In this chapter, once again following Suhrawardī's way of thinking, we shall recapitulate some of the outstanding points of these aforementioned arguments, and then proceed to the presentation of another empirical mode of the theory, the applicability of which passes far beyond the two preceding cases. However, in order to avoid repetition and redundancy, we shall confine ourselves to an explanation of some of the most important developments that occur later in this empirical approach to the theory. Therefore, in returning to some previously mentioned fundamental points, we shall rely upon the understanding we obtained through our first acquaintance with the theory.

A Summary of the Previous Arguments

Concerning the problem of knowledge and human understanding as such, Suhrawardī believed that the first question we as philosophers face is how we can really know ourselves. This question precedes concerns about committing ourselves to the claim that it is possible for us to know something of the external world even before we reflect on the private states of our minds.[3]

Dealing with this question, Suhrawardī proceeded from a summary of his previous arguments to an expanded version of the theory in the following manner:

> In the course of human knowledge man must first make his inquiry into his awareness of himself *('ilmih^{i} bi dhātih^{i})*, then proceed from this step to what is above and beyond himself [the external world].
>
> Thus, we say: the fact that our souls apprehend the reality of themselves *(dhātihā)* does not imply that the apprehension has come to them by a representation *(bi ṣūrat^{in})*.
>
> This is because of the following:
>
> First, the representation that is used by, and appears in, the mind is not exactly the mind as it is in itself *(hiy^{a} hiy^{a})*. But that which is aware of itself is supposedly aware of what its objective 'I-ness' *(li'ayn mā hiya anā'iyyatuh^{u})* consists of, rather than that with which this objective 'I-ness' is in conformity. Any representation taking place in the mind of the knower is, in fact, something added to this reality which, in comparison with that reality, serves as an 'it' *(huwa)* and never as an 'I' *(anā)*.

> Secondly, suppose that self-apprehension is by representation. Now, every representation existing in the self, as an intellect, is universal [in the sense that it is not impossible to predicate it of many]. Even if a complete sum of universals referring altogether to one single individual among others have been gathered together in a unitary complex, it still cannot make that representation cease to be universal. But the fact is that everyone's apprehension of his own reality is with such strict individuality that it can have nothing in common with another. Thus one's understanding of one's own individual reality can never be admitted as being by means of any representation at all.
>
> Furthermore, the self does in fact apprehend its body as well as its imagination and its phantasm. The supposition that these things are apprehended through a representation inherent in the reality of the self, while the representation as such is universal, would imply that the self is the mover of a universal body, using universal mental powers, and has no apprehension of its particular body nor acquaintance with the powers that belong to itself. This [consideration] is obviously not right. For the imagination is ignorant of [cannot apprehend] itself, just as it is ignorant of all the mental powers, and therefore it cannot challenge the effects of these powers in actual operation. Now, if the imagination is not competent to realize either itself or these mental powers, no material power can ever understand the truth of itself. And if the self as an intellect were also not supposed to know anything other than universals, then it would necessarily follow that a man would never know his own particular body, his own particular imagination, and his own particular phantasm, all of which pertain to himself. But this is not actually the case, because in the world of reality there are no human beings who do not know in presence their own particular bodies and their own particular mentalities while using their own particular powers. The conclusion is that man knows all his mental powers with no mediation of any mental image, and knows the entirety of his body in the same manner.[4]

While trying, in this long passage, to sum up his already well-formulated arguments and making his position somewhat clearer and more understandable, Suhrawardī has taken two further steps toward his empirical account:

1. Like self-apprehension, the apprehension of one's own body and all its mental powers and activities must be characterized as a form of knowledge by presence.
2. There is an epistemic criteriology for the universality and particularity of knowledge,[5] which must be taken into account when the problem of private states of mind is in question.

Thus understood, each of these two interesting points is quite an advance and needs to be explained. Let us begin with a brief reflection on the first before we come to an expository presentation of the second.

An Inquiry into Our Private Knowledge

Let us set aside, for the moment, the question of the self-knowledge presented in Suhrawardī's philosophy as the principal step toward the solution of the problem of human knowledge in general. Our philosophy must, nevertheless, answer the question as to how and in what reasonable manner we can be, or are, acquainted with our bodies, our mental powers of imagination and phantasm, and our general sense perceptions. By asking this question and dealing with the metaphysical and epistemological aspects of this problem, it does not necessarily mean that we become unwillingly involved in the psychological evaluation of human mentalities and the ways in which the mind functions. On the contrary, it is rather apparent that the question of how I 'know' my mental powers of understanding is far from being a psychological question, which is implied in probing into what "scientific procedure" governs mental powers, hence determining action and reaction. However, there are two points to be noted in this regard:

The Representative of Body, Imagination, and Phantasm is Universal

The basic premise behind this philosophical issue is that whereas we undoubtedly know our powers of imagination and phantasm, as well as our bodies, we need to understand further how we can characterize this knowledge. Is it that, in order to know our own particular power of imagination, we must in one way or another grasp a representation of that particular power? Hence, does knowledge of phantasm necessitate having a mental image as the representation of that phantasm, and likewise for our body and all the powers operating in our own particular body? If such be the case, then the question will be: How and where does such a representation take place? Does the representation of the imagination appear in the imagination itself, and that of our sense experience in our senses themselves, and hence, of our body in the body itself, etc.?[6]

As the classical epistemic law stands, the representation of these things never occurs in the things themselves, but rather in the higher stage of the self that is called the "intellect," or the power of transcendental understanding. This is because just as sense-perceptions can never perceive themselves, nor can a body ever apprehend itself. Therefore, imagination and phantasm too, cannot imagine and fancy themselves. Starting from this hypothesis, we must come to the conclusion that the representation of the aforementioned things can only appear within the intellectual power of the self and never in any lower mental power of apprehension. Thus all the representations and mental appearances taken from our bodies and mentalities must accordingly be regarded as intellectual, and for that matter, universal. Therefore, no apprehended motion in our body is regarded as particular.

The Intellect Can Only Communicate with the Universal Body

Given that all these representations situated in the intellectual self are abstract, and in that sense, universal, the self as the performative subject can never act upon or be informed by the particular reality of the things represented. This is simply because the self can have no communication whatsoever with these particular things if there is no link between the intellectual universal representations and the particular reality of these things represented. In such circumstances, all that the 'I', as a performative self, can accomplish is to "intellectually" move the universal body, which is the *representation* of my particular body, and operate the universal imagination and phantasm, which are also representations. This is what Suhrawardī pointed out in this empirical theory by saying it "would imply that the self is the 'mover' of a universal body using universal powers."[7] This is, of course, the denial of the most evident, actual motion of our particular bodies that we empirically perform in every intentional act, the absurdity of whose denial must be called a pragmatic contradiction, if not a logical contradiction. For the way of operation and the functioning of our intentional movements contradicts the claim of such a denial that there are no particular motions at all in our bodies and that all our bodily movements are universal.

Criteriology of the Universality and Particularity of Knowledge

Proceeding to the next problem involved in this empirical account, it is easily seen that Suhrawardī has pointed out, quite ostensively, his criterion for distinguishing particular knowledge from universal knowledge.[8] In the above passage, he had implicitly laid down those conditions that must be obtained in order for one's knowledge to be logically particular. He has, moreover, cited those other conditions that must be obtained for one's knowledge to be universal. Now we must explain whether such an attempt can be considered successful. It can be logically restated as follows.[9]

"Universality of knowledge," according to this philosophy, is the quality of an idea or proposition whose application to many individual objects is not logically impossible or contradictory. "Particularity of knowledge," on the other hand, is the quality of an idea or proposition whose application to more than one individual object implies a logical absurdity or contradiction. The contraposition to this definition that is equally valid is that any idea or proposition which is logically impossible or contradictory to apply to many is not universal, but rather particular. Moreover, any idea or proposition whose application to more than one individual does not imply a logical absurdity or contradiction is not particular but universal.

Thus understood, this account that we have extracted from Suhrawardī's passage and interpreted in this way does not, up to this point, serve as a remarkable advance in philosophy. In fact, we can easily find similar views in the statements of a number of philosophers once they arrive at the position of having to make a distinction between universal and particular knowledge. Yet, we should note that the significant achievement of Suhrawardī's criteriology lies in the way in which it states that traditional account within the framework of his own illuminative theory of knowledge by presence. In doing so, he moves forward to saying that every representation existing in the self (of course, the intellectual self which is called the 'intellect') is universal (in the sense that it is not impossible to predicate it of many). Even if the complete sum of the universals referring altogether to one single individual among others have been gathered together in a unitary complex, it still cannot change the status of that representation from being universal.

This means that the specification of an intellectual representation can never result in particular knowledge, for it goes no further than putting some more "restrictions" on that universal representation by gathering together all the universal qualifications applicable to a particular object. As may be expected, this process of specification fails to lead to any logically particular kind of knowledge, because no amount of conceptual qualification and restriction can ever rule out logically the possibility of the representation with all these qualifications to be applied to many. If it is true that the logical possibility of application to many cannot be removed from an intellectual representation, the representation must remain always universal and may never become particular as a result of this kind of specification.

On the other hand, we know, in all factual certainty, that we are acquainted with our particular bodies in such a way that it is impossible or contradictory for that with which we are acquainted to be applied to or shared with others. Therefore, there is no justification for supposing that such particular private knowledge can possibly be obtained by intellectual representation. The possibility of its being obtained through nonintellectual representation, as, for example, in the imagination or by sense-perception, is already ruled out by Suhrawardī when he pointed out that a nonintellectual faculty cannot apprehend itself. It consequently becomes clear that my particular knowledge of my own body cannot possibly be obtained by representation, but rather by presence. It also becomes clear that the criterion for logical "particularity," as opposed to "universality," rests only upon this illuminative theory of presence. And as we shall see next, a distinction must be worked out between "qualification" in terms of restriction or specification, and "particularization" in the sense of individualization.

Qualification and Particularization

As we have just seen in the above argument, a distinction should be made with regard to knowledge between "qualification" or "restriction," and "particularization,"[10] for restricted knowledge is not necessarily particular and private. The former category involves a sort of specification of a universal concept that does not necessarily mean particularization. And the latter is the particularization of the knowledge of an individual object that cannot be applied to many. We have said that the first kind of specification, no matter how far it is pursued, does not have enough force to remove the logical possibility of application to many, even if, as a matter of fact, there may in the external world be no more than one individual object. So a concept specified by any conceptual qualifications always remains universal. However, a particular object instantiated by virtue of presence is truly what is meant by particularization, and this is what characterizes private knowledge by presence. Thus, all our private knowledge is only possible by virtue of presence, because the object of this knowledge is logically particular and hence, cannot be universal. Logical "particularity" in knowledge is equivalent to the meaning of "privacy," which cannot be achieved except through a form of knowledge by presence.

In its application thus far to the private knowledge of our body, imagination and phantasm, as a result of the logical particularity of these elements, this illuminative criteriology has not indicated to us much about its applicability to the knowledge of a particular external object. Within the system of this philosophy, however, must we still remain undecided as to whether or not we are able to have "particular" knowledge of an external individual object?

Taking this question into consideration once again, we must remind ourselves that the words universality and particularity, as well as possibility and impossibility, according to this criteriology, are all to be understood as meaning, neither more nor less than, what is technically meant by them in logic. However, considering the criterion at face value with respect to its applicability to knowledge of an external object, it is apparent that the answer to the question is negative. That is, one cannot have logically particular knowledge by presence of an external object. Therefore, one cannot have logically particular knowledge of an external object at all,[11] for the reason that such an object, being an independent existence, is not present in our mind, and cannot therefore be particularized by this kind of particularization, which is both direct and by presence.

There is, however, an "indirect" particularization, that must be taken into account with reference to our knowledge of an external object. In brief, direct particularization in terms of private knowledge is an intrinsic characteristic of knowledge by presence. Given that the nonintellectual representations of an external object and its sense-data are all present in the mind, they are *directly* particularized by the presence of their unshared individual reality. However, their objective reference, which is not present in the mind of the knowing subject, draws particularization indirectly through the mediation of these representations and sense-data. The objective reference becomes particularly known because it belongs to certain representations and sense-data.

The reasons that the nonintellectual representations of an external object are particularized directly but their objective reference is not are as follows: Firstly, they are present in the mental powers of the self, which are all present in the knowing subject, the performative 'I'. Secondly, the nonintellectual representations of an external object, such as the sense-data, are not by their nature universal, and unlike the intellectual representations are not subject to the process of specification by conceptual qualification. As a result, all nonintellectual representations and sense-data fall into the domain of essentialities of knowledge by presence, and the knowledge of them, like that of the body and the imagination, is private and particular. But the knowledge of the external object represented by these nonintellectual representations is not, according to this criteriology, private and particular in that sense. Rather, it is only particular in the sense that its objective reference becomes particularized indirectly by the presence of its representations in our mind.[12] In other words, the knowledge of an external object is particular only in a derivative sense, and not in a primary and strict sense of particularity.

It should be noted that, as we have indicated at the beginning of this chapter, we are simply calling attention to the magnitude and scope of knowledge by presence in order to remark on the consistency and completeness of our thesis. In accordance with this objective, we felt called upon to consider briefly some modes and instantiations of knowledge by presence. We do not, however, see ourselves further obliged to pass beyond the limits of our subject by committing ourselves to other issues; as for example, saying something about the differences between body, imagination, and phantasm, etc. As far as knowledge by presence is concerned, it seems reasonably sufficient to state the fact that all the aforementioned are private states of mind, sharing in the fact that they are known to us by presence. What differentiates them, however, is not the point at issue for the time being.

SEVEN

An Expanded Theory of Knowledge by Presence: Mysticism in General

ON THE COMMON CORE OF VARIETIES OF MYSTICISM

Mysticism, as a general concept, encompasses an array of intellectual and psychological ideas and experiences. Setting aside, for the moment, all the various forms of mystical experience in different cultures, different religions, and different periods in its long history, there remains at least one common core with which all mystical experiences are associated. This is the conception of "unitary consciousness."[1] It is this basic conception which beckons our attention at this juncture.

The discussion of mysticism, as the term has been understood thus far, need not, at this stage of our thesis, involve itself in a lexicographical examination of each and every particular form and ramification of its inner essence. Therefore, in our present discussion we do not need to concern ourselves with the problem of an *a priori* definition, or that of an empirical family resemblance among the diverse forms of mystical experiences, when the chief objective is understood to be unitary consciousness.[2] Moreover, the subject that we are considering is not a comparative study of mystical experiences, but rather the epistemological dimension of mystical apprehension—that is, a philosophical analysis of unitary consciousness and its validity. We should, therefore, address ourselves directly to our fundamental question, which centers entirely upon the self-objective validity of this consciousness, and examine the question of whether or not it is a truthful consciousness. To be more specific, we aim to put the philosophy of mysticism on a sure path and reestablish it on the basis of our thesis, knowledge by presence. Unless we manage to do this, all approaches to the philosophy of mysticism will fail to be logically consistent.[3]

Mystical Consciousness Is Nonrepresentational

Such being the case, the first question is: How can we identify mystical experience with one mode of apprehension among others particularly in the face of the preceding division of knowledge into knowledge by presence and knowledge by correspondence? In other words, assuming that unitary consciousness is another expression for mysticism as such, our question, in the light of our theory of knowledge, is: Is this unitary consciousness another form of nonrepresentational knowledge by presence, or a peculiar case of representational knowledge by correspondence? Unitary consciousness can also be neither of the two, and act as a deceptive kind of hallucination that falsely presents itself as a mode of transcendental consciousness.

Of these three possibilities, the last one does not concern us, because the possibility of mystical experiences being merely hallucinatory has already been carefully considered by modern philosophers such as William James,[4] R. M. Bucke,[5] and W. T. Stace[6] among others. They have, by and large, reached the conclusion that owing to the orderliness and uniformity of these experiences, it would be highly unjustified to treat mysticism as hallucination, and hence, as merely subjective. Moreover, if we agree with the aforementioned philosophers on the point that mysticism really does enjoy "orderliness" and "uniformity," it would seem to be a sufficient reason for considering mysticism nonsubjective in an important sense. That is, the only logical answer to the skeptical question as to whether order and uniformity justify us in calling mysticism nonsubjective is to recommend the passage through a true mystical experience, one good enough to enable the person to find out if it is really genuine. By analogy, it could be likened exactly to an undiscovered island that has been seen by a few people but is still unseen by others and is therefore legendary to them. All descriptions and information given by these few well-informed people are characterized by orderliness and uniformity.

Now, what response would those few well-informed people give to the skeptical group that does not believe that such and such an island really exists? Could it be anything else but conducting them to the same experience that they have already achieved?

One of the great advantages of mysticism over other metaphysical issues is its being empirical and scientific rather than transcendental. Therefore, by assuming the skeptic's objective to have been previously examined by others, we shall rule it out of our consideration and confine ourselves within the limits of an alternative question: Should a genuine case of mystical experience be ranged among the normal occurrences of knowledge by correspondence that we ordinarily have with regard to external objects, or is it necessary that such an experience be placed under the category of knowledge by presence? Let us first consider the former hypothesis, that mystical experiences are, like our normal sense-experiences, a mode of knowledge by correspondence. That would require the former experiences, like the latter, to have all the essentialities needed to make up the nature of a sort of knowledge that corresponds to its external objective reference. On this account, mystical apprehension would be a peculiar form of knowledge by correspondence demanding a corresponding external objective reference.

Assuming that mystical experiences can be subsumed under knowledge by correspondence, we have already understood that the first essentiality of such knowledge is the existence of a mental representation corresponding to the external object. A simple analysis of this correspondence, however, is sufficient to prove that in addition to the act of knowledge, there is a plurality in this relationship made up of the knowing subject, the representation of the object known, and the independent reality of the external object itself. This is the essential feature of knowledge by correspondence, which is precisely inconsistent with the unitary consciousness of mysticism of any kind and in any degree. It is to this difficulty of representational knowledge by correspondence that Plotinus refers in his remarks that in the case of knowledge, the soul cannot remain a simplex:

> The main source of the difficulty is that awareness of this Principle comes neither by knowing nor by the intellection that discovers the Intellectual Beings but by a *presence* overpassing all knowledge. In knowing, soul or mind abandons its unity; it cannot remain a simplex.[7]

Just as it is the unity and simplicity of knowledge by presence that underlies its strong sense of self-objectivity, so also it is the complexity of knowledge by correspondence that is characterized by double objectivity. Let us agree, for the sake of argument, that mystical experience is a representational apprehension of an external object such as Unity.[8] Taking it as an external object among others, we are inevitably committed to the immediate consequence that there might be among external objects one thing which is Unity, and which is apprehended by the mystic who claims to have had such and such an experience. However, this is certainly not what the mystic himself claims. That is to say, he never says: "I have seen, at a certain point in time, a thing among others such that, if it is momentarily given the name 'Unity', then it is true that Unity is an object and it is undifferentiated."[9] But in our ordinary language we do say, for instance: "I have seen, at a certain point in time, a thing such that if it is momentarily given the name 'X', then it is true that X is a Greek and X is mortal." This is the case because we do ordinarily wish to commit ourselves to the dualism of the 'I-ness–it-ness' relationship peculiar to correspondence knowledge; but a mystic does not. A mystical statement is known and defined to be mystical if and only if it avoids giving any impression of dualism between subject and object, or 'I-ness' and 'it-ness', which is the nuclear point of discourse in our ordinary language. We can put this argument in syllogistic language in the following manner: No unitary consciousness involves the 'I-ness–it-ness' dualism; all correspondence knowledge involves that 'I-ness–it-ness' dualism; therefore, no unitary consciousness is correspondence knowledge.

This argument is sufficient for ruling out any positive grounds for the possibility of mysticism being empirical representational knowledge focused on an empirical objective reference. Moreover, the argument is equally valid for proving that mystical apprehension does not have any marks indicating a family resemblance to theoretical transcendental knowledge. This is because transcendental knowledge, in the sense of abstract universal knowledge, follows the same scheme of the 'I-ness–it-ness' dualism as does empirical knowledge. By having a transcendental phenomenal object, transcendental knowledge also falls within the context of the 'I-ness–it-ness' dictum. It is quite obvious that in this context the opposition and multiplicity of the subject and object can never be overcome to the advantage of mystical unity except through a flat contradiction. Plotinus described how this dualism should be eliminated in mystical language:

> No doubt we should not speak of seeing; but we cannot help talking in dualities, seen and seer, instead of, boldly, talking about the achievement of unity. In this seeing, we neither hold an object nor trace distinction; there is no two. The man is changed, no longer himself nor self-belonging; he is merged with the Supreme. . . .[10]

Stace offered his interpretation of the same point in the following manner:

> We should also note that although at this stage of our exposition of mysticism we speak of mystical experiences as an apprehension of Unity, the mystics of Hindu and Buddhist cultures, as well as Plotinus and many others, generally insist that this is incorrect, since it supposes a division between subject and object.[11]

From all that has been said thus far, it follows that in the essential feature of phenomenal knowledge in which the dualism of the subject-object relation (or in illuminative language, the 'I-ness–it-ness' dictum) is constituted, any sense of mystical unitary consciousness would count for a flat contradiction. The nature of the contradiction is exactly what has been indicated in the above passage of Plotinus: "In this seeing, we neither hold an object nor trace distinction, there is no two." While in mystical apprehension there is no trace of object *vis-à-vis* subject, the dualism of the subject-object relation holds in all kinds of phenomenal knowledge; and this contradiction between the unitary consciousness of mysticism and the subject-object dualism of phenomenal knowledge is not done away with merely by changing the status of the knowledge from empirical to transcendental, depending on a transcendental object.

Let us speak a little more clearly about the important distinction between the interpretation of mystical consciousness and the consciousness itself. Regardless of mysticism itself, which has been viewed by many philosophers as paradoxical, an interpretation of mysticism can also be stated in paradoxical language. The paradox can be presented in this way: If we start interpreting mystical unitary consciousness, we will end up with the multiplicity of the subject-object relation, which is, in a way, a negation of mystical unity; that is to say, if we end up with a multiplicity, we have failed to interpret our mystical unity; therefore, any interpretation of mysticism will imply the negation of what is supposed to have been interpreted.[12]

One solution to this paradox is the two-place predicate analogy that we have suggested in some of our preceding discussions. It is the analogy of the simplicity of the center of a circle and the multiplicity in interpreting the same center when viewed from different angles at the circumference. There is no way in which such a multiplicity at the circumference, though referential to the same center, can be said to contradict or even jeopardize the simplicity of the converging lines at the center. These multiple circumferential lines converging and disappearing at the center are all regarded as a matter of diverse perspectives, which simply cannot be made factually identical with the mere indivisible point at the center. Therefore, the multiplicity of these divergent lines from the innumerable points of the circumference has nothing to do with the mathematical simplicity of the center although they are all "interpretations" of it.

Based on this analogy, let us call all our representational interpretative knowledge of mystical unity circumferential knowledge aiming at the central simplicity of the mystical unity. While beyond any doubt all this multiple interpretative circumferential knowledge is constituted by the plurality of the subject-object relation, it cannot be factually identical with the central knowledge of mystical unity. Were it absolutely identical, it would be unity and not unity, and multiplicity and not multiplicity, which is certainly a double contradiction. It is just the involvement of this contradiction that brings complete failure to those philosophical attempts made thus far for the explanation of the truth of mysticism. Had this problem been carefully examined right at the outset, no philosophers would ever have ventured to contradict themselves in treating mystical consciousness by confusing it with representational knowledge, either empirical or transcendental.

It must be noted that in taking this negative position, we do not intend to advocate the famous doctrine that mysticism is ineffable and impossible to conceptualize in terms of phenomenal knowledge. On the contrary, we will come to the positive position that mysticism, like other modes of presence-knowledge, can be reflected upon and interpreted through the conceptualization and introspection of mystics, and can be taught and spoken of in our ordinary language. But this interpretation and conceptualization should by no means be confused with the mystical unitary consciousness that we are talking about here.[13] Therefore, we have to admit that all interpretation and conceptual understanding of mysticism falls within the domain of phenomenal knowledge rather than knowledge by presence. Yet the rational expression, or language game, of mysticism remains a question that must be decided later on. For the time being, it is necessary to understand clearly that mystical consciousness is quite different from the interpretation of this consciousness. We shall now concern ourselves with the truth and validity of that consciousness and speak about the interpretation and object language of mysticism in due course.

Plato's Intellectual Vision Is Not Mystical

In the above argument we have, as a matter of fact, used the principle of contradiction as a basis upon which to distinguish easily between mystical unitary consciousness and all forms of knowledge by correspondence. We have said that any kind of plurality in knowledge and emotion is inconsistent with the absolute unitary consciousness of mysticism. On this basis we are also able to generalize our position by the following conjunction:

> "No mystical consciousness can ever be identical with any mode of knowledge by correspondence, either in theory or in truth," and "No knowledge by correspondence can ever be identical with any degree of mystical consciousness either in truth or in theory."

Let us examine for a moment, on the basis of this principle, the Platonic notion of intellectual 'vision', to find out if it has anything to do with mystical consciousness. We understand that, in Plato's philosophy, the extended concept of vision has been used to signify human intellectual consciousness as distinct from empirical sensory consciousness. In this regard Plato's doctrine of intellectual vision is substituted for the Aristotelian theory of 'abstract' knowledge. It is indeed to be remarked that Plato's intellectual vision, just like our ordinary intellectual knowledge, is essentially characterized by the dualism of the subject-object relationship, and for this reason cannot be identical with mystical consciousness. Let us now refer directly to Plato himself, in order to find out if his intellectual vision really has any bearing upon mystical consciousness at all.

Among many references in different places there are two relatively clear remarks in *The Republic* concerning the doctrine of intellectual vision.

a. In the world of knowledge, the best thing to be perceived and only with great difficulty is the essential Form of Goodness . . . Without having had a *vision* of this Form no one can act with wisdom, either in his own life or in matters of state.[14]
b. They must be made to climb the ascent to the *vision* of Goodness, which we called the highest object of knowledge, and when they have looked upon it long enough, they must not be allowed, as they now are, to remain on the heights, refusing to come down again to the prisoners or to any part in their labours and rewards, however much or little these may be worth.[15]

In both of these two passages there is a clear indication that in his system of vision Plato is chiefly concerned with the thing perceived as the highest object of knowledge. The intellectual vision of this object is therefore the essential feature that makes up the true pursuit of wisdom for the knowing subject. Here again we are faced with the matter of the subject-object distinction, which cannot be applied to mystical vision. For this reason, it is clear indeed that any attempts to push this Platonic doctrine in the direction of a mystical sense of consciousness will end in failure. However, it does not necessarily follow that the interpretation and conceptualization of mystical experiences is also inconsistent with the Platonic vision. Reflecting upon his mystical experience, a mystic can quite positively bear witness to the objective truth of this philosophical theory; this does not mean, however, that mystical consciousness and this intellectual vision are identical.[16]

Religion and Mysticism

Whatever definition is given to the concept of religion, it is certainly understood that "belief in an Absolute power or Absolute will as the highest concern"[17] is the essential nature of this concept in all cultures and in all its variations. Therefore, "faith and belief in what is to be the object of the highest concern of the believing subject" is a shortcut analysis of the hypothesis of religion. On the basis of this understanding, once we accepted the proposition that belief and faith have their place in our ordinary knowledge, the theory of religion and faith naturally fall into the same framework of the subject-object relationship, which typifies all modes of knowledge by correspondence. This is because, on this stipulation, the statement: "X believes in God" implies "X knows God." If this were the case, we would not need to draw any systematic distinction between mysticism and religion other than that which we have already drawn between our ordinary knowledge and mysticism. We would simply say that religion, as a mode of phenomenal knowledge, is involved in the subject-object complexity. It therefore cannot fulfill the prime condition of mysticism, which calls for the total elimination of the subject-object relationship in order to get to the oneness of unitary consciousness, which is a mode of knowledge by presence.

However, if we do not identify the phenomenon of faith with that of ordinary knowledge, we must then open another line of argument, asking the question whether the phenomenon of faith is essentially mystical and whether mysticism is necessarily religious, or whether they are independent of each other.

In the course of this argument, however, we need, first of all, to answer the question: Is religion in principle a *binary* relation or a *unitary* one? Because we shall endeavor to take the position that mystical consciousness is unique in being a unitary relation from which all binary relations are to be set aside, the question as to whether mysticism is by definition identical with religion is crucial. Concerning this question, however, we wish to make it quite clear that while mysticism and religion have in common that each of them is characterized by being a relation to the Absolute, the uniqueness of mysticism is that it is not a two-place predicate relationship. Once we understand this fundamental difference between religion and mysticism, we can easily arrive at the conclusion that it is impossible for a religion to undertake a transformation from the state of being a binary relation to that of being a unitary one without losing its essential significance. How then can we identify religion with mysticism?

We can simplify our answer to this question by comprehending intuitively that mysticism, being unitary consciousness in essence, is not by nature religious, and conversely, religion being a binary relation, is not essentially mystical. But it is hard to restrict oneself to this oversimplification before giving a full account of the unitary relation of mysticism *vis-à-vis* the so-called simplest binary relations, including the concept of religious belief.

As regards the proposition that religious belief is a two-place predicate relation, technically called a binary or dyadic relation, we may propose that the statement:

"X is religious,"

is equivalent to:

"X is a believer in God,"

or, so as to be applicable even to non theistic religions:

"X is a believer in an Absolute Self."

This belief-statement, however, implies that there is (1) a subject (the believer), and (2) an object (the believed), and (3) the act of belief binding these two together in a complex whole. In this analysis, as in that of knowledge, we encounter the feature of subject-object dualism. Now, since it has this sense of dualism in its very essence, religion can never be identified with our prospective theory of unitary consciousness, which calls, as we shall see, for an absolute unitary relation with God and counts for the self-objectivity of mystical consciousness.

At this point it may be objected that such a sharp exclusion of religion from the essential features of mysticism is not consistent with the idea of "union with God," expressed so frequently by some Western religions, especially Christianity, as a religious principle. Furthermore, it has been remarked that the drive toward mystical union is the vital principle of all religious life. "Without it religion withers away in sterile ritualism or arid moralism."[18] Yet, despite all this, when one turns one's attention to the matter of an examination of the meaning of this religious union, especially in comparison with the mystical sense of unitary consciousness, one finds that that which religious authorities try to indicate by the expression "union" is far from being mystical. It is a religious union that is no more than an "association with," or a "devotion to," the divine Will, such that in this union the distinction between subject and object is highly emphasized and is never disregarded. Even if the meaning of religious union were more than this, it could never, on the basis of any understandable hypothesis, proclaim a complete elimination of the subject-object relation, expressed in the "lover-beloved" opposition, or the beatific vision. We shall see next that the sense of mystical unity is no less than an existential union to which religion cannot, at least theoretically, commit itself, although religion and mysticism are not contradictory. However, the major claim of mysticism is a complete dissolution of the finite self into the infinite Unity, such that phrases like "be Thou our guide . . ."[19] are no longer meaningful.

We shall see later that our theory of the unitary relationship of mystical experiences does not fit with the transubstantial identity relation, or union in essence, or even Stace's "Undifferentiated Unity," let alone the religious sense of unification. I regard the remark, "the drive toward mystical union is the vital principle of all religious life," as a typical fallacy of homonymy, resulting from the resemblance of the word union, which is used in different places with different meanings, both mystical and religious.

It must be added that the idea of mysticism as being independent of religion does not necessarily lead us to the conclusion that mysticism is "irreligious," for, such a conclusion would commit us to a pragmatic contradiction in virtue of many historical figures, both in Christianity and Islam, who were both religious personages and mystics at the same time. Hence, it makes no sense to say that St. John of the Cross's *Dark Night of the Soul,* or al-Ghazzālī's *Niche for Lights* is incompatible with religion simply because it is mystical.

In fact, mysticism, having independently proved its own self-objective truth, can be presented as a reliable basis, or even as an empirical eye witness, for the theoretical truths of religion, all of which can only possibly take place after a correct interpretation and introspection of mystical experiences. Conversely, religion can also be a great help to a mystic in ascending to mystical unitary consciousness, once the mystic casts aside his illusory ties with the multiplicity of this life. Yet, the vital point to be made is that mysticism is completely independent of religion in essence, such that one can clearly understand that:

A. "X is religious,"

is not equivalent to:

B. "X is experiencing mysticism."

Obviously, it does not follow from the negation of such an alleged equivalence that statements A and B are inconsistent. We must come to the conclusion that although it is true to say that mysticism in nonreligious, it is false to judge that mysticism is irreligious, or has no sympathy with religious experiences. Just as it is equally false and illogical to exclude mysticism from religion and hold it to be inconsistent with religious belief.

Mysticism as a Form of Presence-Knowledge

So far we have been discussing the hypothesis of mysticism from the negative side, that is, from what mysticism cannot be in essence. From now on we want to consider the question: What kind of knowledge, if any, might mystical apprehension be, if it is not representational?

Since we have already presented our distinction between knowledge by presence and knowledge by correspondence, it will come as no great surprise if we intuitively answer the question posed above, by maintaining that mysticism is a form of presence-knowledge. After a brief reflection on the framework of mysticism we feel justified in treating it as a form of human noetic consciousness in the sense that mystical moods and experiences are assertive and profoundly informative. Mysticism is characterized throughout by an orderly awareness of the world of reality. It puts something before us as the truth of this world. It is, therefore, quite nonrational to rule arbitrarily that it is subjective and hallucinatory. Therefore, it is legitimate to refer to mysticism as a form of knowledge, because it has been agreed upon by quite a number of philosophers that it is a noetic human consciousness.

We have already decided that we are interested in the hypothesis of mysticism only on the assumption that it is another approach of human consciousness to the reality of the world. Thus, since this assumption is presupposed, the discussion about whether mysticism is a mere subjective phenomenon is beyond the terms of this present thesis. We have therefore taken on a further step towards the point that mystical apprehension can by no means be representational. Now, since the possibility that mysticism may be a form of correspondence knowledge has already been ruled out, the only logical alternative is to judge mystical apprehension as an instantiation of knowledge by presence. It is a form of presence-knowledge, because, once it has proved to be nonphenomenal, nothing else remains to accommodate it except a special form of knowledge by presence.

We should, nonetheless, admit the fact that it would be a substantial intellectual shortcoming if we could not specify by an understandable account what sense of presence mystical apprehension is capable of. We would like to suggest that it is presence by "absorption," which constitutes the essential feature of mystical apprehensions. However, first the meaning of absorption must be accurately studied. In our opinion absorption is a derivative notion of "emanation." We must therefore first know what emanation means.

EIGHT

Mysticism in the System of Emanation

THEORY OF EMANATION

Since, as we have just indicated, our theory of "presence by absorption" is based entirely upon the analysis of emanation, we must consider the "descending" relation between the First Principle and its emanative act, on the one hand, and the "ascending" relation between the emanation itself and its Ultimate Principle, on the other.

In the Islamic philosophical tradition, the theory of emanation concerning the descending illuminative relation was originated by Avicenna in the course of his interpretation of the Aristotelian doctrine of the First efficient cause.[1]

In one of his famous works, *al-Ishārāt wa'l-tanbīhāt,*[2] Avicenna mathematically formulated his doctrine of "emanation" in the following manner:

A Remark:

> Emanation *(al-ibdā')* is that by which one existence is issued from another, and is dependent on the other without the intermediation of matter, instrument, or time.
>
> But that which is preceded by nonexistence in time can never dispense with a mediator.
>
> The act of emanation, therefore, has superiority in degree over the act of generation and over contingency.[3]

As we can see quite clearly, this is a lexical definition of emanation by means of which our attention is drawn to the fact that emanation has the advantage over the notion of generation and contingency insofar as it is not mediated, or even preceded, by time, instrument, or matter. Making his language clear, Avicenna proceeds to sketch the metaphysical proof of his doctrine of emanation:

A Remark:

> The notion that a cause is in a position by which A becomes necessary is different from the notion that the cause is in a position by which B becomes necessary.
>
> If the two things [i.e., A and B] are caused necessarily by the one, this one [as the cause] should [from a different perspective] be viewed as having different forms [of causation] and different realities. . . .
>
> Thus, everything that necessitates two things at once, such that none of them is by means and intervention of the other, is divisible in its reality [and never is unique and simple].[4]

A Further Inquiry:

> It necessarily follows that there must be an intellectual substance from which another intellectual substance and a heavenly body proceed. It is [now] clear that [in this case] the two things have proceeded from one [substance], because of having two different features [of causation].
>
> But, regarding the First Principle, this multiplicity of causal value and variation of causation is impossible. This is because the First Principle is absolutely one in each and every [conceivable] sense. For, He is too exalted to have different modes in reality and varieties of truth, as understood previously.
>
> But, this [multiplicity] is not impossible with reference to those that have proceeded and emanated from the First Principle. Thus considered, it is not possible to emanate from the One more than one act of emanation . . .
>
> [Concerning these emanative beings], there is no set of the two distinct modes of reality that has not associated with each and every one of these beings; [e.g.,] every one of them is a possible being if viewed in itself, and [the same thing] is a necessary being if reckoned in association with the First Principle. Also, each of them knows itself, and knows its principle as well.
>
> Thus, by knowing its principle of existence, and by the way in which it is connected to it, each of these emanative beings gives rise to one thing, and by knowing itself as it is, gives rise to another.[5]

The whole point at issue is that the First Principle, as the absolutely simple Necessary Being, provides immediately only one simple being that is entirely dependent upon its principle. In the same manner, the second existence, insofar as its simplicity requires, provides the existence of a third one that is again totally dependent upon its immediate principle which is already dependent upon the First Principle.

Since the whole light of emanation overflows from the First Principle of existence, it follows that every emanative being is characterized by being an immanent effect, or emanative act of its own principle. Therefore, described as immanent acts or effects of their principle, all emanative beings have, according to this doctrine, two things in common: They are possible in themselves in the sense that they are absolutely nothing without their illuminative relation to their principle; and they are all necessary beings if viewed in the frame of their connection to the Principle, which is a Necessary Being in its essence and in its act. The First Principle is unique in that it is a Necessary Being in itself *(wājib al-wujūd bi dhātihi)*, but these emanative beings are all possible in themselves and necessary by the other *(wājib bi ghayrihi)*.[6]

The central point at issue in this rather peculiar doctrine is that the hierarchy of emanation implies continuity and total dependence of the lower mode of emanation upon its immediate principle which is, in turn, totally dependent on its own immediate principle. Just as the first emanation is totally dependent upon the First Principle, so also the second mode of emanation is totally dependent on its immediate principle, which is already totally, and with all its dependent existences, dependent upon the First Principle, and so on. If C implies B, and B implies A, then it is logically true that C implies A. This is the hypothetical syllogism or the rule of transitivity. We see that in this system of emanation it is possible for the whole universe, with all its characteristic multiplicity, to have emanated from and be reduced to God as the First Principle of existence. This is made possible without the intermediary role of matter, space, time or any other element of disruption and discontinuation in the unitary system of emanation. To give more textual evidence of this hierarchial system, we should refer once again to another passage of Avicenna's doctrine:

A Reminder:

> The First Principle illuminates *(yubdi'a)* an intellectual substance. This substance is in fact the illuminated [emanative being].
>
> By mediation of this emanative substance the First Principle

> [again] illuminates another intellectual substance together with a heavenly body.
>
> In this [hierarchical fashion] from that intellectual substance still another intellectual substance and another heavenly body come into being.
>
> This proceeds to a [final] intellectual substance which no longer provides a heavenly body.[7]

The famous mathematically minded philosopher, Naṣir al-Dīn Ṭūsī (d. 672/1274), contributed his comment to this hierarchical doctrine in the following manner:

> Assuming the First Principle A, and that from A proceeds only one thing, B, then B would be ranked as the first occurrence in the range of A's effects.
>
> Then it is admissible that something C proceed from A with respect to B, and from B itself [as dependent on A] something else D . . .
>
> This is the way in which many things, even of the same rank, can spring forth from one single and simple principle [without disruption of its oneness].[8]

Let us for the sake of further clarity refer here to St. Thomas's treatise on this matter. St. Thomas Aquinas outlined Avicenna's doctrine of emanation in these words:

> 53. Therefore, other thinkers, considering these and similar points, assert that all things do indeed derive the origin of their being from the first and highest principle of things Whom we call God, yet they do not do so immediately but in a certain order. Since the First Principle of things is absolutely one and simple, they thought that only that which is one proceeded from Him. And although this effect be more simple and more one than all the other lesser things, it falls short of the simplicity of the First Principle insofar as it is not its own "to be" but is a substance having "to be." This substance they call the First Intelligence, from which they say that it is possible for a plurality of beings to proceed. For according as the First Intelligence is turned to the understanding of its simple and First Principle, they say that the Second Intelligence proceeds from it. Then, according as it understands itself in terms of the intellectuality in it, it produces the soul of the first sphere: but according as it understands itself in terms of that which is potential within it, the first body proceeds from it. And thus, according to a certain order down to the lowest bodies, they determine the procession of things from the First Principle. This is the position of Avicenna which seems to be presupposed in the Book of Causes.[9]

Before proceeding to St. Thomas's position on the idea of emanation, we should note that the word "potential" *(potentia)* used by St. Thomas is not consistent with the word "possible" as used by Avicenna. Perhaps St. Thomas wishes to offer us his own terminology on this problem, but we should be careful of confusion between the two usages of the term. A confusion of this kind may lead to an infringement upon the distinction clearly made by Avicenna, both in his *Physics* and in his *Logic,* between "material potentiality" and "modal possibility."[10] The applicability of the former is confined within the limits of material objects (i.e., spatiotemporal beings), while the latter includes everything that is not a Necessary Being, starting from the first effect to the last part of the possible world. The first effect therefore, never has potentiality within it. Even if St. Thomas really does have a particular terminological use for the word *potentia,* we cannot use it here so long as Avicenna's theory is in question.

Now let us return to the major points made by St. Thomas concerning this theory, so as to find out if they can prevent us from placing a great deal of reliance on the Avicennian doctrine.

> 54. But it is immediately evident that this position is open to criticism. For the good of the Universe is stronger than the good of any particular nature. Since the nature of the good and of the end is the same, if anyone withdraws the perfection of the effect from the intention of the agent, he destroys the nature of the good in particular effects of nature or art. . . .[11]

St. Thomas asked if emanation, in accordance with Avicenna's teaching, is "unintentional." Yet St. Thomas was not really clear here as to what he meant by "intention." It may be interpreted as will and awareness. Accordingly, the objection is that the principle of emanation is not consistent with the emanation itself, being intended and willed by a free agent who is aware of his action. If so, the modal "necessity" on the part of the agent is the factor for this alleged implication that "every necessary act overflowing from a necessary being must be nonrational." In other words, according to this interpretation, emanation differs from an intentional act only in that the act of emanation is a necessary and nonrational operation of the agent, which has not proceeded from the agent's will and knowledge. Intentional action is (a) that which is not a necessary operation, and (b) has proceeded from the agent's will and knowledge. As thus understood, emanation is questionable insofar as necessity is logically or metaphysically incompatible with knowledge and will in principle. Furthermore, if the agent of free and intentional acts is a Necessary Being in his essence, how can the same agent act as a contingent being according to his knowledge and his will?

It seems again that there is a logical incompatibility between the doctrines that God is a Necessary Being in essence, and that God is intentional in acts by His will and knowledge. In other words, the absolute necessary existence implies necessary emanation, and God's will and knowledge implies contingency, both in the emanation and in the Attributes of God. If this were St. Thomas's objection to the doctrine of emanation, it must be said that it is the same serious question that Avicenna and many other philosophers were fully conscious of when they were dealing with the problem of the "Necessary Being."

Can God be a Necessary Being in His essence, but a contingent and possible being in His will and knowledge of the universe and in His creation and, for that matter, in all of His Attributes? This is a question that was asked by Avicenna and by almost all of his disciples immediately after they had posited the doctrine of emanation. The common position that they all took in the face of this question was that being absolutely one and simple, a being that is necessary in its essence is a necessary being in every aspect and attribute of its being *(wājib al-wujūd bi'l-dhāt huwa wājib al-wujūd min jāmi'al-jihāt)*.[12] If this be the case, God's emanation must have necessarily proceeded from God and be necessarily known and willed by God. This is because God as the agent of the emanation is the Necessary Being in His essence and He is thus the Necessary Being in His knowledge, His will and His act. Supposing that the First Principle of things is absolutely one and simple in essence, any lack of perfection, and any occurrence of privation in His essence would of necessity change His state of simplicity and His modal necessity to that of complexity and contingency. The conclusion is that since God is the Necessary Being, He has necessary knowledge of Himself and of the universe and He has necessary will, necessary emanation, and so on.

Yet the meaning of God's "necessary knowledge" of the universe and His "necessary will" contains a twofold question. The part that belongs to the problem of knowledge concerns the subject under consideration here. The other component of the question, however, that is not the point at issue here, but which belongs to the problem of free will and determinism, will be left for consideration in its own proper place.[13] It should be asserted that as far as the matter of God's necessary knowledge of His emanation is concerned, we are in agreement with illuminative philosophy that this is a sort of knowledge by presence and cannot be otherwise. Were it a form of representational knowledge, divine transcendent or otherwise, St. Thomas's objection would be quite plausible.[14] God knows His emanation as we know our sensation, imagination, phantasm, and bodies. God governs and dominates the whole universe as we do in connection with our private bodies and our private powers of apprehension. Conversely, just as we ourselves do not have a phenomenal representational knowledge of our bodies and powers of apprehension except by way of introspection, God also does not have an intentional—in terms of representational—knowledge of His emanation which is the existence of the universe. And He is too exalted to have an introspective knowledge of Himself. Consequently, God's knowledge of the universe is only by presence.

The question as to how God knows the universe as His own emanation is too great an issue to deal with here. It is a problematic issue both in the ordinary language of philosophy and in illuminative philosophy. However, a cursory review of this subject will elucidate the issues at hand.

Naṣīr al-Dīn Ṭūsī the most famous interpreter of Avicenna, gave an answer to the question concerning how things with distinction and order proceed from Him, as the One and absolute simple principle of emanation with intelligence. Ṭūsī first presents his account of how God knew the first effect. Then he moves to answer the next question: How does He know the universe with all its distinction and order? This is an outline of Ṭūsī's famous account:

> We have understood that the First Principle knows Himself without any differentiation through mediation of a representation between His reality *(dhātihⁱ)* and the apprehension of His reality in existence, except in the intellectual evaluation of those who reflect upon His reality [as distinct from the apprehension of His reality].
>
> We have also already decided that His knowledge of Himself is the efficient cause for His knowledge of the first effect. Now, if you are to make your judgment correctly that the two seeming causes, namely, His own reality and His own apprehension of it, are in existence one and the same and cannot be different in truth, you have then committed yourself to making a subsequent judgment, on the same grounds, that the two seeming effects, that is, the reality of the first effect and the form of His knowledge of that reality, are one and the same and can never be different in truth. There is however, no difference whatsoever to be made in truth to distinguish its reality from the knowledge of that reality by attaching the latter to the existence of the former.
>
> The result is that the very existence of the first effect is nothing but the very act of the First Principle's knowing it, with no need for Him to approach it by a representation *(ṣūrah)* interposing in Himself.
>
> Since these separate intelligible substances, including the first ef-

> fect, apprehend everything which is not their own effect through representations in themselves, and on the other hand they all also apprehend the First Principle, and since it is certain that every existence in the world is but a mere effect of Himself, then it follows that all forms of existences, particular or universal, are represented in these substances.
>
> The First Principle knows these intelligible substances as they are: that is, with whatever representations they have stored in themselves. But He knows them not by a representation in Himself but by the presence of the very reality of these substances and the reality of the forms. In this way He knows the world of existence as it is in itself, not as it appears to Himself.[15]

This was how Avicenna's philosophy of emanation was understood by his celebrated disciple and agreed upon by almost all other interpreters and related philosophers. We have seen in this outstanding analysis that the relation of God to His emanation (i.e., the existence of the universe) is not, and cannot be, by intentional knowledge, but rather only through knowledge by "presence." Little reflection on Ṭūsī's account is needed to extract two kinds of knowledge by presence that are attributed to God, that is, presence by identity exemplified in God's knowledge of His own reality, and presence by emanation, such as the knowledge of God in connection with His emanation. Both are knowledge by presence, because in both cases there is no representation or mental image interposed between the reality of the thing known and the sense of knowing.

As for illuminative philosophy, a brief answer to the question as to how things proceed from God involves first the clearing up of an ambiguity in the word "knowledge," possibly meaning only knowledge by representation. It is necessary that one substitute "awareness" for "knowledge," so that it can apply to presence-knowledge, if the theory of knowledge by presence is to be defended. Secondly, as illuminative philosophers, we should agree with the notion that the First Principle must be aware of all this multitude, plus the first effect that He has provided first. Yet, the fact is that since all this range of multiplicity in the universe is, from the standpoint of "continuity" and "dependence," the one expanded[16] emanation of the First Principle, all is known by God in His presence-knowledge. Hence God's knowledge is neither through representation nor contemplation, which are peculiar to knowledge by correspondence and do not make sense as forms of knowledge by presence.

At this point I would like to admit my lack of understanding of the Thomistic criticism of the Avicennian theory of emanation that asserts: "We may not posit that from the First Principle—granting that It is simple in Its essence—there proceeds only one effect, and that it is from another being, according to the mode of its composition and power, that there proceeds a multitude, and so on."[17] Looking at the face value of this interpretation, it seems to be explicitly making the point that Avicenna's opinion is: just as the first principle is the independent efficient cause for the first effect, so also the first effect is to be counted as an independent efficient cause for the first range of multiplicities, and so on. In point of fact, as this Thomistic interpretation of Avicenna stands, there is a hierarchy of independent efficient causes as well as another hierarchy of effects. Hence, the first effect provides on its own, according to the mode of its composition, a multitude that the First Principle cannot do. Therefore, the First Principle has no role to play over the whole multiplicity of the universe.

Now if this is what Avicenna, or anyone else who advocates a doctrine such as this, really wants to say, it is a self-defeating question that denies the whole point of the emanation theory that the doctrine is trying to establish. This is because the meaning of emanation admits of no independent causation at all. If the multitude of the universe proceeds from a being other than Himself, then this being is the efficient cause for the existence of the multitude, and not the First Principle. It necessarily follows that such an independent being in causation is no longer an emanation in the first place. To the best of my knowledge an emanation in Avicenna's teaching is to be characterized as being absolutely dependent on its principle both in its being and in its act. Since it is an immanent act of its principle, it cannot act from its own. To be an immanent act for an agent is to be absolutely present in, and identified with, the reality of that agent. It is also a rule that an immanent act in essence is immanent in all its intrinsic characteristics, among which its causation should be considered here.[18]

The relation between emanation and the agent of emanation, and vice versa, has been philosophically probed by Ṣadr al-Dīn Shīrāzī (d. 1050/1640) when he described how emanation in general should be understood:

> All existences that take "possibility" as their logical modality, and all realities which are related, and belong, to the Other, are to be considered as different values *(i'tibārāt)* and different features of the existence of the Necessary Being. They are rays and shadows of the same Self-Substantive Light. These shadows are, from the standpoint of their individuation *(huwiyyah),* far from being independent. It is impossible even to conceive of them as unrelated and independent entities. This is because 'subordination' and being 'owned by'

> the Other, as well as need and dependence on the Other, are the whole constitution of their reality. It is not however true to suppose that they are something in their essence liable to the occurrence of being related to and owned by the Other, and thus dependent upon the Other; not at all. But rather, the only conceivable truth of their reality is to describe them as a pure 'dependence' on the Other, not even something dependent on the Other. Thus understood, they have no reality in themselves conceivable by our intellectual power other than to be mere subjections and subordinations of one Reality. From this it becomes clear that there is nothing in the world of reality but one single Reality. Anything else other than this counts for nothing but a manifestation, an exhibition, a perspective, a specific manner, a ray of light, a shadow of the luminosity and a visage of the endless profundity of this One Reality.[19]

It is on this theory of emanation that we seek to base our analysis of mysticism. This version of emanation, as it stands, implies several fundamental theses, among which we must specify the following:

1. The matter of the ontology of the One Reality in its relation to the ontology of Its emanation.
2. The relation of the First Principle to the world as Its unitary emanation.
3. The relation of the world as an emanation to its Ultimate Principle.

Leaving out the problem of ontology,[20] which governs almost the whole field of metaphysics and lies far beyond the frame work of our subject, we may rightfully concentrate our attention on the second and the third points of this triad, laying special emphasis on the last one, which is the point at issue in our analysis of mysticism. We shall consider this problem in the following discussion.

Emanation Is Expressible Only by a Prepositional Phrase

Starting with the problem of the relation of the First Principle to the multitude of the universe, what Sadr al-Din's perspective of emanation gives us is simply expressible by a prepositional phrase such as "proceeding from . . . ," "depending on . . . ," "illuminated by . . . ," and so on. All the words that he has used in the definition of emanation stand, as we have seen, for nothing but a pure, immanent act issued by the agent as a manifestation of a substantive truth. So it is permissible to say that the reality of emanation is analogous to the meaning of connectives and prepositions, in that it has no distinct definable sense in itself separated from its substantive principle. Thus it cannot be defined in terms of either verbs or nouns; rather, it can only be understood in the light of the understanding of its Principle, just as a preposition is only accurately and meaningfully understandable if one can connect it to its own appropriate nouns and verbs. However, the essential truth of emanation lies entirely in the truth of its substantive principle, and its whole reality is no more than a prepositional expression such as "by otherness." As a matter of fact, since the status of the act of emanation is by essence thus prepositional, the only independent reality that really is in itself, and can function as a substantive noun to which all prepositional entities are related, is one reality in the whole universe of existence. This is the One that is not in itself the act of another principle and, therefore, not dependent on anything at all. This is the unique Principle of emanative being, and this is the Aristotelian First Cause and the Cause of causes.[21]

Vertical and Horizontal Lines of Emanation[22]

In the theory of emanation there is no possibility of an existential void, that is, an interruption of nothingness between the First Cause and the ultimate things that emanate from the First. Being in the form of manifestation and illumination, an emanation, whether it is of the rank of the first effect or the last one, is entirely held by and dependent upon its immediate principle. This immediate principle, if not the First One, will in turn have been dependent, along with all its depending existences, upon its own immediate principle and so on, until they are all reduced to and absorbed in the First Principle of existence. Therefore, no matter to what extent multiplicity of causes and effects occurs in accordance with the composition and order of the universe, it appears quite certain that the whole multitude is designed as the single manifestation of the Self-Substantive Being. And as a shadow of His face, it always remains entirely dependent upon His light of lights.

This indicates that there is an unbroken vertical line connecting all the multitude of emanation to its First Principle in a strictly existential unity. There also exist horizontal linkages along which things are to be regarded as different from one another and characterized by multiplicity in rank, in essence, in species, and in individuation. We shall call the vertical line the "inner order" of existence, and the horizontal lines the "outer order" of existence. The former is that with which mystical experiences are concerned and the latter is for what philosophy and the sciences account. In dealing with the problem of mysticism, all philosophy can do is to account for the interpretation and conceptualization of mystical experiences. Being representational, these interpretations and conceptualizations will fall into the order of the horizontal linkages, whereas factual mystical experiences always remain in the vertical dimension of emanation and belong to the inner order of the world of reality.

The Diagram of Emanation

As a matter of fact, what has so far been mentioned about the First Principle and His illuminative connection with the existence of the world as His emanation constitutes the cosmology of illuminative philosophy, which can be illustrated by a pyramidal diagram like the one below:

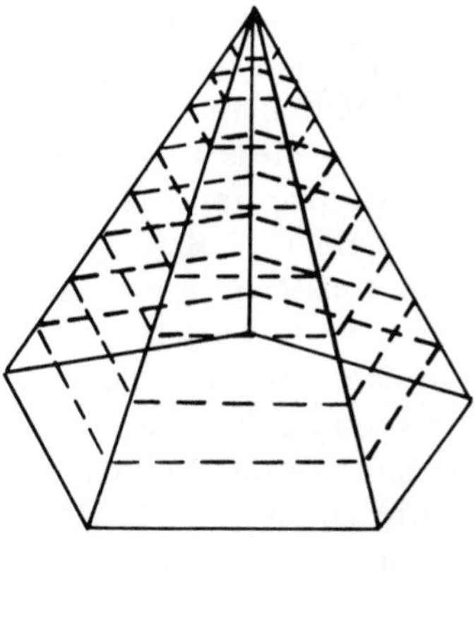

It will be referred to as "the pyramid of existence," because in this system the light of existence flashes out from the source of light at the apex all the way down to the base, which symbolizes the world of material objects. While all the rays and arrows emanate from the simplicity of the First, without any interruption of nothingness or a void, they all enjoy the strongest existential connection and unity with their First Principle at the top. They are, however, widely diversified when they are considered as being at the base or at any point between the base and the zenith where both the horizontal and vertical levels converge into an absolute unitary simplex.

There are two distinct kinds of diversity here which are to be noted. These rays or shadows of existence can be divided by the mind of a philosopher into different fragmentary emanations according to the degrees of proximity to the Highest Principle. Yet this sort of division, being a mere intellectual reflection on the gradation of one simple thing, does not jeopardize the simple unity of the emanation with its First Principle. They are also actually separated and diversified in essence as well as in individuation, etc.; but since this separation and diversity (which occur in the horizontal order) do not happen in the vertical order—the order of unity—they do not drive them asunder and have no impact on the inner system of the continuity of the rays and their unity with the One. In other words, the multitude of the horizontal order has no bearing upon the unitary connection of the vertical order.

This pyramidal diagram of illuminative cosmology, together with the distinction between the vertical and the horizontal linkages within it, must be taken into serious account, not only in illuminative philosophy but also in every philosophical analysis of the question of mysticism. It is of fundamental importance to understand the "inner unity" in relation to the "outer diversity" of this diagram when one meets the paradoxical statements of mystical experiences. This entire system is also of vital importance in elucidating upon the famous Parmenidian principle of "unity in difference," if it is to be handled without contradiction. The contradiction arose from the philosopher's famous disjunctive doctrine "it is or it is not," together with his conjunction "it is and it is not."[23] To all this, the diagram can be an obvious answer.

Finally, the diagram is taken as the major axiom in the theory of the "gradation" of the reality of existence, upon which the school of Islamic philosophy of the primacy of existence has been founded. The problem of "univocity" and the gradational variation of "existence" would need to be pursued in a separate dissertation. Now we must turn to an explanation and interpretation of our diagram.

Setting aside the problem of the Islamic philosophy of the primacy of existence, it seems necessary to emphasize somewhat the philosophical wording and interpretation of our diagram of emanation, over and above its graphical symbolism. There are various ways and approaches by which one can show, both logically and philosophically, the plausibility of the claim of this diagram to demonstrate the existential identity of emanation with the Ultimate Principle. The law of "transitivity" or the "hypothetical syllogism" is one of these approaches that can help us see how the diagram works. The logical form of this law is:

$$\begin{array}{c} A \supset B \\ B \supset C \\ \hline A \supset C \end{array}$$

As we can see, this law is based on material implication as its logical connective.

To apply this law to the theory of emanation, one needs to substitute the emanative notion of "dependence" for material implication. To depend totally, both in truth and in conceivability, on the veracity of another, is taken to mean being overshadowed by and included in the truth of another being. Logically, this existential relation is expressed through material implication, such that the truth of an emanative being consists analytically in the truth of its undetachable principle. Therefore, "dependence" is equated here with the "undetachability" and "indistinguishability" of the emanation from its principle, both in thought and in truth.[24]

Once this argument has been elucidated, any given degree or mode of emanation A, at any point in the lower part of the diagram, will entail by material implication its immediate principle B. Since B is in turn an emanation dependent in the same manner on its own immediate principle, it also logically implies its own principle; the same process continues until the range of emanation ends in the Ultimate Principle C.

In this manner, the unbroken chain of emanation is traced back from the lowest mode of emanation A to the intermediate grade B and, finally, to the ultimate source of emanation C. This is the logical strategy of transitivity. These modes and degrees of emanation, following one upon the other, appear in their own particular stages to be different from one another in terms of their hierarchical standings and extent of proximity and remoteness to the Ultimate Principle. Yet they all constitute only one single and indivisible vertical line from the base up to the zenith of the pyramid of emanation. Therefore, our diagram can be shaped in this way:

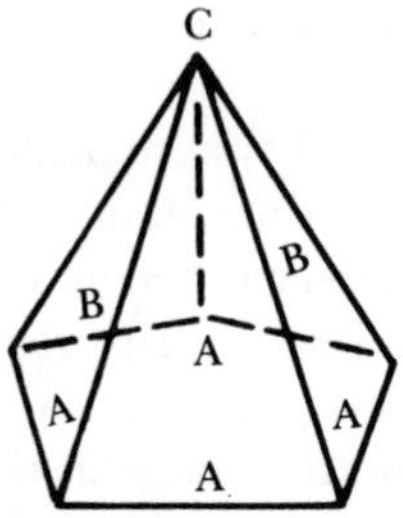

An objection may be made to the notion that the implication of transitivity does not support the claim of the diagram, which calls for nothing other than the existential identity of all the gradations and modes of emanation. All that the rule of transitivity can do is to help us know that there is an unbroken relation between any lower degree or mode of emanation A, through an intermediate mode B used as a middle term, to the Ultimate Principle C. However, whether or not this relation is an identity relation, according to which the whole of the system of the gradations of emanation and its Principle as one existential unity, is beyond the logical perimeters of the hypothetical syllogism.

The answer to this objection is that the existential relation between an emanation and the source from which it has emanated is, as we have already discussed in detail, nothing but an "illuminative relation,"[25] which is unitary and belongs to the order of being and not the order of conception. In point of fact, it is this "unitary" relationship that accounts for the sort of existential identity which the emanation has with the Principle of emanation. Within the context of this unitary relation, we are entitled to apply legitimately the rule of transitivity in order to proceed from one occurrence of this relationship at the base to the ultimate one at the zenith of the hierarchical diagram. In other words, the operation of material implication in the system of illuminative relations results logically in a kind of existential unity progressing from the lower class of emanation right up to the Ultimate Principle of the illuminative causation of emanation, without any disruption or any extraneous mediation.

There also exists another approach to the logic of the diagram. This is the Islamic philosophical doctrine of the "unity of continuity," by which we are able to prove that any continuous unbroken linear system is dominated by an existential unity. We shall consider this thesis in detail, when we come to discuss the notions of absorption and annihilation.

The Meaning of God's Presence in the Universe

In view of the cosmological system under discussion, the issue that now comes to the fore is that the relation of the First Principle to the world, as His emanation, is very much analogous to the emanative relation of the self to its private states. Insofar as knowledge by presence is concerned, God's knowledge of the universe as His emanative act belongs to the same kind of knowledge as that by which the self knows its sensations or imagination. As we have seen in the preceding chapters, the self is acquainted with itself by presence in the sense of self-identity, and is also acquainted with its private states by presence, understood in terms of an illumination and supremacy, called presence by emanation. Here, in this chapter, we arrive at the same division of knowledge by presence—presence by identity and presence by emanation. For we have shown that God's knowledge of Himself cannot be other than the presence of the reality of Himself to Himself, and that it cannot be by representation of Himself to Himself. And God's knowledge of the universe as His emanation is also by His existential presence in the universe, yet it is manifested in the sense of illumination and supremacy over the emanative existence of the universe. Since, as Naṣīr al-Dīn Ṭūsī puts it, God Himself is the cause of the universe, and God's knowledge of Himself, which is the cause of His knowledge of the universe, are absolutely one and the same, hence, the existence of the universe as God's effect, and God's knowledge of that existence as the effect of His knowledge of Himself, are also absolutely one and the same. This means that God's knowledge of the universe can only be by presence in the sense of illumination and emanation.[26]

The overall conclusion is that the One's knowledge of His illuminative act of being is by His presence in that being in the sense of presence by emanation. Presence by emanation is in turn the immanent effectiveness and supremacy of one being over another, in exactly the same manner as is seen with the immanent supremacy of the self over its imagination and private states.

The Modal Status of Emanation

In my opinion there is an argument that is designed to obtain generally the modality of a concept in connection with its truth value and the consideration of its existence, whether the concept is empirical, transcendental, or merely illusory.[27] In other words, given anything as a subject term in an existential form of proposition, we are able to design the modal structure of such a proposition and decide whether that subject is "necessary," "possible," or "impossible." For instance, let us consider the transcendental concept of God in comparison with the predicative concept of existence in the light of this argument. Putting the idea of God as the subject term, and the meaning of existence as the predicate, we get a complete proposition in the form:

"God exists."

Then, from the standpoint of modality, this statement is subjected to the question:

Is God's existence necessary, possible, or impossible? When any two of these alternatives—in the case of God's existence, possibility and impossibility—are ruled out, the remaining one is kept as the truth value of the modality of the proposition. Thus the statement becomes:

"God exists necessarily."

The same modal procedure of decision making can be easily set up for every concept present in our mind, whether it be through our sense-experience, our intellect, or our imagination. If this be the case, it is logically legitimate to say that everything, no matter whether it be in the order of essence or in the order of existence, is either necessary, possible, or impossible. This amounts to the generalization that all forms and degrees of existence will come under the same consideration of modality as all the varieties of essence normally do.

It should be noted that the validity of this argument is based upon an exclusive understanding of this alternation, because it has already been established in this philosophy that all of these primitive terms (i.e., necessity, possibility, and impossibility) are triadically contradictory. For possibility is the negation of necessity and impossibility is the opposite of possibility. A possible thing is one whose existence is not necessary; and similarly, the existence of a possible being is not impossible.[28] In fact, each pair can be reduced and translated into the general form of 'pv-p', which stands for the law of the excluded middle.[29] Thus stated, it is logically impossible that any concept, no matter what it may be, can ever be entirely outside this exclusive alternation. It is equally impossible that a concept can ever assume any more than one of these alternatives. That is, every concept must ["at most" and "at least"] be qualified by one of these primitive forms of modality.

In the language of Islamic logic, this kind of alternation is called 'the complete disjunction' *(al-munfaṣilat al-ḥaqīqiyyah),*[30] meaning that "at least and at most" one of the disjuncts is true. The complete disjunction is to be distinguished from the two incomplete disjunctions. This distinction can be best elucidated by further probing into the structure of disjunctions. First, there is a disjunction in which "at least" one of the disjuncts is true, but all of them may be true as well. This is called 'the inclusive disjunction' *(manīʿat al-khuluw).*[31] Second, there is another disjunction in which "at most" one of the disjuncts is true, even though it may happen that none of them is true. This is called 'the restrictive disjunction' *(manīʿat al-jamʿ).*[32] The complete disjunction may be exemplified by two or more exclusive disjuncts. An example of two exclusive disjuncts is:

"Every number is either odd or even,"

which implies that no number can be both and no number can be neither.

The truth table of all three forms of disjunctions can be seen in this diagram.

Inclusive Disjunction			Complete Disjunction			Restrictive Disjunction		
p	q	p∨q	p	q	p∨q	p	q	p∨q
1	1	1	1	1	0	1	1	0
1	0	1	1	0	1	1	0	1
0	1	1	0	1	1	0	1	1
0	0	0	0	0	0	0	0	1

The same pattern of complete disjunction can be exemplified in a three-disjunct formula like this:

"Everything is either necessary, possible, or impossible."[33]

According to the exclusive sense of the complete disjunction, this statement is taken to mean that ["at least and at most"] one, and only one, of these modal predicates is true of a thing.

The three-disjunct form of the complete disjunction can be applied to the existential feature of an emanative entity, where we are entitled to distinguish intellectually between the essence and the act of existence of that entity. Setting aside the problem of its essentiality, we arrive at the point where we can direct our disjunctive question to the pure existence of the emanation issued forth from its principle. The question, however, is not whether a being such as the self is necessary, possible, or impossible. Rather, it deals only with the actual existence of the self as it has specifically issued forth from its principle, regardless of its essentialities, which belong to the order of its conceptual definition. The question asks if such a form or degree of existence can be qualified by necessity, possibility, or impossibility. In other words, if the existential feature of an emanation be considered as a thing distinct from essence, then what is the truth value for its modality?

Surely such an existence cannot be placed in the rank of Necessary Being which has no causal connections with anything. The very meaning of emanation implies that it is a form of existence that has supposedly proceeded from another being that stands as its principle of causation, or as the source of its emanation.[34] Therefore, the possibility that an emanative existence is a Necessary Being may be ruled out. Similarly, the notion that it could count as a logical impossibility should also be dismissed. There are no grounds, however, for rendering a form of existence characterized by such positive qualities to be impossible. In fact, reflection on all implications that justify reference to a form of existence as emanative enables us to decide that this hypothesis is not contradictory. The only alternative that can be considered with regard to the existence of an emanation is possibility. That is to say, there exists no alternative except to take the position that such an existence must enjoy the modality of possibility. More specifically, we must consider an emanation as a possible being.

A great difficulty arises from this conclusion: What is the meaning of possibility in reference to the question of the existence of an emanation? After all, emanation is supposed to be an intensive mode of existence that has come to the world of reality without the mediation of time and matter.[35] If so, what can the meaning of possibility be when it is applied to the question of the existence of an emanation? It would be appropriate to inquire as to whether the application of possibility to the universal concept of emanation renders a hypothetical being as possible. However, does it really make any sense at all to say that a particular form of emanative existence that really exists, no matter how low its degree of emanation, is a possible existence? Again, an essence, as opposed to an existence, can quite conceivably be said to be a possible being, because it is existentially neutral *(quidditas tantum)*. In other words, it can come into the light of existence by virtue of causation from its principle, and it ceases to exist when the principle withdraws itself from causation. To characterize an essence by possibility is just another way of reflecting upon its state of neutrality between coming into the world of reality and ceasing to exist in that world. Therefore, the very meaning of essence is existentially neutral.[36]

Yet, in terms of the Avicennian interpretation of possibility, how can it be true of an emanation that is a single form of existence to say that it is "existentially neutral"? Can a degree of existence in the form of emanation be existentially neutral? If the subject under consideration is emanation, which is taken to mean that a pure light of existence has issued forth from the principle of reality, then how is it understandable if we modify it by the predicative phrase "existentially neutral"?

There is much to be said concerning the problem of the essence-existence relation, but for the most part this problem does not concern us in the subject under consideration—existential possibility. There is only one important point that might shed some light on the matter under discussion, and that is the distinction between what is existentially neutral and what is not. It has been generally understood that an essence can be subject to the disjunction "either it is or it is not," therefore, it is existentially neutral in terms of "liability" to this disjunction. Existence, on the other hand, is not liable to this disjunction nor, for that matter, to nonexistence (i.e., "it is not"). On this account, essence is characterized by existential neutrality and existence by the state of self-certainty.

Assuming that the meaning of possibility is the state of equilibrium between existence and nonexistence, which is the meaning of the above disjunction, and, furthermore, assuming that the meaning of emanation is substituted for "X" in the following argument: "X is a form of existence, but is X existentially neutral?", this becomes a self-defeating question in the same way that "X is a rectangle, but is X neutral in having four sides?" is a self-defeating question.

Hence, although the modality of possibility is the only conceivable modality for emanative existence, the implication of its existential neutrality is not meaningful as a characterization of this sort of existence. Thus, the pertinent question is: What is the modality of such pure existence as that called emanation?

This argument leads us to the conclusive generalization that the modality of possibility, in its primitive sense, is irreconcilable with the existential part of any form of possible being, whether it is an emanative or nonemanative being, that is, whether we do, or do not, have an emanation. Consequently, we cannot rely on this modal argument in making our decision about the species of the modality of the existential component of any kind of being, or of the existence of the universe at large. The only benefit that we do derive from this argument is the knowledge that we cannot leave the existential feature of the universe undecided and indeterminate from the standpoint of its modal constitution. If we do so, that is, if we leave the existential state of the universe undecided, it will be an infringement of the law of "exclusive disjunction" and, in a way, ultimately an infringement of the law of the "excluded middle." The original question concerning the existential status of an emanation widens when asked of the existential structure of the universe *in toto.* That is, this question can no longer be regarded as a restricted issue concerning the emanative status of the self. Rather, it is a most fundamental point concerned with the major problem of the ontology of the world of reality as a whole.

Under these circumstances we are driven to the situation in which we must distinguish between two species of possibility. One sense of possibility is that which characterizes the essential feature of a being as distinct from its existence. This possibility, of course, belongs to the order of essence and is taken to mean that an essence is existentially neutral. The other possibility is that which qualifies the very constitution of the existence of any form of being that has issued forth from another. This meaning of possibility is not existentially neutral as it stands for a positive relation between a higher rank of existence and a lower one. The first possibility is called "essential," and the second "existential," according to the subject under consideration.

At this juncture it can be established that what is meant by "existential possibility" as distinct from "essential possibility" is none other than the sense of "dependence" of one existence "upon" another,[37] for essential possibility is the state of equilibrium with respect to existence and nonexistence. Thus the logical truth of a possible being is to be defined as that which may either be or not be. This is the meaning of the existential neutrality of a conceivable essence.[38] Existential possibility means total dependence on the other.

Ṣadr al-Dīn Shīrāzī, the founder of the Islamic philosophy of the primacy of existence and the originator of existential possibility, clarifies the meaning of this possibility:

> On the matter of the possibility of a pure essence from the concept of which all the implication of existence is withdrawn, it consists of the negation of the necessity of being; together with the negation of the necessity of not being, with reference to the conceivability of the essence in itself.
>
> But, concerning the possibility of the very reality of existences, it is to be taken to mean that the reality of these existences is absolutely related to, and dependent upon, another reality, such that they are conceivable only in terms of pure relation to the substantive reality of the other.
>
> Thus the reality of possible existences is merely prepositional and

> is understandable only in the light of the radiation of another existence. They are, moreover, devoid of any sense of independence both in conception and in factual truth.
>
> That is not the case when a universal essence is taken into consideration. Although it is true that essences do not stand for anything before becoming involved in some degree of existence, they are nevertheless entities conceivable in themselves in the sense that one can think of them independently insofar as one can present them in one's mind. . . . This means that, despite the reality of existences, the conceivability of essences is not to be dependent on another being as prepositional functions of that being. It is this conceptual sense of independence that enables us to direct our mind to essences and make our judgment about them as to how they are identical in themselves and how they are different from one another.[39]

A similar philosophical development came about concerning the problem of the existence of God and His "existential necessity" long before this discovery of existential possibility took place. It was Avicenna who took the initiative in asking the question: What is the meaning of the modal "necessity" in God if He has no essence or if His essence is absolutely united with His existence? His answer to this question is again a turn in direction from essential necessity to existential necessity, called by him "absolute necessity," and by his disciples "eternal necessity," in order to distinguish carefully between the two necessities. In his *Logic,* Avicenna wrote:

> As for the modality of "necessity," it is either "absolute," like our statement (in speaking of God) "God is existent," or "conditioned." This condition is the duration of the existence of an essence, such as we say: "Man is necessarily a rational thing." By this we do not intend to say that man eternally and everlastingly is a rational thing, because if we do so, this judgment becomes false with regard to the fact that no individual man is eternal. But rather, by such a statement we should intend to mean that man under the consideration of his being in existence, and insofar as his essence continues to be an existing object, is a rational thing.[40]

This distinction between two kinds of necessity was clearly illustrated by the most celebrated interpreter of Avicenna, Naṣīr al-Dīn Ṭūsī in the following passage:

> He [Avicenna] is now dealing with different species of necessity. He has first divided necessity into absolute and conditioned necessities.
>
> By absolute necessity he means that kind of judgment the truth of

> which is unconditionally eternal without any stipulated condition or any possibility of negation. . . .
>
> Then he proceeds to spell out these conditional necessities. They are: that which is conditioned by the existence of the essence of the subject given in a judgment [i.e., essential necessity], and that which is conditioned by the existence of the qualifications of that subject. . . . [41]

By now enough has been said to show that our present analysis of the connection of an emanative existence, such as the reality of the self, to its principle is the consideration of the relation between eternal necessity and existential possibility. Within the limits of this consideration, any account of the conceptual feature of the self that belongs to the order of essence and stands for the relation between the essential possibility of the universe and the essential necessity of its principle would be beside the question.

It should be noted that in the light of this notion of eternal necessity we are capable of developing a strong version of the ontological argument for the existence of God. An ontological argument based on this pattern of necessity has the merit of being invulnerable to the criticisms of Kant and others. If we could succeed in attaching another meaning of necessity to the doctrine of the Necessary Being, it would surely, right from the beginning, render the philosophical issue of divine ontology less problematic. Yet, this is not the right place to enter into a prolonged discussion of the problem of ontology in general, or the problem of the ontological argument in particular.

The most important consequences for consideration are (a) to lay out the ontological relation of an emanative being, such as the self, to its principle through the existential modality of possibility; and (b) to acknowledge how this meaning of possibility, despite essential possibility, identifies the reality of the self with the necessary illumination from eternal necessity, and how this existential union implies that any occurrence of a void, or interruption between the necessary existence of the principle and the possible existence of the self, is impossible.

The Reality of an Emanation Is Prepositional

The argument thus far has led us from complete disjunction to the point where we can say that the only modality applicable to the existential truth of an emanative reality is *existential possibility*. Now the time has come to make it clear that an emanation, by the very nature of its existence, is a continuously "absorbed" reality. For an emanation to exist means the manifestation of being held by another and the maintenance of a situation of dependence on another. That is to say, it can never be detached from its principle and stand by itself as an independent entity, either in the mind or in the world of reality.

It is not true to say, on the basis of a false interpretation, that an emanative existence could have issued forth from its principle and could continue to exist while no longer having existential dependence on its source of being. This false interpretation of possibility would mean that a possible existence was possible when, and only when, it had not yet come into existence through its principle. However, as soon as that same possible existence came into the world of reality, it would change its basic status from that of essential and existential possibility to that of essential and existential necessity. That is, it would no longer remain as a possible being, but would, in the continuation of its existence, become a Necessary Being.[42]

This idea of possibility is by no means valid because if a being becomes, even for the briefest moment of the continuity of its existence, unneedful of and independent from its principle, it means that it is, *at that very moment,* a self-sufficient being with no basis for being. Whatever a self-sufficient being might be, it ought by definition to mean a necessary self-grounded existence. This existence then, even though it is at that very moment continuing in existence, is no longer an emanation and has become a Necessary Being that does not rely for its existence upon another being. This is a transmodification from possibility to necessity. Yet emanation is by definition a form of being that emerges from, and is held by, another being, both in coming into existence and in continuing to exist.

Concerning this problem, a metaphysical question arises: Why is a certain being, say the universe, possible, and another being, say God, necessary? The answer is that the very nature of the former is to be dependent on and held by another, and the latter is to be absolutely groundless and independent. Accordingly, the analogical extension of the relation of the design to the designer, or the building to the builder, to the emanative connection between the maker and the made is logically false and pedagogically deceptive.[43] For one thing, the act of emanation is undoubtedly an immanent act and can never be a transitive one, whereas building and designing are bound to be acts of a transitive nature. Furthermore, as we have said before, when we are speaking of emanation we are not dealing with a being constituted by the essence-existence relationship, but rather with that very simple indivisible entity, the whole nature of which is to be known as a manifestation of the principle of being. This is the meaning of the prepositional state of being that characterizes the reality of emanation. A simple thing that has no definable identity or reality except as a mere issuance from and a manifestation of another is only possible in truth, and conceivable in the mind, if it is preserved by the other. It would be a fake emanation, as well as a fake shadow of the light, if we were to visualize the former as a distinctive reality and the latter as an original light in itself.

The question as to how such an entity can, from another point of view, be spoken of as distinguished by essence and horizontally diversified is analogous to the question as to how a prepositional entity can be spoken of and defined as distinguished from its noun, pronoun, verb, adjective, etc. The answer to such a query is that when we speak of a preposition, say the word "from" for example, describing it in terms of "used to introduce the place, point, person, etc., that is the starting point," we are, beyond any doubt, speaking of the preposition in a very important sense; but at this particular stage of language we are not using the expression "from" in its prepositional function. On the other hand, if we use it in its genuine prepositional sense in a sentence such as "the cat jumped down from the wall," it then quite definitely functions as a true working preposition. This time, although it is being implicitly used and meant as accurately and meaningfully as it can be, it is not laid out as the direct object of our concern. It is, instead, in this case that which binds together the whole structure of our sentence, without which the meaning of our language would break down. Here, its independent conceptualization has not been spoken of at all. In other words, while it is used with its correct meaning in the sentence, it is far from being spoken of in that sentence. Once, through conceptualization, it has been put in the form of an independent entity to be spoken of as the subject of discussion, it completely loses its initial meaning of preposition and is elevated to the state of having a somewhat nounlike meaning. To speak of a preposition, however, is to use an introspective language, and is indicative enough for the depiction and presentation of its definition and all the essentialities of its grammatical evaluation as far as its theoretical meaning is concerned.

This analogy, though primarily linguistic, would seem logically profitable enough as a pronouncement of the linguistic problem of the prepositional nature of emanation, its similarity to prepositional entities in language, and the difficulty and the solution that both have in common.[44]

Absorption as a Derivative Form of Emanation

I hope that it is by now, to some extent, clear that the very description of the ways in which one can explain the meaning of any given emanation is enough to show how its prepositional truth—by another—should be understood. In this way we also arrive at a position of understanding as to how to legitimately use the words "absorption" and "immersion" that are so frequently employed in mystical language. When the whole reality and truth value of emanation is nothing but being held "by another," the state of absorption or immersion in another does not seem odd, or, to use a stronger word, inconceivable. Absorption or immersion in the principle of being in the sense of dependence on and being held by another is not accordingly an accidental fulfillment to be achieved by a mystic through his mystical experiences. Rather, it is the whole existential feature and truth value of the self as a pure, emanative existence to be immersed in another. It is its very existence that is not even possible to think of, except in the light of thinking of its principle, which is its substantive ground for being.

An objection may be raised concerning this line of reasoning since the fact that we can always think of our selfhood independently of thinking of any principle denies the validity of such an analysis of the selfhood as a pure, emanative existence absorbed in another. If it were the case that the self, due to its being totally dependent on another, could not even be independently understood and thought of, it would be impossible for us to have ever had the impression of our selfhood on its own. Yet the fact that we do have the idea of our selfhood on its own counts as sufficient reason for believing that the self is not totally dependent on another in this extreme sense of absorption. Therefore, the self is not an emanative existence.

Illuminative philosophy's answer to this objection is that this so-called impression of the selfhood is the introspective self that comes into the mind through the conceptualization and introspection of the factual performative truth of the self. The emanative self is the performative one that talks, feels, thinks, wishes, judges, decides and has sensation, imagination, and intellection. It is, moreover, acquainted with all these acts and powers of its apprehension. The performative self is that which always acts and perceives and is never acted upon or perceived, by itself or by another, except through conceptualization. Everyone can, by way of introspection, conceptualize the factual reality of his own selfhood as well as those of others. Despite this understanding, it should not be maintained that our impression of the self is the very reality of the self or even a real and truthful representation of it. The analogy just drawn between the reality of the self as an emanative existence and the objective reference of prepositional phrases makes this point somewhat clearer.

If we make a pedagogical statement by saying, for example, " 'by another' is a prepositional phrase," the phrase "by another," as the subject matter of this particular statement, is not really being used in its proper meaning. This is not a substitute instance of a preposition at all; and, for that matter, it cannot be a true representation of the objective reality of "by another." Rather, it is a merely introspective conceptualization of that reality which we speak of in the factual circumstances of our ordinary language. But if I say, in a normal instance, that "I am sitting by the window," or "I am dependent on another person," I have truly used these prepositions with their own objective meanings. This is because their truth value is illustrated by given examples instead of by generalization and conceptualization.

If an emanation, such as the self, is expressible only in terms of a prepositional phrase—for example, "by another" or "on another," and so on—its objective truth too, like any other preposition, will not be understandable unless it is absorbed into the meaning of its principle. As we have just understood, an introspection and representation of a prepositional phrase is a complete distortion and, in a way, a falsification of the objective truth of such a linguistic entity. Likewise, an introspection of the self is an illusory representation of its existential reality, and cannot be taken as its true representation. In illuminative language, the word "illusory" is frequently used to signify this, that is, to conceptualize and interpret the unitary truth of a reality that can never be truly and exactly represented.[45]

In the preceding chapter we saw that Suhrawardī denies, with considerable clarity, any possibility that the self can ever know itself, and still less to be known by others, through representation. Thus the independent impression that we may have from the selfhood of ourselves can never characterize the truth value of the reality of the self as it exists in another. This reality, as we have seen in the preceding chapters, can only be apprehended through knowledge by presence.

Therefore, my conclusion is that an emanative entity such as the self, the truth of which is more or less analogous to the truth value of a connective or a preposition, cannot be thought of accurately as distinguished from its principle. As it stands, the existential value of pure dependence upon another gives rise to the notion of a kind of existential absorption. This means that the truth of an emanative entity is to be known as something overabsorbed in the substantive truth of the other, that is, its principle. Consequently, this mystical sense of absorption is directly derived from the existential meaning of the prepositional truth of emanation, namely, "depending on . . . ," "proceeding from . . . ," "held by . . . ," and so on.

Emanation and Absorption

So far we have considered the two concepts emanation and absorption as distinct from each other, although it has already been shown that emanation is a primordial concept from which the notion of absorption is derived. Now, let us proceed to the question as to whether or not they are veritably identical.

It would seem that while emanation and absorption are linguistically asymmetric, in that the former stands for the descending light of existence from the First Principle and the latter for the ascending light to the Principle, they are in reality one and the same. That is to say, there is no possibility of distinguishing between the two as separate entities, the one emanating from the Principle, and the other being absorbed in the truth of the Principle. Just as it is true that the evening and the morning star are one and the same, meaning that they are numerically one and the difference is only in the manner in which the same thing is described, so it is true that emanative and absorptive beings are one and the same, meaning that they are identical in reality, and that they are distinct only when described from different angles. It is not, therefore, surprising that the self, as an emanation in all its simplicity, can be viewed from two different perspectives: one as a descending ray of light from the Principle, the other as an ascending one turned toward its Principle. This identity in truth, together with the difference and asymmetry in conception, constitutes a sufficient reason for supposing that each of these two concepts logically implies the other in such a way that there is a double implication connecting one to the other. If the implication is true on either side, it must be taken as a material equivalence. That is to say, whatever is true of an emanation is true of an absorption, and conversely, whatever is true of an absorption is true of an emanation. One of these things that is a characteristic of an emanation known by God is knowledge by presence. We have said that God knows His emanation through knowledge by presence. We arrive, thus, at the point where it is clear that since an emanative being is present in God, an absorptive being that is the same as an emanative being, must also be present in God.

From this we can quite legitimately advance our analysis of mysticism by attributing to man in his relation to God whatever we are entitled to attribute to God in His relation to man. That is, if God knows man as His emanation by presence, man as an absorptive being should know God by presence as well. Yet there are two different senses of 'presence', insofar as there are two different descriptions for one single reality of emanation. We shall see next that although there is only one single presence of emanation, the same presence conceptually varies according to two different descriptions: emanative and absorptive. The presence is emanative in that it overflows from God, and the same presence is absorptive in that it is absolutely dependent on God.

Nine

Mystical Unity

The Twofold Sense of Presence

We have come to the point that whatever is true of an emanation is true of an absorption, and whatever is true of an absorption is true of an emanation. We have also shown that God knows by presence what has emanated from Himself. That is, an emanative being like the self, proceeding from God and absorbed in His overwhelming light of Being, is present in God. He, therefore, knows the self not by the sort of presence of self identity as He knows Himself, but by the presence of His supremacy over His overflowed emanation as His immanent act. This is the same manner in which the self knows its body, imagination, and phantasm through presence by causal supremacy. Thus, an emanation is present in the very existential supremacy of its principle; and so also, by the equivalence between emanation and absorption, it is an absorption present in that in which it is absorbed—God.

As we have already pointed out there is only one simple entity, but it is described in two different ways: emanation and absorption. This is also true of the sense of presence. In point of fact, there is only one disposition of presence, but it can be described firstly as presence by "illumination" or "emanation," if one wants to specify the kind of presence that the principle is possessed of by its supremacy over its emanative being. In this aspect we say that the cause or principle is present in its immanent effect or act in the manner of emanation or illumination.[1] Secondly, the same state of presence is called presence by absorption if one's explanation approaches it the other way around. One may be in a position to specify the manner of immersion and the degree of dependence and absorption for which an emanative entity is fitted. In these circumstances one must change the expression as one has changed the perspective. However, this is the same presence by illumination that is expressed as presence by absorption and immersion in mystical language.

Setting up these two senses of presence, we can legitimately say that the self, as a substitute instance of emanation, enjoys kowledge of God by the presence of absorption. We can, for the same reason, say that the self is known by God through knowledge by presence in the sense of illumination. Because of the identity of these two senses of presence in reality, they are also identical in their proportionate degrees of presence. That is to say, to the same degree that God has presence by illumination in the reality of the self, the self also, to the same degree, enjoys its presence in God in the sense of absorption. Thus, in that particular stage of being, God and the self are identical.[2]

The conclusion is that in the case of emanation there is only one real state of presence, but it can be viewed from two different perspectives, and described by two different expressions. It can be stated as "presence by illumination," if the presence of God in the self as His emanation is taken into account; and the same thing can be called "presence by absorption" if the relation of the self to God as its principle of reality is under consideration. But, as we have understood, the objective reference of these expressions is one simple emanative entity that is nothing but the reality of the self. The truth of the self is therefore the unitary simplex of God's presence in the self and the self's presence in God.

The Meaning of Mystical Unitary Consciousness

Now let us turn our attention to the relation of the emanation to its ultimate principle. In illuminative philosophy this relation is, as we said before, called "the ascending ladder" of existence *(al-silsilat al-su'ūdyah).*[3] A mystic ascends to unitary consciousness and becomes united with God in the sense of absorption.

The great problem facing us when as philosophers we deal with the theory of mysticism is the problem of the consciousness of "unity" with God. What is really meant by the word "unity" or "union" with God, or with the Universal self,[4] unanimously used by authorities of mysticism, becomes the prime question in the philosophy of mysticism. According to the various methods of interpretation given to the word unity, there are different answers to this question. These answers are linguistic, philosophical, religious, psychological, and so on. Even despite all this variety of interpretation, one can know for certain that none of them is systematically adequate. For one thing, this form of unitary consciousness, which calls for unity in difference and difference in unity, still remains absolutely paradoxical. None of these interpretations has so far provided a satisfactory solution, for none of them enables us to resolve the problem of this particular kind of unity and hence, answer the main paradoxical questions involved in that problem. It is not, however, the concern of this work to bring these considerations forward and subject them to cross-examination with the objective of demonstrating their shortcomings.

To begin with, we already know that none of these various attempts is based systematically on the authentic foundation of mysticism. An authentic foundation can be nothing other than the theory of knowledge by presence which we have already sketched out in principle. Yet it is our primary interest to concentrate on our solution to the problem of mysticism and to try to introduce an appropriate systematic meaning of the term "union" or "unity" with God according to our thesis of knowledge by presence.

Before coming to our final logical solution, we feel it is necessary to restate systematically the crux of the problem. The chief problem of mystical unitary consciousness is the question of how the two different realities—the reality of an individual self as an emanative being and that of its Principle—become one and the same in the process of mystical experience. Of course, it is a flat contradiction that any two different beings, with two different statuses of existence, could suddenly break into one single existential unity and become really one and the same without undergoing a true process of generation and decay. How can this unity be possible, if it is not purely emotional or hallucinatory?

All we can do in the face of this great problem is to develop, on the basis of the theory of knowledge by presence, an expanded theory based on an illuminative interpretation of the hypothesis of mystical unity. By this I do not mean to assert that, while acknowledging all the other theories, this analysis is unique in being complete and invulnerable to any prospective criticism. I do, however, believe that this doctrine, considered within the confines of its principles, is systematic enough to play an antithetical role in the presence of the above contradiction and those difficult paradoxical questions that are raised against the hypothesis of mysticism.

Unity in the Sense of Self-Identity

Let us begin here by addressing the following question: What is wrong with the supposition that mystical unity is a complete unity with God by nature, in which the meaning of unity is as strong as it can be? Such a supposition implies that a genuine mystic knows the whole reality of God by presence-knowledge, exactly as he knows the reality of himself by presence-knowledge on the grounds of the criterion of "self-identity." In this case, as Nicholson interpreted it, "the Sufi mystic rises to contemplation of the divine attributes and ultimately when his consciousness is wholly melted away he becomes transubstantiated in the radiance of the divine essence."[5]

In dealing with this question, it should be pointed out that we have already acknowledged the two different species of knowledge by presence: presence by self-identity and presence by emanation or illumination. It has also been mentioned that as the self is possessed of both of these two species of knowledge by presence, God must similarly, and on the same basis, have these two senses of presence as well. God's presence-knowledge of Himself by virtue of self-identity has the meaning that the reality of God is absolutely present to and identical with Himself. God's presence-knowledge by illumination and supremacy is, on the other hand, taken to mean that He is present in His immanent act of emanation. Hence, there is no possible interruption or break in His illumination and supremacy over the emanation such as to cause a separation between Himself and His act of emanation.

Now, if we were to take the view that an individual self, such as that of a mystic, becomes identical with God by nature, it would necessarily mean that he knew God exactly as he knows his own selfhood, by the criterion of self-identity. Conversely, it would also mean that God knew this individual self exactly as He knows Himself by the same principle of self-identity. This is the cardinal virtue of the relation of identity: that it is symmetrical, reflexive, and transitive.

Neither of these two equivalences, however, could be true. That is, neither could God know an individual self exactly as He knows Himself by self-identity, nor could an individual self know Him in this way. This is because a relation of self-identity is the most restrictive equivalence that each individual bears to itself and to nothing else. In this relation, any transubstantiation of one essence to another is a flat contradiction and points to a logical absurdity involved in the thesis. The principle of the identity relation does not show anything more than the tautologous truths that "God is God" and "the self is the self." It does not admit of any transformation of one of these two separate natures into another. In the unity of self-identity there is no determinate idea of God distinct from the self. There is not, therefore, any reason why the self should be God or God the self.[6]

To the advantage of the famous Platonic distinction between 'being' and 'becoming', neither the Divine Being nor an individual self that belongs to the order of 'becoming' could transubstantiate from the radiance of the nature of one to that of the other. This is simply because the order of 'being' cannot be transformed into the order of 'becoming'. From the standpoint of God this transformation is impossible because there is no potentiality whatsoever in God to enable Him to pass from one nature to another. On the part of the self, although there is always a potentiality of transcendence, in the sense of proportionate closeness to the First Principle, it is not possible to suppose that this transcendence could ever take the nature of the passing of the self so as to become identified with the nature of the undifferentiated Godhead. Were there such a possibility in the essential nature of the human being of becoming God by nature, the reality of God would be the last form of human consciousness instead of being the First Principle of being. In other words, God can indeed be the final cause for human beatitude, but cannot be the last formal cause produced by the eventual causation of human experiences. This would be like the Hegelian notion of the "Absolute consciousness" as the final result of human phenomenal consciousness.

It is to be noted that the divine pattern of being may, of course, be designed as the ultimate object for human felicity. This does not, however, mean that the reality of God is the last consequence of human causal antecedents. It may, therefore, be concluded that it is a lack of acquaintance with the meaning of the technical term *fanā' al-fanā'*[7]—"annihilation of annihilation"—that causes these kinds of unwarranted interpretations of mystical identity. In the following section we will talk about the terminology of *fanā' al-fanā'* in dealing with the mystical implications of annihilation. In the face of these interpretations, we see that all the authorities of mysticism, from Plotinus to Eckhart and al-Ghazzālī, as well as those in Eastern mysticism, are in agreement regarding the fact that a mystic has the ability to be united with the One, or the Universal Self, in his trance, and to subsequently return to the world of multiplicity. Were his momentary transcendence a genuine process of transformation in nature, there would be a further absurdity in that both God and the mystic would be of such a "transcient nature" that the essential feature of each could occasionally break through to the other. This makes both the idea of God and that of the self a contradiction in terms.

With regard to our system of knowledge by presence, the impossibility of substantial transformation is quite straightforward. We have already mentioned that the existential reality of the self as an emanative entity is analogous to a mere prepositional function that can never arrive, even in the imagination, at the radiance of the nature of its substantive basis. Just as a true preposition cannot function as a substantive noun, so also an emanative being such as the self cannot be transubstantiated into the nature of its principle.

The upshot of our argument is that this proposed sense of identity for mystical knowledge, which is, according to our principle, based upon presence-knowledge by self-identity, involves these several points of absurdity. For this reason the doctrine of mystical knowledge through presence by self-identity, or transubstantiation, is to be ruled out as inconceivable.[8] A doctrine such as this, which implies numerous absurdities, is to be judged not only as lacking in logic and being insufficient, but also as being meaningless.

Within the confines of the theory of knowledge by presence the only alternative left to be considered is unity through presence in the sense of illumination and absorption, not in the sense of self-identity. Unity in the sense of absorption is a sort of unity that we can also ascribe to the prepositional function of our linguistic connective and preposition. A preposition is really united with its substantive nouns and verbs, in terms of not being independently observable, and it has no independent meaning at all. We have already discussed the idea of the prepositional nature of emanation, and we shall be more specific about it later, to a degree in that emanation will no longer remain still unresolvedly paradoxical.

Unity in the Sense of Absorption

In the preceding discussions we arrived at the point at which "the self as an emanation of God is a unitary simplex of the presence of God in man and the presence of man in God." We also considered that the nature of this unitary simplex of presence was not that of a phenomenal occurrence, which can take place eventually in the psychological course of meditation or through some intentional method of contemplation. It is purely existential, arising from the First Principle of being, by which He brings the world of possibility into the actual state of reality on the basis of His necessity: His necessity of being, of knowing, of willing, and of acting.

Strictly speaking, in accordance with the theory of emanation and the doctrine of knowledge by presence, the emanative system of the existence of the self is a simple unitary stage of being where necessity and possibility meet. It is a necessity because emanation is a necessary action of God, which overflows from His necessary existence and necessary knowledge.[9] It is also an existential possibility, because an absorption is nothing but total dependence on God. This "unitary simplex" of presence (i.e., the presence of the Necessary Being in the existentially possible emanative reality of the self, and the presence of the self in the Necessary Being) is the defensible meaning of mystical unitary consciousness, which we are now prepared to advocate.

In this sense of identity, God's presence in the self is the same existential state and the same individual unity that the presence of the self is in God. That is, "God-in-self = self-in-God." Yet, as we have already pointed out, it is a matter of different perspectives that rules that one side of this unitary simplex is to be called presence by illumination and supremacy,[10] and the other side presence by absorption and pure dependence. It is not, however, the case that with this difference of perspective the existential unity and simplicity of this stage of being divides into two individual forms of existence, since there is no possibility of an existential void, and disruption or separation between the emanation and the principle of emanation. There is only one expanded unity of existence, but it has to be described as a principle of emanation and the emanation of that principle. Since it is a *monadic* relation, the Aristotelian analogy of the road from Athens to Thebes and from Thebes to Athens as a dyadic relation does not hold with respect to the emanation relationship.

On the basis of this particular mode of presence, neither can God transubstantiate from his undifferentiated Godhead into the form of an individual spatiotemporal selfhood, nor can the self transcend to the radiance of the Divine Essence. Nonetheless, at this stage of illumination and absorption, God and the self are existentially identical, because both are present in this mode of existence. The self is present in the full scale of its reality, and God is present by His illumination and supremacy but is not present in the whole scale of His reality. It is only the lexical sense of presence that varies from one heading to the other.

'I-ness' and 'By-ness' are One and the Same

To further illustrate this extremely subtle and important meaning of identity, we ought to refer once again to the Suhrawardīan doctrine of 'I-ness'. In a previous chapter, which was entitled "The Prime Mode of Knowledge by Presence," we learned from Suhrawardī that this 'I-ness' stands for the reality of self, and is absolutely invariable and existentially simple. It is invariable because it would be completely lost if it could eventually be converted to a state normally expressible by the 'it-ness' dictum. It is also simple because in the state of 'I-ness' there is no trace of 'otherness'; it is the state of the absence of anything except 'I-ness'. 'I-ness' therefore remains ever present to itself. This means that in the existential radiance of 'I-ness' any possibility for constituting a binary relation out of the reality of 'I-ness' is out of the question. In other words, it is impossible to attach any element of otherness to the ontological truth of 'I-ness'.

This peculiarity of the reality of 'I-ness' accounts for its being a typical *monadic* relation that does not depend upon anything but its principle, from which it cannot be separated and toward which it cannot be another. From this it follows that the reality of 'I-ness' is not a composition of "something" which exists in "another," or which is even "held by another" as a separate being. Yet this does not exclude the fact that the whole simplex of its reality is, as Ṣadr al-Dīn puts it, a relation of pure 'by-ness', rather than something "held by," or "related to," another. The whole point is that the emanation relationship is not of the "one-to-another" kind, but rather it is the illumination of the principle itself that is monadic and marked as a "one-to-one" relation. We have in the past sketched out the meaning of "illuminative relation" and what makes it different from the Aristotelian category of relation and relation in general; but, as a further clarification, we can give the following analogy to emphasize the important sense of the illuminative relation and the extremely significant part played by this monadic relation in the understanding of the problem of unity in difference.[11]

Suppose for the moment we consider the contrary thesis that the existential feature of 'I-ness', called by us the reality of 'I-ness', is a dyadic relationship, like that of a color, say redness. In that case, exactly as the color is presumably something in itself which subsists in, or is related to, a material object, say a red carpet, the reality of 'I-ness' must also be something in itself which subsists in another. If this were so, it would not be just an infringement on the private state of 'I-ness' as opposed to 'it-ness', it would also place the whole reality of 'I-ness' in the category of 'it-ness'.

This would in turn give rise to the Suhwardīan problem of contradiction. When the supposed binary relation of 'I-ness' becomes contradictory, its unitary truth value and monadic relationship must exist all the more strongly, should it be directed to any element of 'it-ness'. That is, if the reality of 'I-ness' could, on mere supposition, be placed in the category of binary relation, the function of which is to relate one objective reality to the other, the logical formation of its objective truth would be:

"X is subsisting in Y."

Obviously, this expression implies that although one is inherent in the other, both X and Y belong to the category of 'it-ness', and neither of them is of 'I-ness'. This contradicts the simplex of the reality of 'I-ness'. We must therefore carefully consider such a unique reality as a "unitary relation," which is far from being a "one-to-another" relation, and that rather enjoys categorization as a one-to-one unitary relation. However, since its unitary relation is pure 'by-ness' or dependence, not "something-by-another" or "something dependent-on-another," it cannot be grasped at all except in the light of the recognition of its substantive reality. The result is that the whole reality of 'I-ness' is nothing but a mere unitary relation of 'by-ness'. 'I-ness' and 'by-ness' are therefore truly identical in the monadic form of a relation to its principle. Thus 'I-ness' is not something that holds its dependence on the other; rather, it is nothing but dependence on the other. *This is the meaning of the illuminative relationship.*

Having now seen that there must be such an identity between 'I-ness' and 'by-ness', the question immediately arises that if the reality of 'I-ness' is absolutely unitary, how can its relation with the principle ever be conceptualized and expressed? Any expression given to the pure objective reality of 'I-ness' in connection with its own principle indicates that there is "something" that bears some relation to another, no matter whether this relation be emanative or otherwise. In other words, in the special case of an emanative reality like 'I-ness', it must be admitted that it makes no sense to say that it is "something-in-another." For there is no trace of otherness in the frame of 'I-ness', and any expression standing for its prepositional truth, such as "by another," necessarily implies its relation to another and such an implication causes it to fall into the category of binary relations.[12] Consequently, 'I-ness' becomes 'it-ness'. In short, this question legitimately asks for a distinction to be made between "in otherness," which should be excluded from the state of 'I-ness', and "by otherness," which is identical with it.

The answer to this question must be as extremely ingenious as critical, for it is the nucleus of the truth of mysticism. The subtlety of the answer lies in the uniqueness of the emanative existence of the self as 'I-ness'. The crux of the matter lies in the following argument: an emanative entity is neither separate from nor absolutely identical with the essence of its principle. Let us take a mental entity such as an idea or a sense-perception as a case of something analogous to an emanative entity. It can never be said that the idea or the sense-perception accounts for a certain mental entity distinct from the mind. Our ideas cannot be supposed to have a reality independent of us. An idea without a mind would mean a mental entity without any mentality at all. It would also be false to suppose that our ideas are united with our minds in essence or with the whole factual reality of our minds.

Here again, it is appropriate to bear in mind the difference between an idea as a mental entity and a color as an external object in subsisting matter. While an idea is, both in theory and in truth, constituted by or consistently interrelated with the mind of the agent, a color is also that which cannot exist without subsisting matter, but which can be thought of even without such matter. As a spatiotemporal object, a color only needs a specified subject in which to exist. But it can quite possibly be understood without any relation to a particular subject or to any subject at all. It is quite otherwise with the relation of an idea to its thinking subject. This difference justifies us in saying that the relation of an idea to the mind is a unitary simplex by nature, because it is not something in itself that happens to exist in the mind of the thinking subject. It is a mere radiation and expansion, or in illuminative language, manifestation and appearance, of the mind itself. It is not merely the case that the mind and its ideas are identical in truth, it is also the case that as a mental entity an idea is not even understandable without the implicit understanding of a mind, because an idea is nothing but a phenomenon of the mind. Since the whole reality of an idea is nothing but a manifestation of the mind itself, it seems quite plausible to say that the relation of an idea to its thinking subject is monadic, and not dyadic. In Islamic philosophy it has been given as a rule that the appearance of a thing can never be anything other than the very reality of the thing itself.[13] Otherwise, that appearance would be an appearance of the appearance itself and not of the thing that has appeared to us. And since an idea is a mere appearance of the mind, it cannot be anything other than the mind appearing itself. On the other hand, the relation of a color to its subject matter is binary, because it proves to be something in itself related to and dependent on another in being.

The reality of 'I-ness' as an emanative act, like any other immanent act, cannot be detached from its principle of being, either in act or in thought. Thus no sense of separation or existential void is possible between that which has manifested itself in this emanation and the emanation itself that has been manifested. Like an idea or a sense-datum that cannot be supposed to have an existence independent of us, and cannot be thought of without relating it to a particular mind or to a mind in general, the reality of the self can neither exist nor be thought of without its absorption in the substantive ground of its being. Absorption is, therefore, not a relation of one thing to another, but rather it is a pure unitary relation of "to-or-by-another," with the omission or annihilation of "somethingness." This is what we have called the "one-to-one" relationship.

Once again, a reference to our linguistic analogy of the preposition makes this subtle point somewhat clearer. On this analogy, the reality of 'I-ness' functions as a mere relation but not something that is related. The only difference between this relation and a binary relation is that the role of a normal binary relation is to relate one reality to another, the dualism of which is presupposed and indispensable. In this relation, however, there is no possibility of such a presupposition. The only thing that must be presupposed is the One in which the reality of the self is absorbed and cannot be known except by knowing the One.

Another linguistic analogy is that of the "negation" relationship. Like the negation of something, the manifestation or emanation of something does not imply a two-place dualistic sense of relation. What it does imply is merely a one-sided relation, which is not even conceivable except in the light of the conception of its principle.

Only in this sense of unity of presence ought Plotinus to be interpreted when he says.

> Thus the Supreme as containing no otherness is ever present with us; we with it when we put otherness away. It is not that the Supreme reaches out to us seeking our communion: we reach toward the Supreme; it is we that become present. We are always before it: but we do not always look. . . We are ever before the Supreme—cut off in utter dissolution: we can no longer be. . .[14]

This vitally important passage contains almost all of the fundamental points that we have already discussed. They are: (a) that God is ever present in the self, by His illumination, if not by the whole reality of His self; (b) that we, as the selves, are also ever-present before God, and that we can realize this if we put any illusory otherness away (this clearly means that the purity of 'I-ness' which puts otherness away is ever present before Him); and (c) that in the unitary relation of an emanative being to its principle there is no possibility of an existential void and break, because this sort of void counts for utter dissolution, not just for a dissociation or interruption between the two entities. From this double sense of presence, clearly acknowledged by Plotinus, we can easily draw our theory of mystical unitary consciousness without any paradoxical problem.

The whole point of this discussion is that if there is to be any logical plausibility for the hypothesis of mystical unitary consciousness, it must be established on the basis of the principle of knowledge by presence. Presence, in the sense of self-identity, evidently does not apply to the unitary relation between God and the self; yet presence in the sense of illumination and emanation does apply to this relation. Only in this latter mode of presence does the self know God by presence at the same stage, and by the same degree of presence, that God knows the self by presence. This one single case of presence, however, takes the form of illumination where the presence of God is concerned. Moreover, the same instance of presence is called absorption if the relation of the self to God is taken into consideration. Finally, from the intervening step of this twofold sense of presence, we arrive at our theory of mystical unitary consciousness: because God and the self are absolutely united in this particular form of knowledge, they are also absolutely united in this particular form of being.

In conclusion, we can draw this material equivalence so as to outline our hypothesis of mystical unitary consciousness.

"God-in-self by emanation = self-in-God by absorption."[15]

What Is the Meaning of Annihilation?

On the grounds of the analysis of mystical unitary consciousness that has just been given, one is entitled to raise this question: If it is true that the self is, by its very ontological reality, ever-present in God and God in the self, what is the meaning of the mystical process of "annihilation" or, in the Surfi's expression, *fanā'*? As mystics believe, it is through this kind of experience that they can reach the stage of unitary consciousness. If unitary consciousness were the very reality of the self, it would hold true to say that for every human being "to be" is "to be a mystic." Mystical experiences would be redundant, if God were ever-present in man, and man in God.

As we have just seen, Plotinus briefly dealt with the question in this way: "Thus the Supreme as containing no otherness is ever-present with us; we with It when we put otherness away . . . we are always before It, but we do not always look. . . ."

But the detailed answer to the question, according to the principle of knowledge by presence, is that the reality of 'I-ness' is tied up in this life with 'it-ness', which is the state of conflicting with material objects, though not identical with it. 'I-ness', however, is characterized by its projecting of objects. It is this character of objectification that causes 'I-ness' to go so far even as to objectify itself in terms of 'otherness' in order to make judgments and statements about itself. Surely it is objectification that causes the simplicity of 'I-ness' to be mixed up with and wrapped up in the obscurity of the multiplicity of 'it-ness', and drives its perspective away from this original position toward the world of multiplicity. But since this natural and materialistic drive does not and cannot have an impact on the existential truth of 'I-ness', it can be erased and shaken off through any kind of antimultiple experiences. Experiences are therefore needed to take all these transcient objectifications away and to help the self further concentrate on itself and recover its reality of pure 'I-ness', which is nothing but presence in its Principle.[16]

Unity of Continuity

In the pyramid of existence in illuminative cosmology we have seen that there are two noninterchangeable dimensions that must be taken into account when the analysis of mysticism is in question. These are vertical and horizontal. The vertical dimension of existence identifies all the modes and degrees of the world of reality—through the law of continuity—with the supreme reality of the One, because in that dimension there is no possibility of an existential dissociation and void and no interruption by nothingness. Thus the dimension is, as a whole, continuous and unbroken. Continuity is, moreover, a mathematical principle for this sort of self-identity. In Islamic philosophy, this sense of continuity is given as a criterion of "individuation" and personal identity. That is, the oneness of continuity is equivalent to the oneness of individuality *(al-waḥdat al-ittiṣāliyyah'ayn al-waḥdat al-shakhṣiyyah)*.[17]

On this principle, along the vertical lines, every segment of reality within the pyramid of existence is existentially and individually united with the supreme reality of the First. The reality of the Vertex is also, on the same basis, individually connected and thus united with the reality of every thing that has a share of existence in that pyramid. In the horizontal dimension of the pyramid, however, either at the Vertex or at the base, there is no such continuity. In that dimension things are comparable with one another. The existential void between one thing and another, and consequently the difference between things in general, becomes genuinely understandable and very real. This is because in the horizontal dimension things are not related to each other by the system of efficient causal and hierarchical connections.[18]

Considering these two dimensions we can quite logically account for mystical annihilation. It is a withdrawing from the horizontal dimension and a turning toward the vertical one. In this way annihilation, which in the Sufi path is called *fanā'*, is simply a resignation from one side of the reality and a concentration on the other. This is a simple purification of the self in order to arrive at the simplex of self-realization where there is no trace of otherness and where there is nothing but the identity of continuity.

Such as it is, the process of annihilation has different degrees through which one reaches the culmination of this process of simplification. Undoubtedly annihilation, in all its degrees, is an intentional process of purification that a mystic quite consciously undertakes, but the culmination of this process is knowledge by presence which is never representational. The ultimate degree of annihilation is a "double" annihilation which in Sufi language is called *"fanā' al-fanā'"* meaning "annihilation of annihilation." In correspondence with the logical double negation, double annihilation implies the completely positive state of unitary consciousness, called in Sufi terminology *baqā'*, meaning the unity of continuity with the One. Just as double negation logically implies affirmation, so also double annihilation arrives existentially at complete unity with the reality of the Principle. This is what the self is in itself, which is its ever-presence in God and God's ever-presence in the self. *This is the meaning of unitary consciousness.*

Ten

The Language of Mysticism and Metamysticism

Preliminary Remarks

In modern linguistic philosophy a significant attempt is made to distinguish metalanguage from object language. If, for instance, I were to write a book in English on the grammar of the German language, English would be a metalanguage and German the object language, talked about in English. In that case, English, functioning as the metalanguage, would take German as the object. The metalanguage would raise questions about the object, and then attempt to systematically answer them. In fact, German is the object language only if there is a metalanguage taking German as the object under its consideration. If I wrote a book in English on the grammar of English, English would be both the metalanguage and its object. This can, of course, be the case only when the object language is rich enough in its means of expression to talk about itself. In short, the term object language refers to that specific language which speaks 'of' a certain subject,[1] while "metalanguage," on the other hand, is a language 'of' the language of the subject, which talks 'about', but not directly 'of', that subject itself, whether these two languages are one and the same or are different. In order to differentiate between these two languages when discussing mysticism, we shall from now on call the metalanguage the language 'about', and the object language the language 'of'.

In connection with mysticism, it may be appropriate to give an analogy from ethical theory to help us clearly understand how metamysticism, meaning the metalanguage of mysticism, must be distinguished from pure mystical language, which is the language *of,* but not the language *about,* mysticism. This analogy will also help us understand how the confusion between these two systems of language misleads some philosophers, as well as a great number of historians, causing them to make serious mistakes.[2]

In the opening of Plato's dialogue, the *Crito,* Socrates is asked by his friends to escape from prison and execution by going into exile with his family. He first lays down some points about the approach to be taken: (1) we must not let our decision be affected by our emotions, but must examine the question carefully and follow the best reasoning; (2) we cannot answer such questions by appealing to what people generally think; and (3) we ought never to do what is morally wrong.[3] The way of thinking that Socrates employs here, which may be employed by anyone who asks what is right or wrong, good or evil, is what is called normative ethics; and the kind of language that is employed in such normative questions is the language 'of' ethics, not 'about' it.

There is, however, also "analytic," "critical," "semantic," "epistemological," and "metaphysical" thinking about these normative judgments. This is the sort of thinking we imagine that Socrates would certainly have used if he had been challenged to the limit in the justification of his normative judgments.[4] Thus, any discussion of this sort ought to be called metaethical thought.

In the study of mystical thinking we are confronted with the same variety of methodological approaches. There have been, throughout the history of human thought, some questions, expressions, and principles that are concerned with a semantic, or an epistemological or metaphysical perspective towards mysticism, as well as a number of others that belong directly to mysticism itself. Hence, in order to avoid any confusion of the sort that has frequently marred nonspecialist approaches to mysticism, we are obliged to set up a classification of mysticism that distinguishes between three phases of mysticism under each of which a particular species of mysticism is categorized. These are:

1. Ineffable mysticism: the experience of mysticism that is not conceptualized in terms of public understanding, and therefore has no normal public language at all. It has a peculiar private language, which is not publicly understandable, and is called, in Sufi

terminology, *al-shaṭḥiyyāt al-ṣūfiyyah,*[5] meaning the nonsensical expressions of mystics. This language is supposedly related to the genuine state of mysticism. It consists of apparently blasphemous, and sometimes meaningless and paradoxical, but nevertheless beautiful statements unintentionally uttered by Sufis when they are completely beyond themselves, immersed in the ocean of trance and annihilation. In these circumstances they speak of what they experience, not of what they are thinking of, or of what they are willing to say. This is why we cannot categorize it as a conventional form of language.
2. Introspective and reconstructive mystical thinking as the pure object language of mysticism. This is what we have agreed to call the language 'of' mysticism.
3. Philosophical or scientific metamysticism that talks "about" mysticism.

Here we should note that as the title of this chapter indicates, we are dealing with mysticism and metamysticism insofar as this general linguistic classification is concerned. Therefore, while from among these three aforementioned approaches 2 and 3 can be categorized under the headings of "language of," and "language about" respectively, 1 falls under the heading of "pure empirical mysticism." Although 1 differs from the others in that it has no language at all, so to speak, 2 is taken as the object language of mysticism proper, and 3 is designed metalinguistically to approach mysticism from various angles; semantic, logical, epistemological, metaphysical, scientific, and so on.

Mysticism and the Theory of Knowledge by Presence

In this section we shall present the primary explanation of the logical relation connecting these three species of mysticism (as discussed thus far) one with another, as well as *vis-à-vis* the principal distinction made between knowledge by presence and knowledge by correspondence.

Starting with the genuine mystical experience, widely known as ineffable mysticism, we must return once again to the diagram of emanation that was drawn up with the purpose of shedding some light on the meaning of mystical unitary consciousness.[6] In this diagram we showed that the human mind, as a mode of emanation, is designed to make the effort to arrive at the state of its own absolute self-realization. Since the reality of the human mind is existentially linked with the hierarchical principles of emanation and ultimately reduced and absorbed in the supreme light of Necessary Being, the process of self-realization is but a kind of prepositional identity relation with the One.

This self-realization can be achieved by the operation of double annihilation. Just as the logical form of double negation implies total negation-elimination arriving at the absolute sense of affirmation, so also the mystical double annihilation *(fanā' al-fanā')* drives us to the purity of unitary consciousness where nothing is to be observed except the substantive reality of the One.[7]

This unitary consciousness, as we have already stated, is mystical knowledge by presence. Of course, it is not the form of presence knowledge by identity of transubstantiation or unity in essence, but it is rather a unity by presence of absorption and annihilation, which is a derivative form of emanation. We have called this identity "prepositional unity."

Considered as beyond the reach of any conventional language, mystical experiences fall into this category of knowledge by presence, and are thus identified with that kind of presence which is prepositional and absorptive. Since they take their place in the rank of knowledge by presence that is identical with the existential reality of the self, mystical experiences become an existential ground for the efficient causation of the introspective representational knowledge of these experiences once the mystic "returns." By the illuminative relation, this underlying mystical knowledge by presence illuminates its immanent act of knowledge by representation introvertively. This means that when the mystic comes back from his self-realization to the world of phenomenal objects, the multitude of which appears in the horizontal order of emanation, then his experiences of unitary consciousness become efficiently active in providing acts of representation.

Such an immanent act of representation is the operation of the illuminative relationship that we spoke of earlier.[8] As a matter of fact, the experienced unitary consciousness of the mystic is creative enough to reconstruct, through illumination, all the beautiful mystical stages that he has already witnessed in the vertical dimension of emanation during his self-realization. This reconstructive act of representation, which directly and introvertively overflows from the depth of the ineffable mystical knowledge by presence, is the introvertive knowledge by representation (knowledge by correspondence), referred to by the Sufi authorities as "*'irfān.*"

'Irfān is thus a kind of knowledge by representation, illuminated and acquired from mystical knowledge by presence through the illu-

minative relationship.[9] Since this introspective knowledge by representation *('irfān)* was set down for the first time in the history of the Sufi tradition by Muḥyī al-Dīn ibn al-'Arabī (1164–1240) with such thoroughness and in such a systematic way, it quickly became popular and well known as the linguistic science of mysticism.[10]

Obviously such a direct access to the truth of mysticism is not possible through a philosophical way of thinking concerned only with a logical, semantic, and epistemological justification of the truth and falsity of mystical statements and paradoxical assertions. All philosophy can do concerning mysticism is to take that language of the mystics—*'irfān*—as the subject of its investigation. With the presupposition of this object language, philosophy can hold to and comply with its task of thinking and talking 'about' what has been expressed and spoken 'of' by mystics in their subject language of *'irfān*. All philosophical approaches to the problem of mysticism should fall only within this systematic way of thinking and talking 'about'. Hence, all philosophical considerations of mystical experiences must be subsumed under the category of metamysticism.

There are few historical examples of men who were truly both mystics *('urafā')*, those who introvertively and thoroughly reconstructed their own mystical experiences, and philosophers who thoughtfully examined their own articulated language of *'irfān* in a philosophical manner. Among the ancient philosophers, Parmenides and Plotinus were two great masters of both mysticism and philosophical introspection, a place similarly filled by Meister Eckhart in Christianity, and al-Ghazzālī in Islam.

The particular combination of mystical and philosophical orientations varies according to the degrees and duration of self-realization in mystical experience, and also according to the ways and means in which these experiences were undergone. Although these ways and means can be either sacred or profane, mysticism itself cannot be subjected to this very disputable division.

As a scientist, William James once attempted to experience a lower degree of mystical trance through inducing nitrous oxide intoxication.[11] He then reconstructed what he had experienced in his own object language, which would be called, in our terminology, *'irfān*. After he had articulated his interpretation in this language, James reported it in print. When he tried later on to reflect on that reported interpretation through his philosophical or scientific contemplation, such a second reflection then became his metamystical inquiry.

The conclusion that can be inferred from all this is that the metamystical inquiry is a contemplation by reflection upon the object language of mystical experiences. While mystical experiences themselves always remain in the rank of knowledge by presence, *'irfān* and meta-mysticism belong to the order of knowledge by representation, and for that matter, they both count as regular forms of knowledge by correspondence.

Mysticism and Metamysticism

It is safe to assert that thus far no satisfactory attempts have been made to separate the problem of mysticism proper, which in the Islamic tradition is called the science of *'irfān,* from that of metamysticism, on the one hand, and from the ineffable mystical experience, on the other. Therefore, the task demanding our attention at this juncture is that of remedying this hiatus. This consideration is not just imperative so as to differentiate the philosophy of mysticism from the science of mysticism, *'irfān.* It is also fundamental for an understanding of how a single problem can be viewed and treated in two utterly different ways—the mystical and the metamystical.

Jacques Maritain (1882–1973) provides a significant distinction between "communicable knowledge" and "incommunicable knowledge," and fits the ultimate stage of mystical experience, or, as he puts it, "the absolutely privileged case of the beatific vision," into the category of incommunicable knowledge, because, he says, "the Divine Essence itself will actuate our intellect immediately, without the mediation of any species or idea." But all other kinds of intellectual knowledge and experience are, in his opinion, to be placed in the category of "communicable knowledge."[12]

W. T. Stace offers yet another position on distinguishing mystical experiences that are putatively "ineffable" from the "interpretation" of those experiences. He exemplifies his idea through this vague analogy:

> On a dark night out of doors one may see something glimmering white. One person may think it a ghost. A second may take it a sheet hung out on a clothesline. A third person may suppose that it is a white-painted rock. Here we have a single experience with three different interpretations.[13]

Taking this analogy into account, the interpretation of mystical experiences must undergo a further analysis with the objective of discerning either a direct and immediate interpretation of mystical experiences that falls in the class of the language 'of' mysticism, or an interpretation or criticism of that interpretation which belongs to the language 'about' mysticism.

Accepting the validity and soundness of each of these two accounts, neither of them truly satisfies the imperative need for a complete and exhaustive classification of the subject at hand that can be used as a guideline for understanding the different approaches to mysticism to the same degree as the classification presented earlier in this study. This is mainly because neither of these suggested distinctions concerns the question of the linguistic variation involved in almost all kinds of mystical study. As we shall see, the confusion concerning the aforementioned variation between meta- and object language is one of the basic factors that has led to fundamental difficulties and disastrous mistakes. Also the problem of the ineffability, or, in Maritain's terminology, "incommunicability," of mystical knowledge has not been precisely analyzed so that we may understand the sense in which the ineffability is to be interpreted. Thus, concerning ineffability, there are two points to be considered: (a) The reason as to why mystical knowledge is incommunicable; and (b) the meaning of this incommunicability, or ineffability. Both of these problems, or ambiguities, must, in our opinion, be treated on the basis of our theory of knowledge by presence. Yet before we delve into a consideration of these problems and their solution, there is need for asserting that, on the basis of our theory of knowledge by presence, and according to the classification which we have just made, there is in fact an articulated object language of mysticism. This is the introspective and interpretive knowledge of mystical apprehension which is "apprehension" of God, or in Islamic terminology, *'irfān*—knowledge by presence of God. The science of *'irfān* has been designed for use as a conventional object language for mystical apprehension and the various stages of mystical experiences.

Setting aside the stages of the mystical experience, which are taken to be absolutely ineffable and with which we have dealt in the preceding chapters, there are still other kinds of mysticism that must all be subsumed, according to our classification, under two general disciplines of mysticism. These are all mystical, because they are related to the general subject of mysticism in one way or the other, but we must place them in a logical order, distinct from one another, if we are to succeed in a proper understanding of mysticism. In the following consideration we are going to present briefly various approaches that have been typically called mystical.

1. There is the descriptive empirical inquiry into the problem of mysticism which is of the category of language 'about' mysticism. This

sort of inquiry is historical, scientific, anthropological, or sociological. The process of inquiry is therefore carried out by historians, psychologists, anthropologists, or sociologists. There are many medieval as well as contemporary writers who have conducted such empirical investigations of mysticism. They do not, however, take logical, metaphysical, or analytical questions into account, nor do they satisfactorily examine the science of mysticism—*'irfān*—insofar as it is the object language of mysticism proper.

William James, for example, is one of those few famous thinkers who, using this scientific principles, tried to capture four essential but empirical characteristics of mysticism, such that when an experience possesses them, it may be justifiably called mystical. These are:

a. Ineffability
b. Noetic quality
c. Transiency
d. Passivity[14]

It is quite apparent that James, as a psychologist, does not, in his remarkable essay, ask or try to answer any epistemic, semantic, analytic, or metaphysical questions about mysticism. Moreover, he does not concern himself with the quality and quantity of the grades of rapture and unification with the Absolute that obviously belong to a genuine mystical language. His language is therefore an empirically scientific kind of metamystical language, but not a metaphysical one, let alone a directly mystical one, such as we find in *'irfān*. In point of fact, James admits that he is looking upon the subject externally.[15] Perhaps by "externally" he is trying to assert that his language is metamystical, and is not at all an object language dealing with mysticism itself. If so, then *externality* is another characteristic of all metamystical language.

As a historian, R. C. Zaehner must also be ranked among the empirical philosophers of mysticism. Zaehner's approach, as compared with James's, is not scientific however. He talks empirically about the history of mysticism,[16] and occasionally, about the empirical philosophy of mysticism. By taking a metalinguistic approach of this kind, he makes a detailed historical comparative survey of varieties of mysticism from many different cultures, religions, and ages, ranging from Hindu, Buddhist, Christian, Islamic, and Jewish forms to those of modern mystics. To a considerable extent, he is concerned with the problem of the new phenomena of mysticism in Western culture as manifested in the *hippie* culture's allusions to mystical experiences and their claims to attainment of the same mystical states as those attained by the pious saints, only their states being achieved through the use of hallucinatory drugs instead of spiritual discipline and devotion. Although on this problem he tries to present his philosophical treatment objectively, his conclusion makes a religious distinction between a sacred and a profane mysticism, without showing any logical justification for it.[17]

2. There are also analytic, critical, metaphysical, and logical ways of approaching mystical thought. These consist entirely of nonempirical analyses of the problem of mysticism. This approach to a philosophy of mysticism is based on posing questions such as the following: What is the meaning of mysticism? What makes it different from religion? Is there any rational justification for the essential and principal claims of mystical propositions? What is the definition or meaning of mystical expressions and concepts such as "Unity," "the One," "the oneness of existence," the notion of "light," etc.?[18] What is the nature of mystical unity? Is it emotional, noetic, or existential? If existential, how can an individual finite existence become united with the absolute infinite existence? Is mysticism really ineffable? If it is, then any assertion about it, negative or positive, ineffability itself included, is self-contradictory. What is the logical solution for all the paradoxical statements that have appeared in the mysticism of all cultures and religions throughout the history of philosophy?

As we see, these questions are logical, semantic, epistemological, or metaphysical ones. Mystical thinking of this kind does not try to answer questions as to how, practically, we can obliterate our limited selves and unite with the One, although these are typical questions in the mystical language, referred to in Islamic terminology as the science of *'irfān*. Many ancient, medieval, and contemporary philosophers have in one way or another viewed mystical thinking through this approach. They have not, however, thought 'of' mysticism in a mystical manner; they have rather thought and talked "about" the objective truth of mysticism. They have not been interested in knowing, for example, what kind of meditation, or moral and religious experiences can take them closer to communion with the One.

3. Finally there is reflective and introspective, scientific but nonphilosophical, thinking in which a mystic tries by the power of his intellect to reconstruct in a sophisticated way the features of whatever he has already seen or apprehended in the course of his mystical experiences. This is what we have referred to as the genuine mystical language, or the science of mysticism, for the simple reason that it is talking 'of' mysticism not 'about' mysticism, and it is designed to recapitulate the state in which a mystic was already involved. Within the scope of this kind of mysticism, any philosophical or scientific question

'about' mysticism is incoherent to the system, and is regarded as absolutely irrelevant and inadmissible. On the matter of the "incoherency" of philosophy as a metalinguistic approach to this pure mystical language, perhaps the Persian Sufi poet Rūmī's (1207–73) beautiful mystical language provides the most lucid reasoning:

> Those demonstrative philosophers are walking on wooden legs,
> O what erratic and shaky things their legs are.[19]

When a mystic is reflecting upon what he has just witnessed, it is of course a "shaky" question if a philosopher asks: Is your assertion true, or false, or contradictory? This seems justified when we remember our classification of mysticism. For taking this classification into consideration, one is inclined to admit that Rūmī and many other great mystics were absolutely correct when they sharply criticized philosophy by referring to it as "walking on shaky wooden legs," or rejecting it as an inadmissible mode of questioning regarding their mystical language. They were right because philosophy, as a language 'about' mysticism, if it is to be kept coherent, must not be applied to, and should not concern itself with, this most articulated system that is truly considered to be the "language of mysticism." Concerning this account, we shall see later on how the most famous British philosopher of recent times, Bertrand Russell, failed to be relevant when he took issue with Rūmī on the mystical assertion that "time is unreal,"[20] for Russell embarked on this debate before he had understood the object language of mysticism and what the mystic means by this assertion and others.

Object Language of Mysticism

One of the great advantages of this classification of mysticism is that it solves the problem of those questions that seem quite appropriate for one to ask and try to answer within the framework of one system of mysticism, but which do not make sense at all if asked in others. If they are to be meaningful, methodological questions must be related to the particular linguistic system concerned, either mystical or metamystical, but not both. For example, the question as to whether mystical claims are logically true or false does not make sense at all in the realm of an ineffable system of mysticism, nor does it within the scope of a mystical language that is supposed to be merely an interpretation of what the mystic has already seen in his ineffable states. This question is only worth considering when, as metamystical philosophers, we take a mystical assertion under critical examination and try to understand whether or not such a given assertion holds true.

In relation to this issue, there is a dialogue between philosophy and mysticism over the problem of "truth" and "falsity," or "reality" and "imagination," pertinent to the two languages, mystical and metamystical, in Rūmī's Persian poetical mysticism. This debate may be considered as a true reflection of the distinction just alluded to. As the poet wrote in his mystical language:

> The miserable philosopher calls fear 'illusion' *(wahm):* he has wrongly understood this lesson.
>
> How should there be any illusion without reality? How could a false coin gain currency unless there be a genuine one?
>
> How can a lie gain value unless there be a truth? Every lie in both worlds has arisen from a truth.
>
> He [the liar] saw the currency and prestige enjoyed by truth: he thus circulated the lie in hope of [it enjoying] the same.
>
> O [incarnate] lie, whose fortune is (derived) from veracity, give thanks for the bounty and do not deny the truth![21]

The mystic, in principle, and with his appropriate language, tries to annihilate every element of multiplicity and reduce all things which, in metalinguistic words, are bifurcated into truth or falsehood, reality or imagination, to the truth in his own language, which is the truth of the One. The philosopher, on the other hand, taking his own direction, and using his own principles of metalinguistic methodology, can face the problem from an entirely different perspective, and hence present his case according to his own linguistic role, in which the differences between reality and imagination, or truth and falsity, by no means have been dispensed with.

The prime question of mysticism, which is unitary consciousness, is one of those things upon which the totality of the science of mysticism, *'irfān*, is based. In the system of *'irfān* this unitary consciousness is not in question; it is, rather, taken for granted. The same question takes on a completely different meaning when asked in a philosophical and metamystical context. The question is then that of the "apprehension of the Infinite." Plotinus explicitly pointed out how this single question can be dealt with satisfactorily according to one discipline and may remain undecided or problematic according to another:

> You ask how can we know the Infinite? I answer: not by reason. It is the office of reason to distinguish and define. The Infinite, there-

> fore, cannot be ranked among its objects. You can only 'apprehend' the Infinite by entering into a state in which you are yourself no longer. This is . . . liberation of your mind from finite consciousness. When you thus cease to be finite you become one with the 'Infinite'. . . you realize this union, this identity.[22]

In this passage, Plotinus drew a line of demarcation between the question, "How can we *know* the Infinite?" and the question, "How can we *apprehend* the Infinite?" His answer to the first question implies that one *cannot* know the Infinite, and his answer to the second one implies that one *can* apprehend the Infinite. Setting aside his agnostic opinion that the Infinite cannot be known by reason, Plotinus's case presents a single question that can be asked in two distinct ways. First, the question may be asked as a typical metamystical question raised about unity with the Infinite. Second, it may be posited as a genuine mystical question. In the second perspective it has to be considered as the centerpiece in the science of mysticism by means of which the mystic tries to find regularities and arrangements that make his journey to unity with the Infinite possible.

Almost the same distinction between the two methods of questioning over one issue is clearly reflected in Avicenna's philosophy with respect to the problem of unity. In his treatise on the conception of unity between knower and the thing known, Avicenna contemptuously rejected the Porphyrian idea that the act of knowledge, the agent of knowing, and the thing known are all one and the same in their ontological status. He explained how it is impossible for these three entities to be united:

An anecdote:

> There was among them a man called Porphyry who worked out a treatise on the unity of knowledge and the things known. The work was praised by the Peripatetic philosophers. But it was altogether absurd and meaningless. They themselves knew that they could not understand it. Porphyry also was aware of this shortcoming. In fact one of Porphyry's contemporaries defied him by presenting an antithesis and the debate continued such that he, Porphyry, set up a refutation to this anti-thesis. But his later attempt was even worse than the first.[23]

Surprisingly, one can find the same position, which is referred to here as "absurd," expressed by Avicenna himself when he later sought to treat the issue of mysticism. He strongly approved of the idea of the absolute unity and the identification of mystical apprehension with the truth apprehended in mystical knowledge.

He portrayed this mystical strategy of identity with his mystical language of *'irfān* in the following manner:

> One who prefers to learn mystical apprehension just for the sake of mystical apprehension commits himself to the absurdity of dualism.
>
> But those who seek this apprehension *('irfān)* as if it were nothing but the very truth of the thing apprehended *(al-ma'rūf bihi)* can attain the unfathomable depth of Unity.[24]

Here, exactly as in Plotinus's case, we see that by a simple substitution Avicenna took a position completely different from that of his philosophical consideration of the identity of a knowing subject and the thing known. He substituted the system of empirical apprehension—*'irfān*—for the metalinguistic system, so as to move from the absurdity of dualism to the unfathomable depth of Unity. According to Plotinus, we cannot know the Infinite but we can apprehend It.[25] Again, in Avicenna's theory of knowledge, the identity of the knower and the known, suggested in the Porphyrian system, proves to be absurd insofar as the philosophical concept of knowledge is concerned. However, the identity of the agent of apprehension, that is, the mystic *(al-'ārif)*, and the Unity apprehended *(al-ma'rūf-bihi)* is regarded as the highest point to be achieved by (in) human development.

One might legitimately ask: Why such a vast difference? In my opinion this difference is due, in the world of language, to the variety of the systems of expression, and in the world of knowledge to the diversity of the essential features of human intelligence. By different systems we do not mean, as we have already indicated, merely a difference in emotion, or a difference in the motivation for questioning. Neither one of these two points of difference can make an absurd proposition acceptable or even praiseworthy. It is rather the very fundamental difference in the two species of human cognition and communication with the world of reality that distinguishes the science of mysticism from philosophy in general, and from the philosophy of mysticism, or metamysticism, in particular. The kind of awareness that the whole problem of mysticism centers upon, as was seen in the case of Plotinus and Avicenna, is different from the cognition and awareness that we usually obtain through our ordinary intellectual act of knowing. It is a sort of knowledge by presence, which is, as we have seen, identical with the existential truth of the human being. But the system of the logic and expression of this knowledge is the mystical science of *'irfān,* and not our ordinary logic of knowledge by representation.

The Science of *'Irfān*

To understand the meaning of the science of *'irfān,* or the linguistic discipline of mysticism as opposed to the ordinary logic of our everyday understanding, and to avoid any kind of arbitrary or unacademic discussions, we must rely on the insights of those who are the historically accepted authorities in both philosophy and mysticism. Yet we should beware of being misled by excessive reliance upon those authorities, lest we lose our objectivity. In fact, it is necessary for us to remember that excessive reliance on an authority, and blindly accepting its assertive judgments, is the most undesirable ingredients in any kind of philosophical inquiry. However, what we do suggest and shall insist upon in this study is that we keep our communication with the true mystics and their language direct and sufficiently authentic so as to understand the true meaning 'of' their specific language in terms of the object language. In other words, as a necessary condition for any philosophical or scientific study of mysticism there must exist a prerequisite understanding of the object language of the mystical experiences, which is *'irfān.* In terms of this necessary condition, we can venture to declare that insofar as most contemporary historians and a good number of philosophers of mysticism have failed to properly meet this condition, they have not been able to produce a satisfactory analysis of mysticism. In fact, their studies are by and large unsuccessful and at times irrelevant to the truth of mysticism. Without an effort to meet this primary condition, studies of mysticism stand in danger of missing the mystics' points altogether, and hence may be dismissed due to their inconsistency and subjectivity.

To understand accurately what "apprehension" or *'irfān* means in the mystical object language, we must refer to the thorough account given in this regard by Muḥyī al-Dīn ibn al-'Arabī.

Ibn al-'Arabī (1164–1240), the great master of Islamic mysticism (Sufism), and the founder of the science of *'irfān,* provided insights into the manner in which we can differentiate between the method of "apprehension" *('irfān)* and our intellectual knowledge, that is, meta-mysticism.

> (66) There are, however, three classifications of 'knowledge'. First is intellectual knowledge *('ilm al-'aql).* This is what you acquire either through an immediate necessity, or after an inquiry into

a proof, provided that you are acquainted with the way for demonstration of the proof. All questions about this kind of knowledge are of the same nature as the knowledge itself, that is, both knowledge and questions about it belong to the world of thinking which is the appropriate place for this system of cognition. This is why people say: In the world of thinking there is something right and something wrong.

(67) The second kind of knowledge is the awareness of the inner states of the mind. There is no way to communicate with these states except by "tasting" them. Just as no man of reason is able to define these states, so also no reason can be established to prove the truth of these states. For example, the sweet taste of honey, the bitter taste of extract of aloes, the enjoyment of intercourse and love, a feeling of happiness and joy, and the like, are states such as are impossible for anyone to be acquainted with except by being subject to their act of qualification and by tasting them. Again, questions about this kind of knowledge are of the same nature as the knowledge itself in being associated with the nature of taste. For example, those who suffer from the bitterness of bile taste honey as bitter, while in fact it is not so. This is because their sense of taste has been already affected by the bitterness of this yellow disease.

(68) The third kind of knowledge is knowledge of the unseen *('ilm al-asrār)*. It is a transcendent form of intellectually knowing; the form of knowing by emanation from the holy spirit into the mind. Prophets and saintly mystics are privileged with this knowledge. It is of two kinds:

One is that which can be received by the intellect. It is similar to knowledge of the first classification in being intellectual, except that the knower does not in this case obtain his knowledge through reasoning; it is rather a transcendent rank of knowledge that reveals itself to him. The other is divided into two subdivisions, one of which is associated with the second classification, knowledge by taste, but is of a higher degree and a nobler quality. And the other is that which is ranked with descriptive knowledge. This descriptive knowledge is by its nature susceptible to truth and falsity, but it is the truthfulness and infallibility *('iṣmah)* of the narrator; i.e., the narrator of the descriptive knowledge, that is being attested by the audience. Those descriptions given by Prophets (may peace be upon them) about God, and also their assertions about paradise and what things in paradise would be like, all count in one way for descriptive knowledge.

(69) Consequently the assertion of the one who is in possession of knowledge of the unseen that there is a paradise is an example of descriptive knowledge. His claim that on the day of resurrec-

> tion there will be a lake, the water of which is sweeter than honey, expresses his knowledge by taste. And finally his statements that God was there and nothing else was with Him, and the like, exemplify his intellectual knowledge of unseen reality, the sort that can also be thought of by reason.[26]

In referring to the above passage in general, we can see precisely that these philosophical mystics or mystical philosophers did in fact appropriately provide a scientific linguistic method for the communication of mystical knowledge. This knowledge is in Ibn al-'Arabī's[27] language called "knowledge of the unseen" *('ilm al-asrār)* as opposed to our phenomenal representational knowledge of observable objects. This is knowledge of the unseen, as well as the unspoken, world, insofar as it remains unreflected upon by the power of our intellect. But the intellect can, and has the power to, so Ibn al-'Arabī believes, introspect and reformulate this knowledge and bring it into the world of phenomena. When the intellect has carefully taken this step and reconstructed and translated the ineffable knowledge within the frame of the phenomenally representational form of knowledge, then it stands as our regular intellectual knowledge that, like our ordinary knowledge, becomes conceptual and understandable, and can, for that matter, be easily spoken of in our ordinary language. It is therefore the power of the intellect, writes Ibn al-'Arabī, that can make such a transition from the knowledge of the unseen to the intellectual knowledge of the world of phenomena. Translating this statement into our terminology, it is the commensurability of intellectual consciousness that provides such a *transexistentiation* from mystical knowledge by presence to phenomenal knowledge by representation. This is a first-glance reflection on this passage, bearing the theory of knowledge by presence in mind. As regards the linguistic classification, one can easily translate all of Ibn al-'Arabī's modes of knowledge into our dualistic linguistic method—language 'of', and language 'about' mysticism.

The linguistic methodology of this introspective knowledge is the science of *'irfān*. The linguistic science of *'irfān* should, in our classification, be placed in the category of object language, because it speaks 'of' the apprehension of God and the ways and rules that make such a unique apprehension possible. *'Irfān,* then, is a systematic object language designed to express the laws and principles of the vertical system of the introspected mystical knowledge dealing with all problematic questions concerning the knowledge of the unseen or divine objects[28]—*'ilm al-asrār*.

Dealing with a further analysis of the text we have just quoted at length, a little reflection is needed in our opinion to pick out from among the many fundamental points in this most constructive passage only those that are related to the subject with which we are at present concerned. These are:

1. Within the frame of the human mind there is another type of human awareness that makes human conciousness mystical. This is the awareness of the unseen object. If this kind of awareness is to be called knowledge at all, it can only be acquired by the unity of emanation and illumination, not by virtue of contemplation and abstraction. This position amounts to what we have already called presence-knowledge through the existential unity of emanation and absorption.
2. This form of knowledge, like ordinary knowledge, is intellectual, that is, it can be reflected upon and conceptualized and understood by the human intellect when introverted. Thus it is intelligible when reconstructed and introspected. This is so because, as the author puts it, it "can be received by the intellect." It is similar to the knowledge of his first classification (in being intellectual) except that the knower does not in this case obtain (his knowledge) through reasoning, but by reflection upon what has been already present.
3. These forms of knowledge, sensory, intellectual, and mystical, are also similar in being descriptive, in the sense that they inform us of something concerning the objective reality of the thing described. If the nature of an unseen object belongs to the order of feeling and sensations, the description of this knowledge is analogous to the assertions of information we usually make when we are describing our normal feelings and sensations to others. If the object of that knowledge is absolute Unity, or other unseen objects, the description must resemble our logic of pure transcendental understanding of an intellectual object, and so on. In short, parallel to our ordinary knowledge, empirical or transcendental, there is a different species of knowledge related to unseen objects such that it can sometimes be introspected by our pure intellect, and sometimes by our feelings and sensations.

These are the theses with which we are concerned in this study. Substantial parts of them were involved in our theory of knowledge by presence, presence by self-identity, and by emanation and absorption, and have already been discussed and fairly defended. Now in this section we shall meet the other part of these theses that belong to the problem of mystical and metamystical language. Since it has been emphatically maintained in this passage that all forms of knowledge of the unseen are describable, we are called upon to show how this character or describability is to be correctly understood. This point is of particular importance when we are face-to-face with problem of the ineffability of mysticism.

The Problem of Ineffability

We have come to understand that there is at least one kind of mysticism called Sufism, which does indeed have an object language designed to express its own self-object knowledge. Hence, mystical knowledge should not be called an incommunicable knowledge or an ineffable experience. The question then arises as to why mysticism should be marked by mystics themselves and by interested philosophers and many others as in essence an "ineffable" experience.

On the basis of our theory of knowledge by presence, the answer to this question is clear and straightforward. That is, since knowledge by presence is by essence self-object knowledge in all its forms, it is identical with the existential reality of the thing known. Moreover, it has been asserted that mystical knowledge is a species of knowledge by presence. Therefore, mystical knowledge is identical with the reality of the thing known. From this it has been concluded that mystical consciousness is the unitary simplex of the presence of God in the self, and the presence of the self in God. Belonging to the order of existence and not to the order of conception and representation, this unitary simplex is primarily incommunicable and therefore ineffable. Such is the case insofar as it remains nonintrospected and not reflected upon.

To illustrate this sense of incommunicability we need to point out that mystical knowledge in its original form—commonly called mystical experience, as an instantiation of knowledge by presence—proves to be nonphenomenal. Furthermore, it must be asserted that unlike our representational knowledge of external objects, knowledge by presence cannot serve as a part of our public knowledge. It is therefore incommunicable in the sense that it can never be shared and communicated with other individuals—even with those who are already engaged in their own mystical experiences—except by vague analogy. It is a private state of the individual reality of the self as knowing subject being united by presence with the reality of the object known. Like knowledge of the self and knowledge of the private states of apprehension and sensation, the representation of which can never stand for the objective reality of the thing known, mystical knowledge, too, cannot truly be represented by means of conceptualization. For this reason it cannot be spoken of like public knowledge. The only way to speak of and make assertive mystical expressions is to turn the mind inward upon itself and bring about an introspective knowledge of those mystical experiences witnessed by the mystics themselves.

Again, just as the introspective knowledge of the self and that of private states of mind must be demonstrated by an analogous representation of the objective truth of these realities, similarly, the introspective knowledge of mystical truth provides a mere analogous representation of the self-object knowledge of mysticism. Mystical knowledge is therefore in its original form absolutely unconceptualized and incommunicable. It is the introspective knowledge of mysticism that is manipulated in concepts and expressed by the articulated object language of *'irfān;* the primary form of mystical knowledge remains unconceptualized and ineffable. Thus, according to our theory, the evident answer to the question as to why mysticism is ineffable is that as a form of knowledge by presence, mystical knowledge belongs to the order of being, not to the order of conception. Succinctly put, mystical knowledge is a self-object knowledge in that the act of communicating is the same as the reality of what is communicated. This amounts to saying that in the realm of mystical experience, there is no act of communication distinct from the communicating subject and the communicated object. All of these account for the unitary simplex. This unitary simplex is the only cause of ineffability. Thus mystical knowledge in its primary form is truly ineffable.

From this it follows that the question regarding the meaning of the ineffability of mysticism can also be answered on the basis of the same argument. Based on the assertion that mystical knowledge is an instantiation of presence-knowledge, we can determine the real meaning of ineffability, as it features in this case. Whether it is logical, emotional, or conventional depends on how we are able to characterize the essential nature of mysticism itself.

According to our understanding of mysticism—that it is a form of knowledge by presence—the meaning of ineffability is logical, for it is inconceivable to convert the order of a private state of being into a public understanding of conception. The question, "In what sense is mysticism private and thus ineffable to the public?" is as logical as the question, "In what sense are the states of our mind private and ineffable to others except by mere analogy?" The problem of the ineffability of mystical knowledge does not seem any more complicated than the problem of the ineffability of private states.

To ascertain the meaning of the ineffability of mysticism, we must once again refer to the authorities in the field. The most authoritative explanations of this matter are those made by al-Ghazzālī in medieval philosophy and by William James in modern philosophy. Both thinkers arrived at the same conclusion, that the ineffability of mysticism can mean nothing but the state of privacy of the individual mind.

Al-Ghazzālī wrote:

> Nothing was left to them but God. They became drunk with a drunkenness in which their reason collapsed. One of them said, "I am God (The Truth)." Another said, "Glory be to me! How great is my glory," while another said, "Within my robe is naught but God." But the words of lovers when in a state of drunkenness must be hidden away and not broadcast.[29]

Using the analogy of drunkenness is the Sufis' answer to the question regarding the meaning of the ineffability of their experiences. In effect, they assert that a teetotaler can never understand the pleasure of intoxication for he has never tasted wine. More to the point, a mere lexical definition that wine is the fermented juice of the grape, or a scientific description of the chemical constitution of wine as such and such, does not help him to understand the real exhilaration of the drinker.[30]

Much the same analogy is given by William James in his *Varieties of Religious Experience*:

> That subject of it immediately says that it defies expression, that no adequate report of its contents can be given in words. It follows from this that its quality must be directly experienced: it cannot be imported or translated to others. In this peculiarity mystical states are more like states of feeling than like states of intellect. No one can make clear to another who has never had a certain feeling, in what the quality or worth of it consists.[31]

In these two passages the essential point is clearly made that the meaning of the ineffability of mystical knowledge is nothing but the logical essentiality of that knowledge's being private; pertinent to the order of the existence of the subject, not to the order of his intellectual conceptualization and representation.

Here we must take note that neither al-Ghazzālī's analogy of drunkenness nor James's analogy of feeling in any way bears upon their positions regarding the other characteristics of mystical experience, wherein they view it as noetic, descriptive, and not emotional. As a mere analogy, neither of these two accounts implies any further step than that of discerning a resemblance between mystical knowledge and knowledge of or acquaintance with our feelings and sensations, with reference to the state of privacy. On the basis of our theory of knowledge by presence, it becomes even clearer that since mystical experiences are an instantiation of knowledge by presence, they must, in all certainty, be both noetic and private, just as is the case with knowledge of the self and knowledge of states of feeling. In the existential state of the self all these forms of knowledge share in the fact that they are a sort of awareness of the reality of the object, and that they are private and ineffable to others.

These characteristics of mysticism, among others, belong to the genuine factual mystical experience, which, like the other kinds of knowledge by presence, remains in the state of self-objectivity and inexpressibility. This by no means implies that these experiences cannot be remembered and carefully interpreted by the agent once he has undergone such experiences. If introspected, these experiences will, quite certainly, be analogically represented and conceptualized, like self-knowledge and knowledge of private states of the mind, and then be expressed in an articulated language, as was done by Ibn al-'Arabī in his linguistic science of *'irfān*.[32] Thus, introspective mysticism should be distinguished from mystical experiences themselves. While the latter remains ineffable, the former is perfectly expressed in an object language which talks 'of' mysticism.

The conclusion here is therefore that we do have ineffable mysticism as distinct from introspective mysticism, that the meaning of ineffability is the private state of the existential sense of knowledge by presence, and that an object language of mysticism such as *'irfān* belongs to introspective mysticism, not to any mystical experiences themselves.

The Obligation of Metamystical Philosophy

The point to which we must now draw attention is a consideration of the essential function that a metamystical philosophy must perform in connection with the object language of mysticism. We must, for the purposes of elucidation, return once again to the analogy we made at the beginning of our linguistic study. There, we pointed out that, "If I wrote a book in English on the grammar of German, English would be the metalanguage and German the object-language talked about in English." In this case the task and responsibility to which that metalanguage has naturally committed itself requires, beyond any doubt, the precursory initiation of a correct and authentic study of the object language before it can subsequently discuss and talk about it in some metalinguistic system.

While taking mysticism under critical examination, a metamystical philosopher is also obliged to acquire considerable knowledge of the object language of mysticism in order to make sure what mystics are talking about. Any lack of communication between meta- and object language renders the former extraneous and, in a sense, meaningless. Having agreed on the matter that mysticism does in fact have an introspective language as its own object language, we must study it, no matter how difficult and paradoxical it may be, if we are going to talk about it philosophically and critically.

One of the many mystical features that is expressed in a paradoxical object language is the "elimination of time and space." We have been told by mystics that in the undifferentiated consciousness, time and space, like other kinds of plurality in the universe, become annihilated. Yet it must be ascertained as to what they mean by "annihilation," "unity," etc., before one embarks on a critical examination of this proposition.[33]

Despite this requirement, Bertrand Russell takes part in a mystical language game that lands him in great philosophical puzzlement, which he expresses in the following words:

> The unreality of time is a cardinal doctrine of many metaphysical systems, often normally based, as already by Parmenides, upon logical arguments, but originally derived, at any rate in the founders of new systems, from the certainty which is born in the moment of mystic insight. As a Persian Sufi poet says: Past and future are what veil God from our sight. Burn up both of them with fire! How long will Thou be partitioned by these segments as a reed?[34]

If he had understood, in the first place, that there is the possibility of another kind of knowledge, in accordance with which one can account, fairly clearly, for the apprehension of the reality of the Unseen in which there is no reference whatsoever to the condition of time, Russell would never have asked the question as to how the elimination of time was possible. First of all, Russell, like any other philosopher, must have recognized on what grounds, and by means of what language, the mystical assertion points to the elimination of time, before he concluded so swiftly to dismiss the claim on the basis of his own metalinguistic treatment. Only after we have correctly understood what the mystical 'annihilation' of time and space, or of any other element of multiplicity means, do we have the right to raise the question whether or not such a claim possesses any sense.

A refutation that has no point of contact with the mystical language, such as is proposed by Russell, in no way blights the position of mysticism, nor does it even meet the conditions required for it to be called a refutation in the first place. This is so chiefly because Russell's method of argumentation is completely outside the tenets of the mystical science. The proposition, "time is unreal," like the proposition, "the agent of apprehension and the thing apprehended are one and the same," together with many other mystical dictums, must be viewed from two different perspectives, one mystical and the other metamystical. Since the totality of the former is based on the linguistic science of apprehension—*'irfān*—any account that seeks either a refutation or a justification in terms of the latter can be appropriate and meaningful if, and only if, the language of this science is critically examined and correctly understood.

Concerning the question of communication in general, I do not agree with Wittgenstein when he states that "if language is to be a means of communication there must be agreement not only in definitions but also (strange as this may sound) in judgments."[35] This I do not believe, because this proposition suggests that in order to make contact with mystical language, one must either agree with mystics on whatever they may say, or treat mysticism as altogether meaningless. Neither of these two alternatives is philosophical. In addition, to my understanding, it seems quite clear that the problem of 'truth' is radically different from the problem of 'meaning'; or, as Avicenna wrote in his "Methodology," the question of "what?" (i.e., what a thing means) must not be erroneously identified with the question of "is it?" (i.e., "is it true?") in any philosophical investigation.[36]

In terms of mystical language, Russell, or any critical philosopher, must first of all take the step of establishing contact, at least at the level of definitions, with the mystical language—*'irfān*—and then try to raise questions and bring in critical judgments. This is the sole way in which the problem of mysticism can be met. Otherwise, without a fair definitional understanding of mystical terms such as the 'elimination of time', the 'illusion of multiplicity', etc., any discussion or judgment will fail to be logically meaningful.

Russell may basically be right in this judgment that the contention that time is unreal and that the world of sense is illusory must be regarded as fallacious.[37] However, the pertinent question revolves around the sense in which the mystic means it. If the mystic believes that he, in his mystical state, can apprehend the whole of the reality of the world, such that past and future are present in the very unity of that reality, it does not mean that time is unreal in the sense that it does not exist at all. On the contrary, it may even imply a tacit acknowledgement of a sense of reality for the existence of time. Yet the manner in which a mystic can describe this apprehension of the whole of reality, and what he implies by this experience, is a question that Russell was obliged to ask an authority in mysticism so that he could acquaint himself with the mystical language, before asking his meta-mystical question. The major point of this discussion is, however, to show that the philosophical problem of the unreality of time, like many other problems in mysticism, is subsequent, and even adventitious, to the object language of mysticism, namely the science of mystical apprehension, *'irfān*.

In fact, Russell did ask some basic questions concerning the truth or falsehood of mysticism such as: Is time unreal? Is all plurality and division illusory? What kind of reality belongs to good and evil?[38] As we can see, all of these questions are asked in terms of the object language of mysticism. But, because of the fact that Russell is not acquainted with the grammar and technique of the object language, the necessary condition for his communication with the mystic is not fulfilled. Those who do not know the German language and its grammar can naturally not teach German in English.

It is only a kind of knowledge by presence, in the first place, and its introspective language, in the second, that can justify us in bringing all mystical assertions under the critical examination of our meta-mystical perspective.

APPENDIX

In one of his major works, *Kitāb al-mashāri' wa'l-muṭāriḥāt,* Suhrawardī refers to his famous mystical trance by the following remarks:

> (280) With regard to my opinion concerning this problem [i.e., the problem of knowledge], I have already explained it in my book *Ḥikmat al-ishrāq.* Here is not the appropriate place to discuss it again . . . The best thing on which scholars can rely even before delving deep into the study of *Ḥikmat al-ishrāq* is that *vision* which we have described in [the book] *al-Talwīḥāt,* pertaining to that which happened between myself and the philosopher, the master of thinkers, Aristotle, in the mystical stage called *jāburs.*[1] On this occasion he started talking to me in a vision about the idea that man should make his enquiry in the first place into [the problem of] the knowledge of the reality of himself *('ilmihi bi dhātihi),* and, in the second place, to inquire into [the knowledge of others] which are beyond [the reality of himself].
>
> *(Kitāb al-mashāri' wa'l-muṭāriḥāt,* Suhrawardī, *Opera Metaphysica et Mystica,* ed. H. Corbin, vol. 1, p. 483–84; translation mine)

In the book *al-Talwīḥāt* (pp. 70–74), although Suhrawardī feels he is in a position to disclose in some detail the philosophical dialogue that he had in his mystical experience, we still hear him saying that there were quite a number of other points in this *vision* that he has mentioned elsewhere in different places in the same book. This means that his account is not a complete presentation of what he experienced in the course of this event. However, we would like here to present our expanded translation of this dialogue, not for the mere purpose of the exposition of this mystical trance, but rather for the evaluation of Suhrawardī's illuminative philosophy, the essence of which has been established within the framework of this dialogue.

An Episode and a Trance

I had been in the past extremely preoccupied with thinking over the problem of knowledge, taking extreme care and exhaustive effort. Whatever had been mentioned in books could never settle my mind. One night it happened that I fell into a trance which was like a dream-state. All of a sudden I felt myself to be enveloped in pleasure, engulfed by the blazing flashes of a dazzling light accompanied by the spectre of a humanlike face. Looking carefully at it, I realized it was the hope of the souls, the leader in wisdom, the first master of philosophy [namely Aristotle]. He was in such a glorious aura of splendor that I fell into a state of bewilderment and wonder. [But it did not take long before] I felt that I had been well received [by the master]. He graciously greeted me and made me feel welcome, so that my astonishment left me and I even began to feel a quite friendly atmosphere. Then I ventured to complain to him of the puzzlement in which I was stuck about this problem [of how and why we can know anything at all]. He then said to me:

"Think introvertively of yourself. [If you do so, you will certainly discover that your very selfhood] will then resolve [the problem] for you."

"But how?" I asked him.

"If you are really aware of yourself, then your awareness of yourself will [not] be [anything but] awareness by yourself. For, if it were in any other way, it would mean that there was another acting power [besides your own], or another knowing subject [besides yourself], that operated in yourself in knowing you. [It would not therefore be you who knew yourself; but it must be the case that you know yourself.] Thus we return to the same question [i.e., of whether or not you are aware of yourself by yourself], and this shows itself to be an obvious absurdity [i.e., it would be a flat contradiction].

"Assuming that you know yourself by yourself [and not by anything else, the question then becomes]: is [your knowledge of yourself] through the production of an effect from yourself in yourself?"

"All right [let us assume the existence of such an effect]."

"But if a [certain] effect [which is actuated by yourself] does not correspond with the reality of yourself, then it is not true to say that you really know yourself."

"Then [let us assume]," I said, "that such an effect is a [true] representation of my own reality."

"Does this representation belong to a universal self, or is it appropriated [to your individual self-hood] by [taking on] specific qualities?"

[Of these alternatives] I chose the second.

"Now every representation occurring in the self [as your intellect] is a universal, even if it be qualified by many universal qualities [and restrictions, for] this [sort of multiqualification] does not prevent [such a representation] being shared by [and applicable to, many] individual selves. If it should happen that [a certain representation of this kind] is prevented [from applying to many], it must be for some accidental reason. But [undoubtedly] you know yourself [in such a way that your selfhood], by [its] essential reality, refuses to be shared [by other selves]. Therefore this [particular and unshared] apprehension [of yourself] cannot be by representation."

"[But surely it is obvious that] I apprehend the concept of 'I' [as the representation of myself]."

"The concept of 'I', insofar as it is the mere concept of 'I', is not [essentially] prevented from being shared [by many individual 'I's, so it is a universal concept]. You have learned that [the concept of] 'particular', insofar as it is merely [the meaning of] particular, is nothing but a universal. This is true of all expressions like 'this', 'I', 'we', and 'it'. [All of these] have universal, intelligible meanings, insofar as they are abstract concepts carrying no specific implication for an individual object."

"Well, if the apprehension of 'I' as the representation of myself is, like all concepts, universal, then how can I really know my particular, individual 'I'?"

"Once you have realized that your knowledge of yourself can never be by any power other than the very reality of your selfhood, you will then [be in a position to] understand that you are acquainted with yourself by yourself, not through [mediation of] any other [agent] and not by a representation that may or may not correspond to the reality of yourself. [The conclusion is that] the very reality of your selfhood is thus a simple unity of self- knowledge (by presence), the self- knowing subject, and the self- known object.

"Would you explain a little further?"

"Are you not constantly acquainted with your body, over which you exert control, with the kind of acquaintance from which you are never absent?"

"Yes [certainly I am]."

"Is it [really] because of the intervention of an individual representation [of your body] actuated in your selfhood? Indeed, you have just understood this to be absurd."

"No [this cannot be], but why should it not be because of my acquaintance with some of the general qualities applicable [to the particular state of my body]?"

"While, [on the one hand] you move your own particular [and unshared] body, with which you are acquainted as a particular private bodily state, it is understood, [on the other hand] that whatever representation made by yourself is not [in itself] prevented from being shared [by others].

"It therefore follows that it cannot be true to say that your apprehension of such [a representation] is in any sense the apprehension of your own body, the concept of which cannot conceivably be true of anything else [but your own body].

"Furthermore, have you not read in my books that 'the self functions in thinking by employing the faculty of thought whose job is to compound and separate particulars as well as to arrange [and organize] middle terms [for the formulation of arguments]', and that 'the faculty of imagination cannot have access to any universal concepts, simply because it is a material faculty'?

"Now, if [it is true that] there is no [direct] communication between the self and particular objects, how can the self ever compound premises [for its own judgments], and in what manner can it obtain universals from particulars? Besides, in what other way is the faculty of thought supposed to be used [if not in the way of employment by the self]? Again, how can [the self] ever receive [anything] from the imagination, and what would be the value of [a consideration of] the act of separation [and compounding done] by the imagination? And how is [the thinking self] to prepare itself by virtue of contemplation to arrive at a conclusion? [Setting aside all this, assuming the fact that] the faculty of imagination is a material power, how can it apprehend itself [in particular] while [as we have just understood], the representation of it existing in the self is universal? But you know [that it makes no sense to doubt] your imagination and phantasm *(wahm)* in their particular beings, and you also know [that it makes perfect sense to suppose] that your phantasm can doubt [and ignore both the truth of itself and of the imagination]."

"May God reward you with the best of knowledge. Will you cast some further light upon this problem so that you may lead us to the way of truth?"

"If you understand that the self is known not by intervention of a mental image corresponding [with its reality], nor by any [other kind of] representation, you may then know that intellection *(ta'aqqul)* is the 'presence' of the thing known in a nonmaterial subject which is free from matter. You can also say, if you wish, 'not being absence from' instead of 'presence of'. This correction renders the account somewhat more understandable, because it includes [both cases]: that the self apprehends itself, and that it apprehends others. [This change therefore serves as a safeguard against the linguistic objection] that a thing cannot be [said to be something] 'present' to itself."

"But, [taking this objection into account, a thing] cannot be 'absent' from itself [either]. However [as far as the reality of] the self [is concerned, the fact that] it is an immaterial being [suffices for it] not to be absent from itself, in the same sense that it is not in something which is foreign to itself. Thus, to the extent that it is independent of matter, [the self] knows itself simply by virtue of not being absent from itself. But [as for] those [external objects] that are absent from the self, it is true that the reality of these things, like the sky and the earth and the like of them, cannot be present in the self, but their representation can. The particular objects [viz. these external things] are represented in the faculties [of sense-experience] which are [all] present in the self.

"But the universal concepts, precisely because of the quality of universality [they have] in themselves, cannot leave an impression in these material faculties, and so they are conceived by, and present in, the very reality of the self itself. However [in either case, universal or particular object], the thing known is always actually the representation [of these objects], which is present in the mind of the knowing subject, not [the objects themselves] that lie beyond the objective reality of that subject. Even if these external objects are commonly termed 'known', they should be understood as [belonging to] a second degree of knowledge.

"However, the reality of the self is never absent from itself, nor is its [particular] body as a whole, and neither are the faculties of perception [which are related] to its body as a whole. Just as the [power of] the imagination cannot be absent from the self, so also the imaginary representations [viz. illusionary forms] cannot be absent either. They are [known and] apprehended [by the self] only because of their presence, and not because of their representation, in the reality of the self. And, just as, if it were the case that [the self] had more freedom [and more disentanglement] from matter, its apprehensions of itself would be more intense and much deeper; likewise, if the [self's] domination [and supremacy] over the body were stronger, the presence of the [body together with all its] powers and faculties [in the domain of the selfhood] would be more complete [and stronger]."

Here [Aristotle gave all his attention] to me [and] said: "Note well, knowledge [as such] is a perfection of existence insofar as the meaning of [the words] is concerned, but [in reality even] this [slight] difference between knowledge and existence does not obtain. This is the reason that knowledge is necessary where existence is necessary."

By this remark, Aristotle pointed to [the doctrine] that I had already [worked out and] set down under the title of a *comprehensive Principle of Being*.[2]

"Necessary being is that whose reality is [absolutely] independent of matter and is therefore a pure and simple being. And the [other] beings are [all] present in it [His Being] on the basis of [His] predominating emanative relationship [to them]. This is because everything [overflowing from Him] is [a] necessary [emanation] from His reality *(lāzim[u] dhātih[i])*. [Therefore] neither His reality nor His necessary emanation can be absent from Himself. [As a result,] the nonexistence of [His] being absent from His reality as well as from His necessary [emanation], together with [His condition of absolute] separation from matter are [the two essentialities which constitute the essence of] His knowledge. [All this is] according to what we have remarked in [our book called] *De Anima,*" Aristotle said.

"With regard to [the theory that] all of knowledge [in general] centers upon [the one idea] that a thing cannot be absent from an immaterial subject, no matter if [that thing] is a representation or anything else, it is permissible that relations and negative [attributes] be applied to God without His divine simplicity and oneness *(waḥdāniyyatuh^{u})* being compromised [by it]. Thus [the truth of] His multiperfection of names is based upon these negative attributes and [this kind of] illuminative relationship. [In consequence], nothing is left absent from His knowledge, not even the weight of a speck of dust in [all] the heavens and the earth.[3]

"If [we were to maintain that] we could have such an overruling [relationship] with [any other thing] apart from our body, just as [we do have] with our body, we would [certainly] have [the same kind of] acquaintance with that thing as we do with our body in accordance with [the same process that] has already been described, [that is to say, a kind of acquaintance] that does not need the support of any representation [as an intermediary in the apprehension of the object known].

"From all this it becomes clear that [because of having this kind of overruling relation with others], He encompasses [by His existence] all things, and [for that matter] has [by His knowledge] acquaintance with all the numerous units of existence [the meaning of] which is [nothing but the sheer] presence [of that reality] in Him and His supremacy [over it] with no interposition of a form of representation *[min ghayr^{i} ṣūrat^{in} wa lā mithāl]*."

[Aristotle] then told me: "This is sufficient for you to know." He further directed me to many other points, some of which I have stated [in different places] in this book.

[As the final question] I asked him: "What is the significance of the 'continuity', and [the nature of] the 'identity', of the souls with one another and with the active intellect [if any]?"

"As long as you are in your [material] world, you are veiled [and disconnected]. But as soon as you leave that world [provided that] you have become perfected, you will enter [into the state of] identity and eternal continuity."

"But we have refuted the groups of those who hold [the theory of] 'abstraction', and those philosophers [who advocate this opinion], over the generalization of 'continuity' [to all things, when] it does not hold true except of physical objects."

"Have you not noticed that [sometimes] you conceive, in your intellectual analysis, of a 'continuity' between two universal intelligible things, and that you also apprehend intellectually [all] the parts of [for example] one single animal in continuity [and conjunction with one another]?"

"Yes [I have]."

"Is there a particular dimensionality or materiality in your mental powers?"

"Of course not [as far as my thinking is concerned]."

"This is then [a kind of] intellectual continuity [which is completely different from spatiotemporal continuity]. Likewise, there is in the divine world, among the [surviving] souls a [kind of] continuity and [a sense of] 'identity' which [like the souls themselves] is intelligible and not physical, [the reality of] which you will be acquainted with as soon as you are separated [from this condition of material existence]."

At this point Aristotle [surprisingly] started praising his master [in philosophy], Plato, [in such a manner that] I was [extremely] astonished, so I asked him: "Has any Muslim philosopher been on a par with him?"

"Not at all, not even," he added earnestly, "with a thousandth of Plato's glorious rank."

I began to specify the names of some of those with whom I was acquainted, but he paid no attention to any of them. Finally, I arrived at the name of Abū Yazīd al-Basṭāmī [Bayazid] and Abū Sahl ibn 'Abd Allāh al-Tustarī and some others [of these typically Sufi philosophers]. [This time] he seemed to become delighted and was moved to the extent that he said:

"These are, however, true philosophers and people of wisdom, since they have not confined themselves within [the limits of] representational knowledge *(al-'ilmal-rasmī)*, but transcended to knowledge by presence [which is the state of] unity and vision. They also did not occupy themselves in material interests; thus, they succeeded in [attaining] the 'near approach and the excellent resort';[4] they have proceeded [in the same path that was taken] by us, and expressed [the same words] that we have already spoken."

At this moment he disappeared from my sight and left me alone, weeping over [the sadness of] being separated from him. Ah! how joyful was this experience.

NOTES

Foreword

1. For further reading in this subject, see H. Corbin, *La Philosophie iranienne islamique aux XVIIe et XVIIIe siècles* (Paris, 1981); H. Corbin (in collaboration with S. H. Nasr and O. Yahya), *Histoire de la philosophie islamique* (Paris, 1986); H. Corbin, *L'Iran et la philosophie* (Paris, 1990); S. H. Nasr, *Three Muslims Sages* (Delmar N.Y., 1979); M. M. Sharif, ed., *A History of Muslim Philosophy,* 2 vols. (Weisbaden, 1963–66); T. Izutsu, *The Concept and Reality of Existence* (Tokyo, 1971); S. H. Nasr, *Islamic Life and Thought* (Albany, N.Y., 1981); S. H. Nasr, *Islamic Philosophy in Contemporary Persia* (Salt Lake City, 1972); and S. H. Nasr, "Theology, Philosophy and Spirituality," in *Islamic Spirituality—Manifestations,* ed. S. H. Nasr (New York, 1991), pp. 395–446.

Introduction

1. See Stace, W. T. *Mysticism and Philosophy,* pp. 146–52.

Knowledge by Presence

1. This is the technical Illuminative *(ishrāqī)* expression that Suhrawardī formally established for knowledge by presence. See H. Corbin, ed., *Kitāb al-mashāri' wa'l-muṭāriḥāt, Opera Metaphysica et Mystica* (Istanbul, 1945) vol. 1, pp. 474–89. Note that in this study references to that concept are according to the appropriate English terminology as follows:

1. Knowledge by presence
2. Self-object-consciousness
3. The theory of self-objectivity
4. The theory of presence-knowledge
5. Self-objective knowledge
6. Nonintentional knowledge
7. Nonphenomenal knowledge

8. Nonrepresentational knowledge
9. The identity of being and knowing.

2. As will be seen later, the language of intellectual vision was used by Plato himself in a number of places, including *The Republic,* and by all Neoplatonic philosophers as well. In Islamic philosophy, it was used by almost all Illuminative philosophers in such terms as *shuhūd, mushāhadah, al-'ayn,* etc. Ṣadr al-Dīn Shīrāzī qualified this idea by the use of the expression: "witnessing from distance." He said that the intellect is in a position to witness these divine objects from an intellectually dimensional distance. This distant witnessing is the designation of the universal ideas in our minds. See *Al-wujūd al-dhihnī* ("Mental Entities" or "The Phenomenology of Mind") in *Kitāb al-asfār,* Journey 1, pt. 1 (Tehran, 1378/1958), p. 289.

3. Plato, *The Republic,* (V. 474, B-480).

4. Ibid., p. 188.

5. Ibid., vol. 7, p. 517.

6. Aristotle, *De Anima,* bk. 3, B. 427–29.

7. *Op. cit.,* ch. 7–8, B. 431–32.

8. Speaking of knowledge by presence, Plotinus sometimes appears to commit himself to a kind of 'knowledge' of the Unity and Principle, such as when he writes:

> Cleared of all evil in our intention towards The Good, we must ascend to the Principle within ourselves; from many, we must become one; only so do we attain to knowledge of that which is Principle and Unity. (*The Enneads,* trans. Stephen Mackenna (London, 1967), VI 9, para. 3)

But sometimes Plotinus openly denied the possibility of "knowing" and "awareness" of this Principle by stating:

> In knowing, soul or mind abandons its unity; it cannot remain a simplex: knowing is taking account of things; that accounting is multiple; the mind thus plunging into number and multiplicity departs from unity. (*The Enneads,* VI 9, para. 4.)

All this means that he really did not distinguish between the two kinds of knowledge. Yet the extent of such a distinction and how it should be sketched out logically do not appear in *The Enneads.*

9. Al-Fārābī, *Harmonization of the Opinions of Plato and Aristotle, Kitāb al-jam' bayn ra'yay al-ḥakīmayn* (Beirut, 1969), pp. 105–6. Author's translation.

10. Al-Fārābī, *Kitāb al-fuṣūṣ,* Dā'irat al-Ma'ārif, Hyderabad Daccan, India, 1926, p. 13. Author's translation.

11. Al-Fārābī, *Philosophy of Plato and Aristotle,* trans. Muhsin Mahdi (Glencoe, 1962), p. 4.

12. This is the Aristotelian theological argument:

> If there were an infinite regress among 'efficient causes', no cause would be first. Therefore all the other causes, which are intermediate, would be suppressed. But this is manifestly false. We must, therefore, posit that there exists a 'first efficient cause'. (*Aristotle's Metaphysics,* la, 2 (994a))

13. Aristotle, *Nichomachean Ethics,* bks. 1, 6, and 10, trans. M. Ostwald (Indianapolis, 1962).

14. St. Thomas, *Summa Contra Gentiles,* bk. 3, pt. 1, ch. 37–49 (New York, 1977).

15. *(Qā'idat al-wāḥid lā yaṣdur^u^ 'anh^u^ illa al-wāḥid)* literally means the principle that from one, no more than one can issue forth. This principle is taken to be the logic of the Avicennian system of emanation. From this principle Avicenna himself developed the principle of the hierarchy of emanation called the rule of the "nobler possibility" *(qā'idat imkān al-ashraf).* Referring to the principle of the hierarchy of emanation, Avicenna pointed out:

> Notice how the reality of existence emerges from the nobler principle down to the next (which is of less nobility) until the hierarchy of nobility" terminates (at the lowest degree of existence,) in matter. ("On Abstraction," in *Kitāb al-ishārāt,* pt. 3, ch. 7, ed. Sulaymān al-Dunyā (Cairo, 1960), p. 241. Author's translation)

16. *"L'âme humaine,"* in *Le Livre des directives et remarques,* trans. A. M. Goichon (Paris, 1951), pp. 324–26. Since there are some fundamental differences between this translation and my understanding of the text, I present here my own translation directly from the Arabic text for purposes of comparison:

> Of the soul's [intellectual] powers concerning [its] need to transcend its substance [from potential intellect] to the actual intellect are [the following]: First, the power of receptivity *(quwwat isti'dādiyyah)* toward intelligibles called by some philosophers the material intellect. This is the niche *(mishkāh)* [of lights]. Next to this, is another power obtained by the intellect when the primary intelligibles appear in it. The occurrence of these primary intelligibles is the basis on which the secondary intelligibles can be acquired. [This process of acquirement] is brought about either through contemplation, which is [called] the olive tree, if the mind is not sharpwitted enough, or by surmise called fuel [the oil of the olive tree], if the mind is exceedingly shrewd.

[In either case] this power called the habitual intellect is as transparent as a glass.

The extreme nobility of this power is the divine kind whose oil is as if it lights itself up without fire touching it.

Then, there comes to the intellect a power and a perfection: The perfection counts for the ability to acquire the intelligibles in action such that the mind can perceive them as they are pictured in the mind. This is a light upon lights. The power consists in that the mind is in a position that, without any need of new inquiry, it can obtain the previously acquired and presently forgotten intelligible as if perceived, whenever the mind wants to. This is the lighted lamp.

The agent which causes the mind to set out from the habitual intellect to the state of the complete act, and from the material intellect to the habitual intellect, is the Agent Intellect. This is the fire. (*Al-Ishārāt,* pt. 2, p. 390)

17. As Naṣīr al-Dīn Ṭūsī states in his Commentary, this analysis of human intelligence has been taken from the Quranic verse on the matter of divine light, the text of which is as follows:
Sūrah, 24; v. 35

Allah is the Light of the heavens and the earth. The similitude of His light is as a niche wherein is a lamp. The lamp is in a glass. The glass is as it were a shining star. (This lamp is) kindled from a blessed tree, an olive neither of the East nor of the West, whose oil would almost glow forth (of itself) though no fire touched it. Light upon light, Allah guideth unto His light whom He will. And Allah speaketh to mankind in allegories, for Allah is Knower of all things.

To my understanding the Avicennian philosophical interpretation of this Quranic verse has actually been the intellectual source of inspiration for al-Ghazzālī's brilliant achievement in his systematic account for the problem of mysticism, the *Mishkāt al-anwār.*

18. Al-Ghazzālī, *Mishkāt al-anwār, The Niche for Lights.* Trans. W. H. T. Gairdner (London, 1952).

19. *Op. cit.,* p. 81.

20. *Op. cit.,* p. 83.

21. Avicenna's doctrine of the "suspended soul" has quite accurately been interpreted as the prime mode of knowledge by presence. This interpretation was first given by Naṣīr al-Dīn Ṭūsī in his *Commentary on al-Ishārāt* where he characterized self-knowledge as the identity of knowing and being. Ṭūsī says:

That Avicenna made the stipulation for the suspended soul to be in absolutely temperate air means that the soul in this condition does not sense anything extraneous to itself . . . It is in these circumstances that the soul is oblivious to everything except its pure reality and the fact that it exists. (Footnotes to *Kitāb al-ishārāt,* ed. Dr. Sulaymān Dunyā, pt. 2, p. 344. Translation mine)

22. The Latin translation of this sentence is: *"non est generabilis et corruptibilis."* There is, according to our text, no negation sign or negative sense in the Arabic version of the text to support such a translation. See Averroes, *Kitāb tafsīr mā ba'd al-ṭabī'ah, The Long Commentary,* ed. Maurice Bouyges (Beirut, 1967), p. 1489.

23. *Op. cit.,* pp. 1486–90. Translation mine.

24. In the following chapters, we shall discuss the meaning of the illuminative relationship, and how it is different from the Aristotelian category of relation.

25. As we shall see, the notion of 'absorption' is a derivative notion obtained from 'emanation'.

26. Transubstantiation in such an important sense as used by Averroes is that on the basis of which the existentialist doctrine of "substantial motion" has been established by Ṣadr al-Dīn Shīrāzī. This doctrine is officially called *(al-ḥarakat al-jawhariyyah)* to which we sometimes refer as "transexistentiation."

27. To the "descending" system, Avicenna, as we have just seen in footnote 15, assigned the principle of 'nobler possibility', and to the "ascending" system, Suhrawardī provided his rule of 'posterior possibility' *(al-imkān al-akhaṣṣ).* See Suhrawardī, *Kitāb ḥikmat al-ishrāq,* ed. H. Corbin (Paris/Tehran, 1952), pp. 154–85. Also, *Kitāb al-talwīḥāt,* ed. H. Corbin (Istanbul, 1945), pp. 50–1.

28. Averroes, *Tafsīr māba'd al-ṭabī'ah, The Long Commentary* (Beirut, 1967), p. 886. Translation mine.

29. In the last chapter of this study, we shall discuss the problem of *'irfān* as a linguistic science of mysticism which genuinely speaks 'of' mystical experiences as contrasted with metamysticism which speaks 'about' that object language of mysticism. *'Irfān* literally means "apprehension," or "knowledge." Yet, in Islamic philosophical language it is always used in the sense of an apprehension that is not identical with, or even applicable to, our normal sense of knowledge in a strict sense; *'irfān* should not be used technically at all in the sense of a philosophical knowledge of divinity. Rather, it is designed to be used in the meaning of a kind of apprehension attained only through mystical experiences. This apprehension is called by Islamic mystics *"shuhūd"* or *"mushāhadah."*

30. See Muḥyī al-Dīn ibn al-'Arabī, *Fuṣūṣ al-ḥikam,* ed. Abu'l-A'lā 'Afīfī,

(Beirut, 1966), pp. 32–35. See also the major work of Ibn al-'Arabi, *al-Futūḥāt al-makkiyyah,* ed. O. Yahya, (Egypt, 1972), on ch. 1–3.

31. Monorealistic existence is the literal meaning of *waḥdat al-wujūd* which admits of no plurality or dualism in existence, much less the plurality of theism or pantheism.

32. Suhrawardī's dialogue with Aristotle in a "Mystical Stage." See the appendix. Suhrawardī, *Kitāb al-talwīḥāt,* p. 70.

33. Self-objectivity is the essential characteristic of knowledge by presence. Ṣadr al-Dīn Shīrāzī describes this matter thus:

> It is understood that in this kind of knowledge what is actually known by the knowing subject and what is really existent in itself is one and the same. *(Kitāb al-asfār,* Journey I, pt. 3 (Tehran, 1378/1958), p. 313)

34. See the commentary by R. Qumsha'i in Vol. 1, pp. 13–16 of the *Kitāb al-asfār* (Tehran, 1378/1958).

35. See the meaning of *"al-tashkīk fi'l-wujūd", Kitāb al-asfār,* Journey I, pt. 1, ch. 1.

36. *Op.cit.,* ch. 1, 2, 3.

37. *Op.cit.,* ch. 10, "On knowing and the known."

Immanent Object and Transitive Object

1. In his course on "Intentionality" at the Pontifical Institute in Toronto in the academic year 1975–76, Professor A. C. Pegis, when interpreting the Aristotelian philosophy of knowledge, distinguished two kinds of human action: 'immanent action' and 'transitive action'. His illustration of the former was human knowledge that is present in the mind of the knowing subject; and of the latter, those actions that actually pass through the mind and become stable independently among external physical objects in the external world, such as building a house, writing a book, etc. On the basis of this distinction, it seems quite admissible to derive two pertinent kinds of objects that organize and determine our act of knowledge. These are the immanent object and the transitive object of our knowledge.

2. C. J. Ducasse. *Truth, Knowledge and Causation* (New York, 1959), pp. 94–5.

3. St. Thomas, *The Commentary on Aristotle's De Anima II, IV* (New Haven, 1951), 303–05.

4. Regarding the efficient cause, Aristotle says:

> For it is unnecessary to add this qualification: when nothing external hinders it; for the agent has the potency insofar as it is a potency for acting. (*Metaphysics of Aristotle,* [1047b31–1048a24], vol. 2, p. 670)

5. St. Thomas, *Commentary on the Metaphysics of Aristotle,* vol. 2 (New Haven, 1951), pp. 1648–80.

6. *Op. cit.* On the matter of the difference between the efficient and the final cause, St. Thomas interpreted Aristotle in this way:

> . . . such a cause [the efficient] is investigated as the cause of the process of generation and corruption. But the other cause [the final] is investigated not merely as the cause of the process of generation and corruption but also of being . . . And inasmuch as the goal moves the agent through his intending it, it is also a cause of generation and corruption. And inasmuch as the thing is directed to its goal by means of its forms, it is also a cause of being. (Vol. 2, l. 17: C. 1648–1680)

7. Aristotle, "Final Cause" and "End," in *Metaphysics,* vol. 1, pp. 177–79.

8. Ṣadr al-Dīn Shīrāzī, *Kitāb al-asfār,* Journey I, vol. 1, pt. 3, p. 112.

9. G. W. Cunningham, *The Problems of Philosophy* (New York, 1924), p. 97.

10. *Op. cit.,* p. 102–03.

11. C. J. Ducasse, *Truth, Knowledge and Causation* (New York, 1959), p. 63.

12. *Op. cit.,* pp. 93–5.

13. This distinction can also assert another point by accounting for the difference between the problem of science and the problem of logic. Scientific experimental verifications hinge entirely upon the fact that science tries further to acquire reliable correspondence between subjective objects and objective objects; whereas logic is not by its nature involved in the implementation of such a verification.

14. Shīrāzī, *Kitāb al-asfār,* Journey I, vol. 1, pt. 3, ch. 2, pp. 466–70.

15. Aristotle's *De Anima:*

> Speculative knowledge is the same as what is knowable in this way. (III, IV, 724–7, p. 421)

16. St. Thomas, *The Commentary on Aristotle's De Anima:*

> So the understanding and the understood are one being, provided the latter is actually understood; and the same is true of the object and subject of sensation. ([New Haven, 1959]. III, IV, 724)

17. *Kant's Critique of Pure Reason,* Trans. N. K. Smith (New York, 1965), A-302, B-421.

18. Shīrāzī, *Kitāb al-asfār,* Journey I, vol. 3, pt. 10, ch. 7, p. 313.

19. B. Russell, *The Problems of Philosophy* (London, 1976), pp. 37–8.

20. *Op. cit.,* p. 41.

21. Shīrāzī, *Kitāb al-asfār,* Journey I, pt. 10, pp. 313–15.

22. *Op. cit.,* p. 280. Translation mine.

23. *Op. cit.,* p. 313.

24. See W. T. Stace, *Mysticism and Philosophy* (Philadelphia, 1960), pp. 146–52.

Knowledge by Presence and Knowledge by Correspondence

1. In the language of Islamic philosophy, knowledge by correspondence is called *al-'ilm al-ḥuṣūlī al-irtisāmī,* meaning representational, acquired knowledge. This is in contrast with knowledge by presence, *al'ilm al-ḥuḍūrī,* which is not acquired from the external object by representation. Our translation of *al-'ilm al-ḥuṣūlī al-irtisāmī* might have been "knowledge by acquired representation"; but the reason that we suggest "correspondence" instead of "representation" is that in almost all versions of Islamic philosophy, from Avicenna down to Ṣadr al-Dīn Shīrāzī, the notion of "correspondence" is taken as the prime condition of this kind of knowledge. In his *Commentary on Kitāb al-ishārāt,* Ṭūsī says:

> 'Representation' is of two kinds: that which corresponds to the external objective reference, and that which does not. The former representation is 'knowledge' and the latter is 'ignorance'. *(Kitāb al-ishārāt wa'l-tanbīhāt,* ed. Sulaymān al-Dunyā, pt. 2, p. 363. Translation mine)

2. An external object can be called known if there is in the knowing subject a representation corresponding to it. See Suhrawardī's *Kitāb al-mashāri' wa'l-muṭāriḥāt,* ed. H. Corbin (Istanbul, 1945), p. 479.

3. See *Kitāb al-ishārāt wa'l-tanbīhāt* and Ṭūsī's Commentary on the definition of knowledge as such and the notion of *"ḥuḍūr"* and *"shuhūd"*, mean-

ing "presence" and "apprehension" respectively. Ed. Sulaymān al-Dunyā, pp. 363–65.

4. This kind of knowledge is given the name in our terminology of presence-knowledge by "identity," as compared with presence knowledge by "illumination" and "absorption." The first is supremacy, and the second dependence.

5. Avicenna: "There was among the Peripatetic philosophers a man called Porphyry who believed knowledge and the thing known to be one and the same." *Kitāb al-ishārāt wa'l-tanbīhāt,* Metaphysics, *'namaṭ'*. 3.

6. Ṣadr al-Dīn Shīrāzī, *Kitāb al-afsār,* Journey I, pt. 3.

7. Suhrawardī, *Kitāb al-talwīḥāt* (Istanbul, 1945), p. 72.

8. B. Russell, *The Problems of Philosophy,* ch. 12, "Truth and Falsehood" (London, 1976).

9. Avicenna, *Kitāb al-najāt, 'Logic',* ch. 2 (Cairo, 1938).

10. By nonphenomenal we mean that it has no connective connotation in the sense that it 'shows' itself to us. Rather, this version of truth, like the very meaning of things in themselves, has its pure objective reality in presence, even though it may not have shown itself to us.

11. This phenomenal representation is called in Islamic Iluminative language *al-āthār al-muṭābiq li'l-wāqi',* meaning the mental effect that corresponds to the objective reality of the object. See *Kitāb al-mashāri' wa'l-muṭāriḥāt* (Istanbul, 1945), p. 479.

12. This is the typical Islamic sense of the phenomenology of mind. See *Kitāb al-asfār,* Journey I, vol. 2, pt. 4, (Tehran, 1964).

13. Mullā Hādī Sabziwārī, *Sharḥ-i manẓūmah,* 'The Problem of Human Mental Existence' "Metaphysics", (Tehran, n.d.), pp. 58–85.

14. This kind of opposition is called ' 'adam wa malikah'. See Sabziwārī, *Sharḥ-i manẓūmah,* p. 153.

15. For a full-scale treatment of all the important senses of 'truth', see al-Farabi's consideration quoted by Sabziwārī *Manẓūmah,* p. 170.

16. Suhrawardī, *Kitāb al-mashāri' wa'l-muṭāriḥāt,* pp. 487–89.

17. Suhrawardī, *Kitāb al-talwīḥāt,* p. 70.

18. *Op. cit.,* pp. 71–80.

19. Mehdi Ha'iri Yazdi, "Introduction," in *Kawishhā-yi 'aql-i naẓarī* (Tehran, 1969).

20. B. Russell, *An Outline of Philosophy,* ch. 16 (London, 1976), p. 170.

21. *Kitāb al-asfār,* Journey I, vol. 3, pt. 3 (Tehran, 1964).

22. *Op. cit.* "The Problem of Knowledge," Journey I, pt. 3.

An Empirical Dimension of Knowledge by Presence

1. This is a pedagogical device for starting with what seems more understandable to the minds of students. As Naṣīr al-Dīn Ṭūsī put it, this might be the reason that the first master of philosophy, Aristotle, started his teaching with physical and empirical matters, and then shifted into metaphysics, which is less familiar to our average understanding. See Ṭūsī's *Commentary on Kitāb al-ishārāt,* Section One, Physics, on the problem of 'The Constitutive Elements of Matter'.

2. B. Russell, *The Problems of Philosophy* (London, 1976), ch. 12.

3. It may be proposed that knowledge by presence is just another way of describing Russell's knowledge by acquaintance, and that there is no difference. This section has been specifically included to answer this criticism.

4. Suhrawardī, *Kitāb al-mashāri' wa'l-muṭāriḥāt,* p. 485.

5. Russell, *The Problems of Philosophy,* ch. 5.

6. For more information about self-objective knowledge, see the interesting debate between the two distinguished interpreters of Avicenna's *De Anima,* Naṣīr al-Dīn Ṭūsī and Fakhr al-Dīn al-Rāzī in *Kitāb al-ishārāt,* pt. 2, pp. 359–66.

7. Henry Bergson, *Introduction to Metaphysics.*

8. Wittgenstein, *Philosophical Investigations,* trans. G. E. M. Anscombe (New York, 1968), para. 246.

9. On the same topic, see Ṣadr al-Dīn Shīrāzī, *Kitāb al-asfār,* Journey I, vol. 1, pt. 3.

10. *Philosophical Investigations,* para. 247.

11. Russell, *The Problems of Philosophy,* pp. 46–7.

12. If we follow the line taken by these illuminative philosophers, it is possible to reduce all perceptions and conceptions to illuminative acts of the knowing subject, and this, of course, makes all these perceptions and conceptions, including sense-data, a form of knowledge by presence. See Ṣadr al-Dīn Shīrāzī, *Kitāb al-asfār,* Journey I, vol. 1, pt. 3.

13. In a later chapter, we present another empirical feature of knowl-

edge by presence which makes our theory complete and consistent. There we shall speak of the knowledge of the private states of the mind, including our knowledge of our body, imagination, and phantasm.

14. It has become almost a matter of course for modern writers and scholars in the field of Islamic thought to translate the Arabic *dhāt* synonymously with *māhiyyah* or "essence." This translation is accurate enough in a context where the distinction between essence and existence is under consideration and has already been made, but where such a distinction has not been made and is not relevant such a translation makes no sense and is even misleading. I would suggest as the best choice in such contexts the translation of *dhāt* as "reality." Since we have already understood that the essence-existence dichotomy does not hold in the case of God, to use the word *dhāt*/essence as existentially neutral would make no sense. We therefore use the word "reality" as the more suitable translation of *dhāt* when reference is being made to the very content of the existence as opposed to the form of essence, be it in relation to God or to the performative self.

15. *Kitāb al-mashāri' wa'l-muṭāriḥāt,* p. 485, para. 612.

16. This is a kind of argument that became known in Islamic thought as the argument for an already acquired conclusion *(taḥṣīl al-ḥāṣil)*. It may be thought of as an equivalent of the ordinary sense of tautology, but not of logical tautology.

The Prime Mode of Knowledge by Presence

1. In this and the following chapters, our major reference is Shihāb al-Dīn Suhrawardī's illuminative philosophy *(ishrāq)*. We agree with him in principle on his notion of the self. According to this, our definition of the self does not initially categorize it as a material or immaterial substance, nor is it generally placed under the heading of "objects" at all. This is because, as we shall see, it is not an object in the sort of way in which one can refer to it using such expressions as "it," or "this," or "that," etc. It is simply a performative subject. It is on the basis of this performative self that we wish to establish our prime mode of knowledge by presence. See Suhrawardī, *Kitāb ḥikmat al-ishrāq,* ed. H. Corbin (Paris/Tehran, 1952), pp. 106–10.

2. L. Wittgenstein, "Family Resemblance," in *Philosophical Investigations,* trans. G. E. Anscombe (New York, 1968), pp. 65–77.

3. Avicenna, "Logic," in *Kitāb al-ishārāt wa'l-tanbīhāt,* ed. Sulaymān Dunyā, pp. 249–66.

4. Avicenna, "A Treatise on the Point that No Definition can ever be Obtained from a Deductive Argument", Logic, *Kitāb al-najāt.*

5. Suhrawardī, *Kitāb al-mashāri' wa'l-muṭāriḥāt* (in his *Opera Metaphysica et Mystica,* ed. H. Corbin vol. 1). It starts with this opening sentence:

وهو يبحث الانسان عن علمه بذاته ثم يرتقى الى ....

6. As we mentioned in the preceding chapter, the word *dhāt* which can normally be translated as "essence" must be translated as "reality" when reference is made to the factual existence of a thing rather than to its essence or essentialities by definition. A similar observation is made by Sabziwārī in his *Metaphysics*. See *Sharḥ-i manẓūmah,* pp. 56, 60–90.

7. Suhrawardī, *Ḥikmat al-ishrāq,* sec. 2, p. 106.

8. *Op. cit.,* pp. 106–7.

9. On the matter of the language of light, see al-Ghazzālī, *The Niche for Lights,* trans. H. T. Gairdner (London, 1952).

10. Suhrawardī, *Ḥikmat al-ishrāq,* pp. 107–8.

11. *Op. cit.,* p. 108.

12. *Op. cit.,* pp. 107–8.

13. *Timaeus, Plato's Cosmology* (London and New York, 1937), para. 27–28D.

14. In Islamic philosophical language, the following words are used synonymously to refer to the mental image of an objective reference.

1. *mithāl:* meaning analogue.
2. *ṣūrah:* meaning form.
3. *al-wujūd al-dhihnī:* meaning mental existence.
4. *al-ẓuhūr al-dhihnī:* meaning subjective appearance.
5. *al-māhiyyat al-dhihnī:* meaning subjective essence of object.
6. *al-shabah:* meaning mental image.

The first two are much more frequent in this language than the others. For the reason that all of them, especially the first two, are extremely ambiguous, and quite often homonymous, we have chosen the Kantian term 'representation' as our translated technical term for the immanent or subjective object.

15. Suhrawardī, *Ḥikmat al-ishrāq,* p. 111, para. 115. Translation mine.

16. It is the indirect awareness of myself which is implied in that sentence but not asserted and spoken of in terms of the use and meaning of language.

17. Sabziwārī, *Sharḥ-i manẓūmah,* pp. 60–3.

18. By "phenomenalist" theory we mean the phenomenon of representation. We could also have said "representationalist" theory. In general, phenomenon and representation are interchangeable in our terminology.

19. *Qiyās al-khulf,* see "Logic," in *Kitāb al-ishārāt,* pp. 461–64.

20. Ṣadr al-Dīn Shīrāzī, *Kitāb al-asfār,* Journey I, pt. 3, pp. 465–9.

21. By "pure existence" or "pure light," Suhrawardī meant that feature or degree of existence that has been divided by intellectual analysis from the essence. Although such an analysis or division cannot possibly be achieved in the world of reality, our intellect can concentrate on the existential component of the self alone and be oblivious to its essence. On this hypothesis, the purity of the existence of the self is a postanalytical purification that applies only to the state of its factual existence, not to the state of its conception and intellectual essence.

22. Suhrawardī, *Ḥikmat al-ishrāq,* p. 111. Translation mine.

23. *Op. cit.,* pp. 111–2.

24. Suhrawardī, *Kitāb al-talwīḥāt* (*Opera,* vol. 1), p. 72.

25. *Ḥikmat al-ishrāq,* p. 112. Translation mine.

26. *Kitāb al-mashāri' wa'l-muṭāriḥāt* (*Opera,* vol. 1) pp. 474–80.

27. See *Kitāb at-talwīḥāt,* p. 72.

28. Our interpretation of the word "performative" is based on Suhrawardī's frequent emphasis on such words as *al-mudrikiyyah, al-shā'iriyyah,* etc., which denote the acting, knowing subject, or the position of knowing subjectively.

29. *Ḥikmat al-ishrāq,* p. 112. Translation mine.

30. In the ontological background to this thesis, it has been assumed that there is an important distinction between an "existence-in-itself" and an "existence-by-itself." The former mode of existence does not necessarily imply the latter. Many Aristotelian substances can truly be said to be beings-in-themselves but not beings-by-themselves. Being-in-itself together with being-by-itself would only be applicable to the existence of God as the Necessary Being. With regard to the existence of the self, its substantiality means simply a being-in-itself in terms of not being in another. But as an emanative being, it is far from being by itself, as we shall discuss next. This important distinction does not appear in the Aristotelian doctrine of *'being'*.

31. Our conceptual definition of things must only be given according to this standard if we are to be concerned with logically valid definitions. Then

we are in a position to see how distant this process of definition is from an *a priori* definition.

32. On the same subject, see *Kitāb at-talwīḥāt,* p. 115.

33. *Kitāb al-asfār,* Journey I, vol. 1, pt. 3.

An Appendix to the Theory of Knowledge by Presence

1. We can see, almost exactly, the same methodology at work here as that which was used by Avicenna, when he moved to the explanation of private states of our minds and the mind's immanent actions, immediately after he formulated his well-known doctrine of "the suspended soul." See *Kitāb al-ishārāt wa'l-tanbīhāt,* pt. 2, pp. 350–8.

2. This pedagogical method is characteristic of Islamic thought as a whole. Naṣīr al-Dīn Ṭūsī believes that this is the reason why the *Metaphysics of Aristotle* has acquired such a name. That is to say, a study of the observable things of the universe has natural pedagogical priority over those intellectual issues with which the first philosophy is concerned. See Ṭūsī's *Commentary* on *Kitāb al-ishārāt wa'l-tanbīhāt, op. cit.,* p. 149.

3. See the last appendix. See also Avicenna's *Kitāb al-ishārāt wa'l-tanbīhāt,* pt. 2, pp. 348–9.

4. *Kitāb al-mashāri' wa'l-muṭāriḥāt,* p. 485. Translation mine.

5. Notice that this is the problem of the particularity and universality of knowledge, which is quite distant from the particularity and universality of things. The former is a question of epistemology, and the latter a question of ontology.

6. I think it is imperative to understand that these mainly epistemological questions do not necessarily engage us in the fundamental problem of the mind-body relation. Whether this relation is categorized as a matter-form relationship, or a substance-accident relation, does not concern us insofar as we focus our attention on the existential feature of the performative 'I'. As we have seen in detail, the performative 'I' belongs entirely to the order of the reality of existence in the radiance of which any kind of 'otherness' becomes totally obliterated.

7. Suhrawardī, *Kitāb al-mashāri', op. cit.,* p. 485.

8. *Op. cit.,* p. 486.

9. It should be understood that by particular knowledge we, as Muslim philosophers, do not mean a particular proposition in logic. A logically partic-

ular proposition is a proposition quantified by a term such as "some," "at least there is one thing," etc. But particular knowledge is that which has no more than one single objective reference and which cannot be applied to many.

10. In Islamic existential philosophy, it is an existential norm to say that particularity in terms of individuation hinges only on the objective existence of a thing but quality, quantity, position, time, etc., cannot make a thing individual. See Sabziwarī, *Sharḥ-i manẓūmah,* (Tehran n.d.), litho. ed., p. 58.

11. In Avicenna's *Metaphysics,* there exists a material equivalence between the concept of 'existence' and the concept of 'oneness', carefully drawn and stated. But whether or not this oneness is an individual oneness or generic oneness is not clear. Later, in Ṣadr al-Dīn's philosophy, it becomes clear that this equivalence holds only between the reality of existence, as opposed to the concept of it, and actual individuation. See *Kitab al-shifā'*, *The Metaphysics,* ed. G. C. Anawati (Cairo, 1960), ch. 5.

12. Suhrawardī, *Kitāb al-mashāri' wa'l-muṭāriḥāt,* p. 486.

An Expanded Theory of Knowledge by Presence: Mysticism in General

1. By unitary consciousness we do not wish to understand any specific mode of unity and identity. Whether it is a unity with the personal One as claimed by Western mysticism—Judaic, Christian, and Islamic—or with the Universal One, such as in the case of Oriental mystical experience, does not make any difference to our theme which is "unitary consciousness." Unitary consciousness is rather a rational state of identity in which no multiplicity of any kind can be considered. In this state even the epistemic dualism of the subject-object relationship, the metaphysical dualism of the existence-essence distinction, or the religious devotion involving a worshipper-worshipped relationship do not appear to be meaningful.

2. See W. T. Stace, *Mysticism and Philosophy* (Philadelphia, 1960), ch. 2, pp. 41–133.

3. That is so for the good reason that any kind of consciousness other than self-object consciousness, which is true only of knowledge by presence, is inconsistent with mystical unitary consciousness.

4. William James, "Mysticism," in *The Varieties of Religious Experience* (New York, 1936), pp. 370–420.

5. R. M. Bucke, *Cosmic Consciousness* (New York, 1923), p. 12.

6. W. T. Stace, *Mysticism and Philosophy,* pp. 146–52.

7. Plotinus, *Enneads,* trans. S. MacKenna (London, 1967), VI, 9, para. 4.

8. *Op.cit.,* para. 10.

9. It would be a self-contradictory claim if a mystic were to say, "I have seen at a certain point of time one thing among others such that it is Unity and it is undifferentiated." For if it were really Unity and undifferentiated, then it would not be an object among others to be seen by a perceiving mystic.

10. Plotinus, *Enneads,* VI, 9, para. 10.

11. W. T. Stace, *The Teachings of the Mystics,* p. 15.

12. The paradox of interpretation was also noticed by Plotinus for he warns us in his above passage: "No doubt we should not speak of seeing; but we cannot help talking in dualities . . . "

13. W. T. Stace, *Mysticism and Philosophy,* p. 31–8.

14. Plato, *The Republic,* VII, 516–7.

15. *Op. cit.,* VII, 519.

16. Plato, *Sophist,* trans. F. M. Cornford (New York, 1957), 266B.C.

17. This definition is at least implicit in various definitions made in the contempdorary philosophy of religion. See William P. Alston, "Religion," in *The Encyclopedia of Philosophy.*

18. L. Dupré, "The Mystical Vision," in *The Other Dimension* (New York, 1972), ch. 12.

19. This is a symptomatic expression of the worship relationship which designates the dualism of the worshipping subject and the object worshipped.

Mysticism in the System of Emanation

1. Just as Avicenna developed the system of the "descending order" of existence within the doctrine of emanation, Suhrawardī, agreeing with him in principle, tried to take the initiative in establishing the system of the "ascending grades" of light in his mystical philosophy of illumination. The descending order of emanation is called by Avicenna the principle of "the nobler possibility," and the ascending grades of light is called by Suhrawardī the principle of "posterior possibility." See Suhrawardī, *Kitāb al-talwīḥāt,* pp. 50–54.

2. Avicenna, "Metaphysics," in *Kitāb al-ishārāt wa'l-tanbīhāt,* pt. 3, p. 95.

3. *Op. cit.,* p. 97. Translation mine.

4. *Op. cit.,* p. 102. Translation mine.

5. *Op. cit.,* pp. 216–22. Translation mine.

6. According to this doctrine, an emanative being is a unitary simplex wherein the two opposite modalities, i.e., possibility and necessity, meet. The matter of modality follows next in our discussion.

7. *Op. cit.,* pp. 229–30. Translation mine.

8. Ṭūsī's Commentary on Avicenna's *al-Ishārāt,* 'Metaphysics,' (Egyptian ed.), pp. 217–20. Translation mine.

9. St. Thomas Aquinas, *Treatise on Separate Substances,* trans. F. J. Lascoe (New York, 1976), ch. 10, p. 92.

10. Avicenna, *Kitāb al-ishārāt, Physics,* pt. 2, pp. 149–81.

11. St. Thomas Aquinas, *Treatise on Separate Substances,* p. 93.

12. Avicenna, "Metaphysics" in *Kitāb al-ishārāt,* pt. 3, pp. 44–76. Also, *Kitāb al-shifā',* ed. G. C. Anawati (Cairo, 1960), vols. III–IV, pp. 37–170.

13. A thorough treatment of God's will and God's knowledge can be found in Ṣadr al-Dīn Shīrāzī, *Kitāb al-asfār,* Journey III, vol. VI. "The Problem of the Existence of God," and "God's Attributes."

14. St. Thomas sharply criticized this Avicennian doctrine:

> And because things proceed from Him as from a principle with an intellect, which acts in accordance with concerned forms, we may not posit that from the first principle granting that It is simple in its essence then proceeds only one effect; and that it is from another being, according to the mode of its composition and power that there proceeds a multitude, and so on. (St. Thomas, *Treatise on Separate Substances,* p. 93)

15. Ṭūsī, Commentary on *Kitāb al-ishārāt,* pt 3, pp. 283–85.

16. Suhrawardī, *Kitāb ḥikmat al-ishrāq* (Tehran/Paris, 1952), pp. 154–58.

17. St. Thomas, *Treatise on Separate Substances,* p. 93.

18. Besides, we have just been told by Avicenna himself that:

> By mediation of this emanative substance [the first effect] the First Principle [again] illuminates another intellectual substance together with a heavenly body.

It means that the whole system of emanation issues from the First Principle within this hierarchical order.

19. Ṣadr al-Dīn Shīrāzī, *Kitāb al-asfār,* vol. I, p. 45.

20. The problem of ontology and the meaning and reality of existence has been treated so thoroughly and so systematically in this philosophy that the whole area of this philosophy is characterized by the sense of existence.

21. For more explanation of the notion of "the First Cause" or "the Cause of causes," refer to Avicenna's philosophy of causation in *Kitab al-shifā'* and *al-Ishārāt.* But because of the fact that the latter has been authentically interpreted by two outstanding authorities in philosophy, namely al-Ṭūsī and al-Rāzī, we preferred to make our major references to it instead of the other work of Avicenna. See *Kitāb al-ishārāt,* pt. 3, pp. 18–55.

22. Our vertical and horizontal lines are obtained from the Avicennian principle of the "nobler possibility" *(al-imkān al-ashraf)* together with Suhrawardī's principle of the "more posterior possibility" *(al-imkān al-akhaṣṣ). Kitāb ḥikmat al-ishrāq,* pp. 154–57.

23. G. S. Kirk and J. E. Raven, "Parmenides," in *The Pre-Socratic Philosophers* (Cambridge, 1976), pp. 269–72.

24. "Undetachability" and "indistinguishability" are other expressions of implication, because a thing implied in another means it is undetachable and indistinguishable from that other. Conversely, a thing undetachable and indistinguishable from another means it is implied by and contained in that other.

25. A description of the "illuminative relation" has been given in chapter 3 where we spoke of the relation between knowledge by presence and knowledge by correspondence. Further explanation on this specific subject can be obtained in Sabziwārī, *Sharḥ-i manẓūmah* p. 571.

26. Ṭūsī's Commentary on Avicenna's *Kitāb al-ishārāt,* pt. 3, pp. 283–85.

27. Ṣadr al-Dīn Shīrāzī, *Kitāb al-asfār,* Journey I, pt. 1, pp. 210–62.

28. *Op. cit.,* p. 201.

29. a. Possibility is the negation of necessity:
"X is possible" = "X does not necessarily exist."
b. Impossibility is the negation of possibility:
"X is impossible" = "X cannot possibly be."
c. The necessity of being exemplifies the negation of the possibility of not being:
"X is a necessary being" = "X cannot possibly not be."
d. The necessity of not being exemplifies the negation of the possibility of being.
e. The necessity of being implies the denial of the impossibility of be-

ing, on the one hand, and identifies itself with the impossibility of not being, on the other.

f. The necessity of not being implies the denial of the impossibility of not being, on the one hand, and is identical with the impossibility of being on the other.

30. Avicenna, *Kitāb al-ishārāt, Logica,* pt. 1, p. 295.

31. *Op. cit.,* 296.

32. *Op. cit.,* 296–300.

33. Ṣadr al-Dīn Shīrāzī, *Kitāb al-asfār,* Journey I, vol. 1, pp. 215–20.

34. Suhrawardī, *Kitāb al-talwīḥāt,* p. 41.

35. *Op. cit.,* pp. 42–43.

36. E. Gilson, *Being and Some Philosophers* (Toronto, 1952), pp. 74–107.

37. Sabziwārī, *Sharḥ-i manẓūmah,* p. 410.

38. *Op. cit.,* pp. 408–09.

39. Ṣadr al-Dīn Shīrāzī, *Kitāb al-asfār,* Journey I, vol. 1, p. 47. Translation mine.

40. Avicenna, *Kitāb al-ishārāt wa'l-tanbīhāt, Logica,* p. 310. Translation mine.

41. *Op. cit.,* p. 311.

42. Suhrawardī, *Kitāb al-talwīḥāt,* p. 42.

43. *Op. cit.,* pp. 42–43.

44. Ṣadr al-Dīn Shīrāzī, "An Inquiry into Prepositional Existence," in *Kitāb al-asfār,* Journey I, vol. I, part 1, pp. 326–80.

45. Berkeley says almost the same thing when he speaks of the active soul:

> We may be said to have some knowledge or notion of our minds, of spirits and active beings; whereof in a strict sense we have not ideas. (Berkeley's *Philosophical Writings,* ed. D. M. Armstrong (London, 1969), p. 98.

By not having ideas of ourselves Berkeley most probably means that as soon as the mind objectifies itself in terms of a notion or an idea setting it up before the subject-seat of its understanding, the idea, counting as a mental object, no longer represents the reality of the acting subject, except in a very vague sense.

Mystical Unity

1. "Illumination," "emanation," "supremacy," and "absorption," all serve to point to the unitary relation of the efficient cause and its immanent effects. As we have discussed in preceding chapters, it is to this particular relation that the so-called "illuminative" relation refers.

2. This unitary consciousness is the logical justification for all those ostensibly paradoxical mystical statements *(shaṭḥiyyat)* in which we sometimes hear such things as: "Adorn me in Thy Unity, and clothe me in Thy selfhood, and raise me up to Thy Oneness . . ." Abū Yazīd of Basṭām. See A. J. Arberry, *Sufism* (London, 1961), pp. 54–55.

3. Ṣadr al-Dīn, Shīrāzī, *Kitāb al-asfār,* Journey I, vol. 1, pt. 1, ch. 1–3.

4. W. T. Stace, *Mysticism and Philosophy* (Philadelphia, 1960), pp. 28, 34.

5. R. A. Nicholson, *The Mystics of Islam* (London, 1914), pp. 149–59.

6. In the matter of the impossibility of the identity of the knowing subject with the object known, Avicenna says: "Notice that the claim that one thing becomes another without undergoing the law of transmutation is a sheer absurdity. . . . " *al-Ishārāt,* pt. 3, p. 272.

7. *Fanā'* literally means annihilation, but technically it stands for the final stage of the ascending journey of mystical experience. See Sabziwārī, "The Stages of Mystical Experiences" in *Sharḥ-i manẓūmah, 'De Anima,'* (Tehran, n.d.), litho ed.

8. We should notice that this kind of transubstantiation is quite different from that of Averroes's transubstantiation in his doctrine of ultimate human happiness. Averroes's ultimate happiness is by way of contemplation and intellectual union with the divine substances, and is far from being an existential identity through mystical experience.

9. Suhrawardī, *Kitāb al-talwīḥāt,* p. 41.

10. The illuminative relation is also expressed as a supremacy relation *(iḍāfah qayyūmiyyah). Op. cit.,* p. 72.

11. Further explanation on the meaning of the "illuminative relation" theory can be obtained in Sabziwārī's *Sharḥ-i manẓūmah,* "Mental Existence."

12. Other examples of the monadic relation are negation and manifestation.

13. Sabziwārī, "Metaphysics," in *Sharḥ-i manẓūmah,* p. 62.

14. Plotinus, *Enneads,* trans. S. Mackenna (London, 1967), vol. 1, 9, para. 8.

15. Only in this sense of the self-being-in-God and God-being-in-the-self ought Abū Yazīd Basṭāmī to be interpreted when he exclaims: "Glory be to me, how exalted I am!" R. C. Zaehner, *Hindu and Muslim Mysticism* (Oxford, 1961), p. 76.

16. Concerning mystical experiences, Avicenna specifies various kinds of actions including prayer, music, singing, etc., in "*Maqāmat al-'ārifīn* (Stages of the Mystics)," in *Kitāb al-ishārāt,* pt. 4, pp. 78–85.

17. Ṣadr al-Dīn Shīrāzī, *Kitāb al-asfār,* Journey 3, vol. I, pt. 1, ch. 2.

18. One of the outstanding features of the vertical relation is the hierarchical system of efficient causation, whereas such a relation does not hold true in the horizontal line. Causation in the horizontal line is not hierarchical; rather, it is spatiotemporal, in the sense of the succession of time at the base.

The Language of Mysticism and Metamysticism

1. G. E. Hughes and D. Londey, *The Elements of Formal Logic* (New York, 1965), p. 48.

2. These mistakes commonly range from imputing those characteristic qualities of mystical experiences to the object language of mysticism, as well as imputing those characteristic qualities of the object language to the metalanguage of mysticism. An example of the former confusion is the problem of the "ineffability" of mysticism, attributed by many to the object language of mysticism by supposing it to be self-contradictory. And a confusion of the latter kind is represented in some misinterpretations of mystical terminology such as "annihilation," "unification," "purification," etc.

3. William Frankena, *Ethics* (New York, 1963), p. 2.

4. Plato, *The Dialogues, Crito,* trans. B. Jowett (Chicago, 1962), vol. 1, p. 427.

5. There is a good deal of literature on these paradoxical utterances of mysticism. See Rūzbihān Baqlī Shīrāzī, *Sharḥ al-shaṭḥiyyāt al-ṣūfiyyah.*

6. See our diagram together with its logical explanation on pp. 126–129.

7. There are numerous interpretations of the mystical meaning of the

One, regardless of those many interpretations made by theology, religion, philosophy, etc. One of the famous Sufi approaches to the definition of the One is that which is ascribed to "theistic tasting," *dhawq al-ta'alluh.* Mullā Hādī Sabziwārī, *Sharḥ-i manẓūmah,* pp. 56–58.

8. The illuminative relation has been described on *op. cit.,* pp. 58–65.

9. For a further definition of *'irfān* and its stages of elevation see Avicenna's *Maqāmāt al-'ārifīn, Kitāb al-ishārāt,* pt. 4.

10. The major works on the science of *'irfān* by Ibn al-'Arabī are *al-Futūḥāt al-makkiyyah,* and *Fuṣūṣ al-ḥikam.*

11. William James, *The Varieties of Religious Experience* (New York, 1936), p. 378.

12. J. Maritain, *The Degrees of Knowledge* (New York, 1959), ch. VIII, sec. 1, p. 331.

13. W. T. Stace, *The Teachings of the Mystics,* p. 10.

14. William James, *The Varieties of Religious Experience,* pp. 371–72.

15. *Op. cit.,* p. 370.

16. R. C. Zaehner, *Mysticism: Sacred and Profane* (Oxford, 1961).

17. Zaehner's final conclusion seems to be conceived in an entirely religious way of thinking. See the last chapter of the book.

18. There is an important glossary by Ibn al-'Arabī called *Kitāb al-iṣṭilāḥāt al-ṣūfiyyah* (Hyderabad, India, 1948) in which can be found all the authentic definitions of mystical terminology.

19. Jalāl al-Dīn Rūmī (1202–73), *Āyinah qiṣaṣ wa ḥikam,* p. 561. Translation mine.

20. B. Russell, *Mysticism and Logic* (London, 1963), pp. 23–26.

21. *The Mathnawi of Jalal al-Din Rumi,* trans. R. A. Nicholson (London, 1926–34), bk. 6, p. 382.

22. This passage is taken from a letter from Plotinus to Flaecus, quoted in Bucke, p. 123. See W. T. Stace, *Mysticism and Philosophy,* p. 112.

23. Avicenna, "On Abstract Beings," in *Kitāb al-ishārāt wa'l-tanbīhāt,* pt. 3, ch. 7, p. 270. Translation mine.

24. *Op. cit.,* ch. 9, "Stages of the Mystics." Translation mine.

25. We take the word "apprehension," quoted here from Plotinus, as having two implications. One implication is the sense of mystical conscious-

ness which is a mode of knowledge by presence. The other implication is a representational knowledge derived from the first kind of knowledge which serves as an introspective knowledge interpreted by mystics themselves. Both will be called apprehension, or "*'irfān,*" as contrasted with our metamystical knowledge about mystical apprehension.

26. Muḥyī al-Dīn ibn al-'Arabī, *al-Futūhāt al-makkiyah,* ed. O. Yahya, (Cairo, 1972), vol. I, pt. 3. Translation mine.

27. Ṣadr al-Dīn Shīrāzī frequently refers to this division of knowledge as Ibn al-'Arabī's theory of knowledge. See "On knowledge," in *Kitāb al-asfār,* Journey I, pt. 10.

28. Ibn al-'Arabī, "Introduction," in *Kitāb al-futūḥāt,* ed. O. Yayha, vol. I.

29. R. C. Zaehner, *Mysticism: Sacred and Profane,* pp. 157–58.

30. *Op. cit.,* p. 159.

31. William James, *The Varieties of Religious Experience,* pp. 292–93.

32. See Abu'l-'Ala' 'Afifi, *Introduction to Kitāb Fuṣūṣ al-ḥikam* (Beirut, 1966).

33. See Ibn al-'Arabī's *Iṣṭilāḥāt al-ṣūfiyyah,* pp. 6–7.

34. B. Russell, *Mysticism and Logic* (London, 1963), p. 22.

35. Wittgenstein, *Philosophical Investigations,* trans. G. E. M. Anscombe (New York, 1968), part 1, para. 242.

36. Avicenna, "A Treatise on Reasoning," in *Kitab al-najāt,* pp. 66–68.

37. B. Russell, *Mysticism and Logic,* pp. 23–28.

38. *Op. cit.,* pp. 22–23.

Appendix

1. *Jāburs* and *jābulq* are two proper names used in the Islamic mystical language which stand for two different stages in the world of "suspended forms" *('alam al-muthul al-mu'allaqah).* The world of these forms is intermediate between this material world and the divine intellectual forms.

Quṭb al-Dīn Shīrāzī, the celebrated interpreter of Suhrawardī, describes what the world of suspended forms is like:

> This is a world of which some ancient . . . philosophers have already spoken when they said that there is in the realm of existence a world that is characterized by pure quantity and is different from this sen-

> sible world. The strange things and communities that exist in this world are infinite in number. From among its innumerable cities one can mention Jabulqa and Jabulsa. These are two great cities, the population of which cannot be calculated ... In this world are all kinds of suspended forms with infinite diversity. . . . (*Kitāb ḥikmat al-ishrāq,* in Suhrawardī, *Oeuvres philosophiques et mystiques,* ed. H. Corbin, vol. II, n. 4, p. 234. Translation mine)

Apparently this is a description of the imaginative and quantitative forms that are produced and held within this sphere. It was believed by those ancient philosophers that the soul of the first sphere had the same faculties of apprehension, and the same characteristics, as the soul of the human being. It also enjoys the power of imagination and phantasm as the soul of man does. Thus, in the spherical worlds of imagination all these innumerable forms exist. Although these forms, like those of pure mathematics, are not of a material nature in terms of subsisting in matter, they are nevertheless held by, and suspended in, the inner state of this sphere.

2. Under this title *(al-ḍābiṭ al-jāmi')* Suhrawardī worked out a material equivalence between 'knowledge' and 'existence', or in modern language, between 'epistemology' and 'ontology'. (See *Kitāb al-talwīḥāt, ibid.,* p. 41, para. 32).

3. Naṣīr al-Dīn Ṭūsī provides an answer to the question as to how things that display differentiation and order are known by God without losing His absolute simplicity. While his treatment of the problem seems, on the face of it, to be typically Peripatetic, it is quite obvious that he arrives at the same point that illuminative philosophy tries to reach, namely, knowledge by presence. However, in dealing with this question, Ṭūsī says:

> We have come to understand that the First Principle knows Himself without differentiation through the mediation of a representation *(ṣūrah)* between His reality *(dhātih')* and the apprehension of His reality in existence, unless it be in the intellective analysis of those who reflect upon His absolutely simple reality.
>
> We have also established that His knowledge of Himself is the efficient cause of his knowledge of the first effect. Now, if we are to make our judgement correctly that the two seeming causes, namely His own reality and His apprehension of it, are in existence one and the same and cannot in truth differ from each other, we are then committed to making the subsequent judgement, on the same grounds, that the two seeming effects, that is, the reality of the first effect and the form of His knowledge of that reality, are one and the same and can never be different in reality.
>
> The result is that the very existence of the first effect is nothing

but the very act of the First Principle's knowing it, without there being any need for Him to approach it through an intermediary representation within Himself. (Avicenna, *Kitāb al-ishārāt wa'l-tanbīhāt* with the commentary of Naṣīr al-Dīn Ṭūsī), ed. Sulaymān Dunyā, vol. III–IV, pp. 715–16.

4. Quran 38:24 and 40.

BIBLIOGRAPHY

Original Arabic Sources.

Averroes (ibn Rushd). *Tahāfut al-tahāfut.* Ed. Sulaymān Dunyā. Cairo, 1964.

———. *Talkhīs kitāb al-nafs.* Cairo, 1952.

———. *Tafsīr mā ba'd al-ṭabī'ah* (the major Commentary on Aristotle's *Metaphysics*). Beirut, 1967.

Avicenna (Ibn Sīnā). *Kitāb al-ḥudūd (Livre des definitions).* Ed. A. M. Goichon. Cairo, 1963.

———. *Kitāb al-ishārāt wa'l-tanbīhāt.* Cairo, 1960.

———. *Kitāb al-mabda' wa'l-ma'ād.* Litho. ed. Tehran, n.d.

———. *Kitāb manṭiq al-mashriqiyyīn.* Cairo, 1910.

———. *Kitāb al-najāt.* Cairo, 1938.

———. *Kitāb al-shifā'.* Ed. G. C. Anawati. Cairo, 1960.

———. *Kitāb al-ta'līqāt.* Cairo, 1973.

Al-Fārābī, Abū Naṣr. *Fuṣūṣ al-madanī.* Cambridge, 1961.

———. *al-Jam' bayn ra'yay al-ḥakīmayn.* Beirut, 1960.

———. *Sharḥ kitāb al-'ibārah.* Beirut, 1960.

———. *al-Siyāsat al-madaniyyah.* Hyderabad, 1346 A.H.

Al-Ghāzzālī, Abū Ḥāmid. *Iḥyā' 'ulūm al-dīn.* Cairo, 1348 A.H.

———. *al-Iqtiṣād fi'l-i'tiqād.* Cairo, n.d.

———. *Maqāṣid al-falāsifah.* Cairo, A.H. 1331.

———. *Mishkāt al-anwār.* Cairo, 1964.

———. *Mi'yār al-'ilm.* Cairo, 1961.

———. *Tahāfut al-falāsifah.* Beirut, 1927.

Ibn al-'Arabī, Muḥyī al-Dīn. *Fuṣūṣ al-ḥikam.* Ed. Abu'l-'Alā' 'Afīfī. Beirut, 1966.

———. *al-Futūḥāt al-makkiyyah.* Ed. O. Yahya. Cairo, 1972.

———. *Iṣṭilāḥāt al-ṣūfiyyah.* Hyderabad, 1948.

———. *Kitāb al-tajalliyyāt.* Hyderabad, 1948.

Ikhwān al-Ṣafā'; *Rasā'il Ikhwān al-Safā'.* Beirut, 1957.

Rāzī, Fakhr al-Dīn. *Commentary on Avicenna's Kitāb al-ishārāt.* Istanbul, 1869.

———. *al-Mabāḥith al-mashriqiyyah.* Hyderabad, 1922.

———. *al-Muḥaṣṣal.* Cairo, A.H. 1323.

———. *Talkhiṣ al-ishārāt.* Cairo, n.d.

Ruzbihān, Baqlī Shīrāzī. *Kitāb sharḥ shaṭḥiyyāt al-ṣūfiyyah.*

Sabziwārī, Mullā Hādī. *Sharḥ-i manẓūmah.* Litho. ed. Tehran, n.d.

———. *Sharḥ-i manẓūmah.* Tehran/McGill, 1969.

Shīrāzī, Ṣadr al-Dīn, *Kitāb al-asfār.* Tehran, 1378/1958.

———. *Kitāb al-ḥikmat al-'arshiyyah.* Tehran, A.H. 1278.

———. *Kitāb al-mashā'ir.* Tehran/Paris, 1964.

———. *Kitāb al-shāwahid al-rubūbiyyah.* Tehran, A.H. 1286.

———. *Sharḥ al-hidāyah.* Tehran, A.H. 1313.

———. *Sharḥ uṣūl al-kāfī.* Tehran, n.d.

———. *al-Ta'līqāt.* Tehran, A.H. 1315.

Suhrawardī, Shihāb al-Dīn. *Opera Metaphysica et Mystica.* Vol. I. Ed. H. Corbin. Istanbul, 1945 (contains *Kitāb al-mashāri' wa'l-muṭāriḥāt,* and *Kitāb al-talwīḥāt*).

———. *Oeuvres philosophiques et mystiques.* Vol. II. Ed. H. Corbin. Paris/Tehran, 1952 (contains *Ḥikmat al-ishrāq* and *Qiṣṣat al-ghurbat al-gharbiyyah*).

Ṭūsī, Naṣīr al-Dīn, *Commentary on Avicenna's Kitāb al-ishārāt.* Tehran, 1951.

———. *Naqd al-muḥaṣṣal.* Cairo, 1964.

———. *Taḥrīr uqlīdus.* Tehran, n.d.

———. *Tajrīd al-i'tiqād.* Tehran, n.d.

English Sources.

Arberry, A. J.. *Sufism.* London, 1950.

Aristotle. *Basic Works of Aristotle.* Ed. R. McKeon. New York, 1941.

———. *Categories and De Interpretation.* Trans. J. L. Ackrill. Oxford, 1974.

———. *De Anima* and *The Commentary of St. Thomas.* New Haven, 1959.

———. *Ethics.* Ed. and trans. J. Warrington. New York, 1973.

———. *Metaphysics.* Chicago, 1961.

———. *Nichomachean Ethics.* Trans. M. Ostwald. Indianapolis, 1962.

———. *Prior and Posterior Analytics.* Ed. and trans. J. Warrington, New York, 1964.

———. *The Politics of Aristotle.* Trans. E. Barker. New York, 1958.

Ayer, A. J. *The Foundations of Empirical Knowledge.* London, 1971.

———. *The Problem of Knowledge.* London, 1956.

Bergson, H. *Introduction to Metaphysics.* London, 1913.

Berkeley, G. *Berkeley's Philosophical Writings.* Ed. D. M. Armstrong. London, 1965.

Bucke, R. M. *Cosmic Consciousness.* New York, 1923.

Buber, M. *I and Thou.* Trans. W. Kaufman. Edinburgh, 1970.

Chisholm, R. M. *Theory of Knowledge.* Englewood Cliffs, N.J., 1977.

Cunningham, G. W. *The Problems of Philosophy.* New York, 1924.

Descartes, R. *Descartes Philosophical Writings.* Vol. I. Ed. E. S. Haldane and G. R. T. Ross. London, 1967.

———. *Discourse on Method and Meditations.* London, 1960.

Ducasse, C. J. *Truth, Knowledge and Causation.* New York, 1959.

Dupre, Louis. *The Other Dimension.* New York, 1972.

Edwards, P. (ed.). *The Encyclopedia of Philosophy.* New York, 1967.

Frankena, W. *Ethics.* New York, 1963.

Gairdner, H. T. *The Niche for Lights* (trans. al-Ghazzali, *Mishkat al-anwar*). London, 1952.

Gilson, E. *Being and Some Philosophers.* Toronto, 1952.

Hamlyn, D. W. *The Theory of Knowledge.* New York, 1971.

Hegel, F. *Hegel's Logic.* trans. W. Wallace and J. N. Findlay. Oxford, 1975.

———. *The Phenomenology of Mind.* Trans. J. B. Baillie. New York, 1964.

Hughes, G. E., and D. Londey. *The Elements of Formal Logic.* London, 1965.

Hume, D. *A Treatise on Human Nature.* Ed. L. A. Selby-Bigge. Oxford, 1978.

———. *An Inquiry Concerning Human Understanding.* New York, 1975.

———. *Dialogues Concerning Natural Religion.* Ed. A. Wayne Colver, Oxford, 1976.

Husserl, E. *Cartesian Meditations.* Trans. D. Cairns. The Hague, 1960.

———. *Ideas.* London, 1931.

James, W. *Essays in Pragmatism.* New York, 1977.

———. *The Varieties of Religious Experience.* New York, 1936.

Kant, I. *Kant's Critique of Pure Reason.* Trans. N. K. Smith. London, 1965.

———. *Kant's Critique of Practical Reason.* Trans. L. W. Beck. New York, 1956.

Kirk, G. S., and J. E. Rave. *The Pre-Socratic Philosophers.* Cambridge, 1976.

Maritain, J. *The Degrees of Knowledge.* New York, 1959.

Moore, G. E. *Principia Ethica.* London, New York, 1978.

Morewedge, P. *The Metaphysics of Avicenna.* New York, 1973.

Nicholson, R. A. *The Mathnavi of Jalal al-Din Rumi.* Trans. London, 1926–34.

———. *The Mystics of Islam.* London, 1914.

Otto, R. *Mysticism East and West.* Trans. B. L. Bracey and R. C. Payne. New York, 1972.

Plato: *The Collected Dialogues.* Ed. E. Hamilton and H. Cairns. New York, 1961.

———. *The Dialogues.* Trans. B. Jowett. Chicago, 1962.

———. *The Republic of Plato.* Trans. F. M. Cornford. Oxford, 1942.

———. *Theory of Knowledge: The Theaetetus and the Sophist of Plato.* Trans. by F. M. Cornford. New York, 1957.

———. *Plato's Cosmology; the Timaeus of Plato.* Trans. F. M. Cornford. London, 1957.

Plotinus. *The Enneads.* Trans. Stephen Mackenna. London, 1967.

Rist, J. M. *Plotinus: The Road to Reality.* Cambridge, 1967.

Russell, B. *Mysticism and Logic.* London, 1963.

———. *An Outline of Philosophy.* London, 1976.

———. *The Problems of Philosophy.* London, 1976.

Stace, W. T. *Mysticism and Philosophy.* Philadelphia, 1960.

———. *The Teachings of the Mystics.* New York and Scarborough, 1960.

Thomas Aquinas. *Being and Essence.* New York, 1937.

———. *Commentary on the De Anima of Aristotle.* Trans. K. Foster and S. Humphries. New Haven, 1951.

———. *Commentary on the Metaphysics of Aristotle.* Trans. J. Rowan. Chicago, 1961.

———. *Summa Contra Gentiles.* New York, 1977.

———. *Treatise on Separate Substances.* Trans. F. J. Lascoe. New York, 1976.

Veatch, H. B. *Aristotle: A Contemporary Appreciation.* Bloomington and London, 1974.

Wittgenstein, L. *Lectures and Conversations.* Los Angeles, 1966.

———. *Philosophical Investigations.* Trans. G. E. M. Anscombe. New York, 1968.

———. *Tractatus Logico-Philosophicus.* New York, 1961.

Zaehner, R. C. *Mysticism: Sacred and Profane.* Oxford, 1961.

French Sources.

Corbin, H. *Avicenne et le recit visionnaire.* 3 vols. Paris and Tehran, 1954.

Goichon, A. M. *Le Livre des directives et remarques.* Paris, 1961.

———. *La Philosophie d'Avicenne et son influence en Europe mediévale.* Paris, 1944.

Persian Sources.

Avicenna (Ibn Sīnā). *Dānish-nāma-yi 'alā'ī, (manṭiq, ilāhiyyāt).* Tehran, 1950.

Ha'iri Yazdi, M. *Kāwishhā-yi 'aql-i naẓarī.* Tehran, 1969.

Rūmī, Jalāl al-Dīn. *Mathnawī.* Tehran, 1952.

———. *Dīwān-i Shams-i Tabrīzī.* Tehran, 1960.

Sabziwārī, Mullā Hādī. *Asrār al-ḥikam.* Tehran, 1959.

———. *Sharḥ-i Mathnawī.* Tehran, n.d.

Ṭūsī, Naṣīr al-Dīn. *Asās al-iqtibās.* Tehran, 1955.

———. *Akhlāq-i nāṣirī.* Tehran, 1932.

INDEX

Absence, 89; state of, 37

Absorption, 156, 195*n25*, 199*n4*; existential, 141; knowledge by, 175; presence by, 67, 114, 145–146; relation to emanation, 140–143, 145; by union, 21

Abstraction, 8, 9, 175; Aristotelian theory, 9, 16; object in, 39–40

Absurdity, danger of, 80

Accidentality, 86

Acquaintance: bodily, 96; knowledge by, 58–61, 65–67, 200*n3*; meaning, 65–67

Action: immanent, 27, 52, 196*n1*, 204*n1*; transitive, 27, 196*n1*

Active Intellect, 13–14, 17

Agent: acting, 28; of emanation, 123; mind of, 53; nonrational operations, 119

Agent Intellect, 17, 18, 19; divinity, 21

Al-Fārābī, Abū Naṣr, 10–13

Al-Ghazzālī, Abū Ḥāmid, viii, 149, 163, 178; treatise on light, 15–17

Annihilation, 3, 19, 156–157, 210*n7*; of annihilation, 3, 149, 158; in mysticism, 149, 158; in self-realization, 162; of time and space, 180

Apparentness, 90

Appearance, of sense-data, 66

Apprehension: 212*n25*; of God, 165, 174; of Infinite, 169, 170; mystical, 22, 41, 71, 103–104, 105, 107, 113, 114, 165; nonrepresentational, 68; object, 67; of the One, 9; and perception, 14; powers of, 121; by presence, 9; presence of reality in, 67; reality of 'I-ness', 81; representational, 60, 94, 95; of self, 72, 95; stages, 94; theory, 16; of Unity, 9

Appropriation, 85–86; representation in, 85

Aristotle, 6, 13, 24, 152, 184, 187, 197*n6*, 200*n1*; efficient cause, 11, 12; final cause, 12; on objects, 8; rejection of Platonic ideas, 8, 10–11; system of causation, 28; theory of abstraction, 9, 16; theory of knowledge, 7, 10; thesis of identity, 32–33

Ascent, 22

Attributes, 83–85

Attribution, to self, 76

Averroes, vii, viii, 12, 23; theory of beatitude, 44–45; theory of ultimate happiness, 17–22

Avicenna, x, xi, 46, 120, 121, 136, 170, 171, 181, 195*n27*, 199*n5*, 204*n1*, 206*n1*; Agent Intellect, 17; analysis of emanation, 13; criticism of, 15; interpretation of possibility, 134; niche of lights, 15; on *a priori* arguments, 70; theory of emanation, 12, 21, 24, 115, 116, 117–119, 122, 193*n15*; theory of knowledge, 13–15

Awareness: disintegration, 5; empirical, 8; of experience, 60; nonphenomenal, 16; preepistemic, 16; by presence, 24; of reality, 26, 87; of